THE END OF LITERATURE

THE END OF LITERATURE

Essays in Anthropological Aesthetics

Richard van Oort

The Davies Group, Publishers
Aurora, Colorado

Library of Congress Cataloging-in publication data:

van Oort, Richard.
  The end of literature : essays in anthropological aesthetics / Richard van Oort.
    p. cm.
  Includes bibliographical references and index.
  ISBN 978-1-934542-05-7 (alk. paper)
  1. English literature–History and criticism–Theory, etc. 2. Literature–History and criticism–Theory, etc. 3. Literature and anthropology. 4. Literature and science. 5. Anthropology–Philosophy. 6. Literature–Philosophy. 7. Anthropology in literature. 8. Science in literature. I. Title.
  PR21.V36 2008
  820.9–dc22

                              2008017412

Cover: Old paper textures © Iloveotto | Dreamstime.com

Printed in the United States of America
0123456789

For Sheila

CONTENTS

Introduction

It may seem somewhat peculiar for someone trained in literary studies, as I have been, to argue that the end of literature is anthropology, but that is precisely what this book—in however piecemeal and tentative a fashion—seeks to do. The current buzz among critics for all things cultural is no mere passing fad. There has of course always been some faddishness attached to new programs like cultural studies, concerned as they are to legitimize themselves vis-à-vis their intellectual precursors. In this sense, the current scene is no different from previous ones. The very idea of intellectual progress, upon which the modern university is based, depends on this antagonism between present and past, between scientific or scholarly progress and a "conservative" tradition that is regarded, often unfairly, as intolerably backward and unenlightened. In this familiar spectacle of rivalry between young and old, the challenge is to remain focused on the essential intellectual conflict and not to get distracted by the more voluble but less illuminating disputes taking place within each particular discipline or, in some cases, subdiscipline.

What, then, is the essential conflict? The conflict is over texts and how they are to be interpreted. Among animals, humans alone produce texts. In the social sciences this peculiar fact is usually taken for granted. Texts are a useful means for the scientist to gain access to reality, whether this reality exists internally in the minds of individual subjects (psychology) or externally in the structures of social organization (sociology). For scholars in the humanities, on the other hand, texts are far from being a straightforward means of data collection. They are, on the contrary, independent objects that must be studied for their intrinsic aesthetic or cultural worth. What is "sacred" for the humanist—what forbids easy assimilation or reduction to preexisting patterns of cognition or social organization—is the text, which is regarded as *inviolable*. Conflicts over which texts deserve most attention depend upon this notion of inviolability.

Today the idea of the inviolable text has expanded considerably. For example, interpreters in cultural studies hold that since all culture can be defined as a text, it follows that there must exist considerable latitude in the selection of one's subject matter. No longer beholden to the tyranny of the old ritual center, the critic is now free to range over cultures high and low, elite and popular, avant-garde and commercial, sacred and profane. At the beginning of the twentieth century, Durkheim suggested that culture was founded on the distinction between sacred and profane. But today the old high culture is gone. In its place is popular culture, the culture of the marketplace. Hence culture, like the global marketplace itself, is everywhere, which is the same thing as saying it is nowhere.

Since the romantics, humanists have taken a rather dim view of the market, which appears to short-circuit the aesthetic sublimation of desire by delivering not merely imaginary but worldly satisfactions. Whereas the artist produces, the people merely consume. There is some truth to this doctrine, but it remains partial. Culture and the market, aesthetic production and material consumption, are not separate ontological entities, to be analyzed according to separate methodologies or paradigms. Economic exchange is from the beginning mediated by cultural exchange. The proliferation of the market for consumer goods in the postwar era spells the demise of high culture only in the sense that in a world organized by peripheral rather than central exchange, the very notion of what is "high" depends on the a posteriori forces of the market rather than the historical inertia of ritually controlled distribution systems.[1] This is not to deny that inquiry in the humanities still requires an arduous and disciplined training in Western and non-Western letters. But this inherently "conservative" concern for tradition is balanced by an obligation to reaffirm the relevance of the humanities *in the present*. This function is performed, no doubt imperfectly with many a false prophet, by the marketplace.

Despite frequent and all too predictable protestations to the contrary, the market is not a single homogeneous entity with a well-defined (and hence authoritarian) center. It is a collection of centers, each corresponding to a potentially infinite number of participants. The university provides a minimal model of how markets function within the intellectual community. Within the context of each particular discipline, researchers compete for the attentions of their peers. Despite the often intense pressure exerted by these specialized intellectual markets, what guarantees the entire enterprise—and, more pertinently, what prevents it from descending into a crisis of undifferentiated rivalry—is the sense of inviolability each group attributes to its particular disciplinary center.

If for the humanities scholar the center's "violence" has become an increasingly textual phenomenon, for the scientist it has been forgotten altogether. From the scientific viewpoint, a particular text's historical uniqueness—its originarity or sacrality—is subordinate to its referential power, where reference is here understood to be *empirical reference.* Signs ultimately refer not to other signs, but to objects in the real world. When a humanities department persuades its dean that it is better off in the social sciences, it is declaring its commitment to the empirical. The history of the social sciences is a history of such defections from the humanities. The success of science depends upon this evolution from textual to empirical inquiry. (Imagine a department trying to persuade its dean that it would like to move from the social sciences back to the humanities—once won the empirical is unlikely to be abandoned.)

The tremendous historical success of the physical and life sciences in the modern era has granted considerable prestige to the notion of scientific method. But I do not think that the steady erosion of the humanities, which once occupied the center of the university in the idea of the "liberal arts" degree, should be regarded as a one-sided victory of the scientific worldview. On the contrary, in shedding the contingent accretions of the empirical, we only sharpen our understanding of that which is fundamentally human.

The rise of theory in the humanities should be understood in this context. "Theory" is the umbrella term we use to describe the persistence of the anthropological in the wake of the inexorable triumphs of the empirical sciences. It is no accident that Jacques Derrida's powerful rhetoric of deconstruction was appropriated by literary critics keen to consolidate the anthropological territory upon which they operated, even if this territory was never made the object of an explicit anthropological hypothesis. Instead, crippled by a general skepticism concerning the revelatory power of Western culture, critics remained content to sacralize in more modest fashion the minimal text as the unacknowledged horizon of anthropological criticism. But the seed of anthropology had been sown in deconstruction's idea of textuality. When critics of literature adopted Derrida's style of interpretation, they were contributing to this development of anthropology from the ashes of a moribund literary culture. What was originary about literature was not merely its obvious anthropological content, but the fact that this content was self-consciously presented as an artifice of a more general linguistic or symbolic form.

In contrast to the gradualist orthodoxy of scientific accounts of human origin, the cultural critic assumes that symbolic reference

it has become very unfortunate
to deem that there is any exigency
unity of humanity

takes place as a culturally generative "originary event."[2] Postmodern "textuality" is an aesthetic attempt to figure this event in language.[3] But aesthetic figuration cannot compete with the minimalist rigor of originary thinking. The latter takes the hypothetical event of human origin as its explicit, rather than implicit, point of departure. The postmodern notion of the ubiquitous cultural text is thereby given anthropological specificity and explanatory power. The text is indeed everywhere because the minimal condition of human existence is the originary scene of representation. The expansion of this scene from its minimal beginning to the proliferation of cultural forms so evident today is a tribute to the unprecedented generative power of the event of human origin. But we must not confuse this wealth of cultural content with the origin itself. In particular, we should not expect to find at the minimal origin of human culture the vast diversity of cultures we admire today. It is the unprecedented nature of this origin that makes such an assumption, however agreeable to the contemporary ideal of multiculturalism, implausible in the first place and, in the second, counter to the minimalist rigor of an anthropology. The latter seeks not to justify the singularity of every cultural form, whether in the present or the historical past. It seeks only to explain the generative principle of culture in general. To cite an analogy from the sciences, Darwin's obvious admiration for the immense variety of biological life he encountered in the field did not prevent him from hypothesizing that the origin of this diversity was to be found in a much simpler—which is to say, much less diverse—beginning.

The widespread skepticism that currently greets those who reflect on the ultimate unity of our species has led to a stultifying dichotomy in our conception of the human. From within the humanities, the very idea of a unified scene of origin is rejected as an intolerable constraint on the self-evident reality of a plurality of human cultures. Is it not the ethical function of the humanities to preserve our cultural differences? Yet the unfortunate consequence of this well-intended but shortsighted emphasis on cultural difference is that the anthropological question is rejected by the very group that can least afford to relinquish it. The unintended consequence is to abandon originary thinking to the reductive ontologies of the physical and life sciences. But these ontologies are patently incapable of explaining the cultural differences that the humanities critic would preserve. Having abandoned all dialogue on human origin to the scientists, scholars in the humanities have discarded the very territory from which they could defend, in the strongest terms possible, their position within a university dominated by the empirical sciences.

This book provides such a defense. But defending the originary core of the humanities requires us to widen our focus considerably. It is no longer possible simply to assume that literature is worth preserving without also explaining *why* it must be preserved. And such an explanation, if it is to have any validity at all, must begin from anthropological premises. The very possibility of dialogue on this issue depends upon the assumption that culture is sharable. The task of *The End of Literature* is to grasp literature's relationship to human knowledge in the broadest sense possible. How can anthropology enlarge our understanding of literature? Is the "end of literature" anthropological reflection?

I have divided the essays in this book into three parts. The first part deals with the relationship of literary studies to the human sciences, in particular, to recent developments in cognitive science and evolutionary anthropology. Unlike the humanities, the human sciences have not abandoned the problem of defining the human. We therefore need to consider the answers they have come up with, even if—*especially* if—these answers prove to be unacceptable. The second part seeks to demonstrate the explanatory power of the more "literary" anthropologies of René Girard and Eric Gans. I do this by setting them side by side with the more influential "cultural poetics" of Clifford Geertz and Stephen Greenblatt. Finally, the third part consists of two essays dealing with literary history, the first on Shakespeare and the second on Mary Shelley's *Frankenstein*. I hope those persuaded by my analyses of these "classic" authors will be encouraged to explore the anthropological model for themselves.

Despite the fact that these essays were written separately and over a number of years, they possess an overall unity. I have relied a great deal—some would say too much—on Girard and (in particular) Gans. No doubt this reflects my own personal predilection. But I think it also reflects a genuine lacuna in humanistic studies today. Few have been tempted by Gans's originary hypothesis. Yet this is not because the hypothesis has been tested and found wanting. On the contrary, it has been all but ignored. My hope is that these essays will stimulate further dialogue on these fundamental and pressing issues.[4]

Acknowledgements

These essays were written over a period of roughly six years, from 2001 to 2007. As with all human endeavors, they reflect the specific social networks in which they were born. At the University of California, I wish to thank the late Wolfgang Iser. Many of the ideas and arguments in this book originally took shape as responses to his brilliant seminars. I am also deeply indebted to Eric Gans, whose books on generative anthropology I had read long before he became a personal friend during my studies in Irvine and Los Angeles. I am grateful to J. Hillis Miller and Alex Gelley who have read, in various stages, the entire manuscript and provided support and encouragement over the years. After leaving California, PhD in hand, I spent five years at the University of British Columbia in Vancouver where I was fortunate enough to receive back-to-back postdoctoral fellowships. I am most grateful to the Social Sciences and Humanities Research Council of Canada and to Canada Research Chair Mark Vessey for his generous gesture of personal support. Tony Dawson, Alex Dick, Sandy Tomc, and Adam Frank read parts of the manuscript and provided helpful feedback. A big thanks to the members of the Vancouver *Sparagmos!* group: Andrew Bartlett, Chris Morrissey, and Pablo Bandera. In 2007 I joined the English department at the University of Victoria. I am very grateful to my new colleagues for providing such a stimulating place to finish this project. I also wish to thank my research assistant, Kate Shearer, who did the proofreading and compiled the index. Finally, my greatest debt goes to my wife Sheila. This book is dedicated to her.

The essays in this book have been published previously as follows:

"Cognitive Science and the Problem of Representation." *Poetics Today* 24 (2003): 237–295.

"Imitation and Human Ontogeny: Michael Tomasello and the Scene of Joint Attention." *Anthropoetics* 13, no. 1 (2007), http://www.anthropoetics.ucla.edu/ap1301/1301vano.htm.

"The Critic as Ethnographer." *New Literary History* 35 (2004): 621–661.

"The Culture of Criticism." *Criticism* 49 (2007): 459–479.

"Shakespeare and the Idea of the Modern." *New Literary History* 37 (2006): 319–339.

"A Race of Devils: *Frankenstein*, Romanticism, and the Tragedy of Human Origin." In *Spheres of Action: Speech and Performance in Romantic Culture*, edited by Angela Esterhammer and Alex Dick. Toronto: University of Toronto Press, 2009.

I am grateful to Duke University Press, Johns Hopkins University Press, Wayne State University Press, and University of Toronto Press for permission to reprint.

PART I

THE SCIENCE OF HUMAN ORIGIN

Chapter 1

Cognitive Science and
the Problem of Representation

I. What is the Problem of Representation?

Cognitive science has been making steady inroads into literary studies. Since the publication in 1980 of George Lakoff and Mark Johnson's influential *Metaphors We Live By*, literary critics have been encouraged by the idea of a cognitive poetics—of, that is, a systematic theory of the mind in which literature is not merely peripheral but central to the understanding of human psychology. Much of this cross-disciplinary work, however, has not produced the revolution in literary studies hoped for by its proponents.[1] On the contrary, cognitively informed interpretations of various literary works seem for the most part content to apply the newly acquired terminology of cognitive science to the fundamentally old task of providing original interpretations of literary works.[2] In this sense, cognitive poetics is new wine in old bottles.

Within literary studies, debates over the new cognitive paradigm, both pro and con, have largely avoided the bigger philosophical and anthropological issues. Indeed, one wonders if there is actually any difference in this debate other than the same old conflict about whose theoretical paradigm gets to be used when it comes to interpreting literature. Such debates are testimony to literature's continued (sacred) power over its interpreters.[3]

But I believe there are deeper issues at stake. In particular, I do not think that the cognitive paradigm, at least as it is currently constituted, is ready to revolutionize the study of literature and culture. And this is ultimately because the cognitive model lacks a theory of representation adequate to the task of interpreting human culture.[4] Simply put, the cognitive paradigm has overlooked the anthropology implicit in its approach to the problem of the origin of representation. Or, to put the same point somewhat less charitably, it interprets this origin exclusively in terms of ontogenetic development, thereby failing to recognize that ontogeny can only offer a partial and limited contribution to the *specifically anthropological* problem of language origin and function.

3

What do I mean by representation? And why do I suggest that a specifically "anthropological" approach is needed for a theory of representation? In order to begin answering these two questions, it is necessary to ask what is assumed by anthropology. I take it for granted that anthropology depends upon biology, just as biology depends upon chemistry and physics. In making this assumption, I am not privileging one discipline over another. I am just saying that a lower level of explanation must be assumed by each higher-level discipline. For example, to explain the structure and function of organisms, the biologist assumes the existence of molecules out of which organisms are composed. The biologist's job is not to explain the behavior of the elementary molecules (which is the job of the chemist), but rather to explain the behavior of the macromolecules—in particular, RNA and DNA—that are capable of replication, which is to say, of life. As Richard Dawkins and others have ably demonstrated, Darwin's idea of natural selection is all that is necessary to explain the evolution of an immense variety of life forms, given the reality of a mechanism for self-replication.[5]

As biology stands to chemistry, so does anthropology to biology itself. If anthropology has the right to exist as a scientific discipline, it is because it can provide a systematic answer to questions that the biological level of explanation cannot. That such an answer can be provided is of course controversial. In anthropology (as in the social sciences and humanities more generally), the dispute between "culturalists" and scientists is really a dispute about whether anthropology is an interpretive discipline (Geertz 1973) or can be assimilated to the explanatory mechanisms of biology (E. O. Wilson 1978, 1999).

So, how would a biologist explain the origin of representation? In biology, a trait shared by all members of a species can be explained from four logically independent perspectives, namely, those of mechanism, ontogeny, phylogeny, and function.[6] Mechanistic explanations address the causal mechanisms underlying the trait; for example, one can explain language in terms of the neurological, anatomical, and psychological structures necessary to produce speech. Ontogenetic explanations appeal to the genetic and environmental factors that guide the development of the trait in the individual from the embryo to adulthood, for example, in the stages of language acquisition by the child. Phylogenetic explanations trace the trait's evolutionary history by studying its appearance in (fossilized) ancestors. In the particular case of language, such studies are necessarily limited to speculations about the pattern of brain evolution in early hominids, such as *Homo erectus*, as well as to comparisons with other closely related living primates, such as chimpanzees and bonobos. Finally, functional explanation looks at the fitness consequences of the trait for survival and reproduction; in particular, it offers hypotheses about the selection pressures necessary for the appearance and maintenance of the trait in question.

As Robin Dunbar has argued, although these four perspectives are logically independent of one another, no explanation of a particular trait is complete without being considered from all four of them.[7] We can now see that the particular emphasis of the cognitivist model of representation is on mechanistic and ontogenetic explanations. Neuroscience is making rapid advances in studying the structure of the brain and the brain's role in generating higher cognitive functions like language. Cognitive science takes its lead from neuroscience by studying the causal mechanisms involved in perception and conceptual thought. Cognitive science is also interested in ontogeny because by studying the development of the individual, we get some idea of which cognitive structures are more basic and which require greater interaction with the outside (perceptual, social, and cultural) environment in order to develop. In the case of language, for example, it has long been clear that there is a "critical period" for language acquisition, so that both genetic and environmental factors play a crucial role. It is true of course that evolutionary psychology also promises to balance these well-developed areas of research by offering hypotheses concerning the evolutionary origin and function of higher cognitive functions like language.[8] This takes us into the area of phylogenetic and functional explanation. But it is precisely in this area that the theoretical difficulty of an anthropological definition of language emerges most prominently.

The theoretical difficulty (as opposed to the obvious empirical difficulty involved in dealing with hypothetical rather than living specimens) is that one has to commit oneself to a definition of language in order to know what to look for. But this definition in turn depends upon an observation that is not merely empirical but indeed historical, which is to say, implied by the language user's participation in a linguistic community that ultimately extends back to the very first language users. To ignore this historical continuity in the hope of achieving greater objectivity in the definition is illusory, because it is precisely this historical continuity that defines language and differentiates it from the kind of genetically transmitted signal systems used by many other animals. But many are the scientists and their scientifically minded fellow travelers who have decided that language is fundamentally no different than other animal communication systems.[9] It is this assumption that motivates researchers to claim, for example, that human language emerged from the kind of call system used by vervet monkeys.[10]

On the other side of this debate stand the linguists, who for the most part remain committed to the anthropological specificity of language—to the point where, as in the case of Noam Chomsky, they deny that evolutionary theory can hope to explain the origin of language from animal signal systems. For the linguist, language is distinct from the kind of stimulus associations produced by conditioning or instinct. Alarm calls, such as those used by vervet monkeys, therefore do not qualify as evolutionary precursors because we now understand them to have a different structure and function. Whereas human language has a *symbolic* structure and function, animal signal systems have an *indexical* structure and function. More precisely, the referential function of an index is given by the interpreter's prior experience of the contiguous relationship between the indexical sign and its object. This relationship is most often perceptually learned (e.g., by stimulus/stimulus association or conditioning), but it can also be genetically assimilated, so that the perception of the referent will predispose the perceiver to utter the sign prior to any actual learning. Indeed, vervet monkey alarm calls appear to be genetically assimilated (i.e., "hardwired") examples of indexical signs.[11] Symbols, on the other hand, don't work like this. Symbolic reference is not generated by empirical association between perceptual categories (whether learned or innate). Rather, a symbol is capable of generating a referential function even if we have never experienced the object that the symbol refers to. For example, I may never have tasted haggis before, but if it is described to me as "a large spherical sausage made of the liver, heart, and lungs of a sheep, all chopped and mixed with beef or mutton suet and oatmeal and seasoned with onion, cayenne pepper, and other spices" (*Encyclopaedia Britannica Online*), I get a pretty good idea of what haggis is without having the item directly before me where I can see, touch, and taste it. Indeed, when I come across an object that fits this description, I may readily identify it as haggis. Reference has then been produced not by directly associating the word "haggis" with a real haggis, but by producing a "clear and distinct" idea of the formal structure of haggis (i.e., haggis as a semantic category). In other words, reference to the object (i.e., the real haggis) is mediated by a network of other symbolic relationships (i.e., the description of haggis as a sausage made of lamb, oatmeal, onion, cayenne, and so on). Indeed, because symbolic reference seems to function only by combining symbols, we may decide that this combinatory feature is the distinguishing mark of language. Thus, only a system capable of syntax, including clause and phrase structure, qualifies as true language. In this case, representational systems that are symbolic but not syntactic, having a semantics but no well-defined grammar, are merely "protolanguages" or "pidgens."[12]

Like the linguists, I will be assuming that language can be most broadly defined as symbolic representation. For reasons that will become clearer later on, I also assume that symbolic representation implies syntax. I therefore see no need to distinguish so dramatically, as Derek Bickerton does, between protolanguage and language, between symbolic words and complex sentences. I would claim, with Terrence Deacon, that once you have symbolic representation, you inevitably get syntax. Historically speaking, protolanguage inevitably leads to language, because the definition of protolanguage is that reference is generated symbolically, which means associating the sign with other signs in a minimal syntactical system *before* referring this system as a whole to a nonlinguistic object.

So much for the difference between mechanical, ontogenetic, phylogenetic, and functional explanations, and for language as symbolic representation. But what makes an explanation specifically "anthropological"? It counts as such when its broadest level of application is limited to our own species. For example, if we assume that language is not a specifically anthropological phenomenon, but rather a general communication system with equivalents in the animal world, then we are making a biological claim about communication systems in general. Hence we will be inclined to interpret the function of language as we would any other biological trait, namely, in terms of its fitness consequences for the individual or, more precisely, for the individual's genes.

Ultimately, of course, the human world must answer to the biological world. No specifically anthropological category, such as language, is exempt from Darwinian processes of natural selection. But the peculiar difficulty in explaining the origin of a specifically anthropological institution such as language is that its *anthropological* function (as opposed to its more general biological function) cannot be reduced to the biological level of explanation without at once also evacuating it of its specifically anthropological function. Interpreted in terms of its bio-logical function—its fitness consequences—language can only be seen as a more elaborate way of representing and manipulating the outside world. If I can say to you, "Be careful! There's a bear behind that tree," this saves you from having to discover the bear yourself by actually perceiving it with your own senses. Indeed, this view of representation is precisely what motivates ethologists to see language as simply a more advanced signal system that evolved from the kind of alarm calls used by many other animals.[13] I hope it is intuitively obvious how we can explain the origin and evolution of these types of call systems using only the mechanistic and functional explanations implied by natural selection. I will later elaborate more fully on the relationship between learned behavior and innate or genetically assimilated behavior, but for now it is only necessary to understand that the idea of language as a sophisticated signal system for drawing attention to objective features of the world can be quite easily assimilated to Darwinian principles.

What remains less tractable for this model of representation, how-ever, are precisely those elements traditionally studied in the humani-ties, namely, literature, art, and religion. How are we to explain to our proverbial visitor from Mars the function of religious or aesthetic rep-resentations? It is in the interpretation of these forms of symbolic repre-sentation that we can discover no direct causal (genetic) relationship that would explain the fitness consequences of a particular cultural artifact.

Why is the interpretation of literature, art and religion so intrac-table to functionalist and mechanistic biological explanation? Why do we always get the sense that something is missing, for example, when we are told that religious awe emerges in the individual's natural ex-perience of the might and power of the sun[14] or that "human culture is mainly a set of adaptations for courtship"?[15]

I think the reason for this skepticism is our sense that the causal relationship between the perception of worldly objects and their social-symbolic representation in culture is not a simple one-to-one correlation. For example, as Emile Durkheim realized in his criticism of Max Mül-ler, it is more likely that we experience awe toward the sun not because of its natural properties, the monotonous predictability of which will rather make the sun seem all but insignificant, but because of the sun's sym-bolic significance to a community of worshippers.[16] But this just begs the question of why we should not merely perceive the sun, but experience it as symbolically significant, as something worth worshipping collectively.

[handwritten margin notes: "Draws a distinction between ontology/biology + Biology cannibalism" and "Symbolic layer"]

It is this transition—from perception to symbolic representation—that needs to be explained. And it is precisely the functional explanation of this transition that cannot be reduced to purely biological terms. What we are seeking is rather an *anthropological* explanation, which applies only to those who can participate in the process of symbolic representation. Between the immediate perception of the symbolic object and its causal consequences for survival and reproduction lies a more complex representational relation, not to be transcended or reduced on pain of destroying the very anthropological function of the symbolic sign. It follows that an explanation of the symbolic relation must begin not with the reduction or elimination of this representational relation, but with a minimal account of its origin and function, an origin and function that is, furthermore, unique to our species.

To sum up the preliminary argument, I have defined the problem of representation and laid out some key terms. These key terms include: (1) the fourfold distinction among ontogeny, phylogeny, function, and mechanism in biological explanations; (2) the difference between biological and anthropological levels of explanation; and (3) the importance of a theory of representation for specifying higher-level anthropological categories. The assumption I am working with is that a definition of symbolic representation is also a minimal definition of the human and thus the starting point for an anthropology. As corollary of this assumption, such an anthropology, if it is to exist at all, must be distinct from—irreducible to—the explanatory categories of biology. Hence the explanation for symbolic representation must be in the first place a *functional* explanation, one moreover that recognizes the essential, specifically anthropological functions that symbolic representation performs. Such an anthropological hypothesis must be able to explain not merely instrumental uses of representation (e.g., how it enhances the individual's capacity to manipulate the environment), but also sacred and aesthetic uses of representation (e.g., how it constitutes our sense of moral reciprocity).

II. The Cognitive Model of Representation

Any reasonably complete account of representation must sooner or later address the problem of origins. Where do our representations come from, and how are they grounded in the real physical and biological world? In this section, I will look at two answers to this question: one given by Lakoff and Johnson and another, to be discussed at greater length, by Mark Turner.[17] Though the two answers are not identical, they both adhere to the general assumption that understanding the causal relation between basic perception and higher cognitive functions, like language and culture (i.e., symbolic representation), is the best way to answer this question. As will quickly become clear, I think they take too much for granted in their assumption that there is a natural progression (evidenced in ontogenetic development) from basic perceptual categories to their *re*-presentation in language. Most damagingly, the assumption that there is such a progression leads them to reverse the causal order in their account of the origin of symbolic categories. Instead of understanding the construction of symbolic categories like language, ritual, and art as a consequence of a more general symbolizing function, they see symbolic categories as constructed by "emergent metaphors"[18] or "projections"[19] from more basic perceptual and sensory experiences (e.g., tracking the path of a moving object, placing an object in a container, placing one object in front of another, etc.). But in so doing, they omit precisely what is peculiar about symbolic reference, namely, its "displacement" or "decoupling" from the perceptual associations of direct experience. It is the originating process of displacement or decoupling that needs to be explained, not the subsequent recruitment of perceptual and sensory experiences for symbolic purposes.[20]

Let me illustrate the problem of symbolic displacement or decoupling from an example given by Lakoff and Johnson. In their discussion of metaphor, the authors inevitably get to the question of the "grounding problem," that is, how metaphors refer not just to other metaphors, but to the real world as well. [21] To answer this question, they offer the following examples:

> Harry is in the kitchen.
> Harry is in the Elks.
> Harry is in love.[22]

According to Lakoff and Johnson, all three statements use the concept of a container. But in the first, the concept is not metaphoric but "emerges directly from spatial experience" (*MWL* 59) Only the second and third statements are metaphors because they are dependent upon a mapping or projection from the prior *direct experience* of containment. Thus, the idea of containment is perceived in the first case, is mapped onto the idea of a social group in the second, and is mapped onto an emotion in the third.

But this explanation of how metaphors are grounded in the real world is really no explanation because it assumes precisely what is at issue, namely, the difference between a symbolic reference system and a reference system based on perceptual categorization. Thus, in those examples, a predicate refers to an increasingly abstract concept: first a room (the kitchen), then a social group (the Elks), and finally an emotion (love). Lakoff and Johnson appear to think that the fact that they have pointed out that the idea of a container gets steadily more abstract counts as an explanation of how metaphors are grounded. But in the first, crucial example, they fail to explain the difference between directly perceiving Harry in the kitchen and representing the fact that Harry is in the kitchen, for example, by saying "Harry is in the kitchen." By assuming that the essential problem is fundamentally a problem of *individual* cognition rather than collective representation, they take for granted precisely what needs to be explained: namely, the social basis for higher cognitive processes like metaphor. Thus, they reduce the anthropological problem concerning the social basis of language to a cognitive problem concerning the mechanism and ontogeny of symbolic processes in the individual mind. But the problem of the social basis of symbolic representation—of language—is not simply supplemental to the cognitive structure of metaphor. On the contrary, it is the very origin of metaphor itself.

A second answer to the problem of the origin of representation is given by Turner in his study of "the literary mind." Turner begins by making a series of broad and fundamental claims for his three central concepts: narrative, projection, and parable. He proposes, for example, that narrative is "the fundamental instrument of thought," that it is a capacity "indispensable to human cognition generally," and that it is our means of "looking into the future, of predicting, of planning, and of explaining."[23] The same fundamental status is claimed for parable, which arises "inevitably from the nature of our conceptual systems" (*LM* 5). Turner is quite serious about the fundamental cognitive and biological status of narrative, projection, and parable. At one point he even claims that the "motivations for parable are as strong as the motivations for color vision or sentence structure or the ability to hit a distant object with a stone" (*LM* 5).

These are strong claims indeed, but what exactly does Turner mean by narrative, projection, and parable? It turns out that these three concepts are ontogenetically and dialectically related. Narrative is the primitive or originary concept, because once you have the capacity to construct narratives, you can begin to project one narrative onto another. But by understanding one narrative in terms of another, you have not merely narrative, but parable. As a minimal example of parable, Turner (*LM* 6) cites the well-known proverb, "When the cat's away, the mice will play." The parable works by projecting onto a specific situation (e.g., the behavior of a classroom of preschoolers without their teacher) an easily grasped story concerning our knowledge of the relationship between cats and mice. Cats control mice populations; when cats are not around mice proliferate and cause havoc—they "play" just like preschoolers do without their teacher. We have projected one story, the story of the cats and mice, onto another story, the story of preschoolers without their teacher. Hence Turner's hierarchical triad: narrative → projection → parable (*LM* 5–7).

But of course narrative, as Turner realizes, is not itself an atomic form. It depends on yet more basic processes of pattern recognition, including the ability to recognize objects and events. And the most basic patterns, Turner argues, are those perceptual and motor patterns by which we relate to the world around us. Thus, our cognitive processes appear to bottom out at the level of sensorimotor patterns. Turner calls these patterns "image schemas,"[24] such as perceiving milk flowing into a glass; drinking from a glass; recognizing the similarity between one door and another, one chair and another; sitting on a chair; opening a door, and so on. In other words, at the most basic level we form categories of objects and events. By recognizing the similarity between events, we create basic categories of events. Turner argues that these sequences or "small spatial stories" (*LM* 17) are the basic elements of narrative. One could summarize Turner's developmental schema of cognitive categories as follows: image schema → narrative → projection → parable.

It is important to remember that Turner regards this sequence as ontologically given, in the sense that, given our biological and evolutionary past, there is no way we can prevent our cognitive systems from producing narratives and projecting them to produce parables. This ontogenetic or developmental inevitability is no doubt a guiding assumption for research in cognitive science. In a related discussion, for example, it enables Steven Pinker to talk of a "language instinct." Turner's idea of "the literary mind" is motivated by an equivalent faith in the cognitivist and innatist program. The difference is that, where Pinker argues for a

biologically given language competence, Turner argues for a
cally given literary or aesthetic competence. Just as we are all la.
users, so too are we all poets, because we all possess an innately
literary or aesthetic capacity. In this sense, the separation of poetry i.um
everyday language is a historical contingency rather than a cognitive
necessity; the historical division has nothing to do with the cognitive
reality that underpins our literary capabilities. When Turner claims that
our motivation for parable is as strong as our motivation for color vision
and sentence structure, he is putting forth a version of the strong innatist argument. In fact, he appears to go one better than Pinker, because
he believes that language can be more parsimoniously explained as a
product of narrative, projection, and parable (see Turner, *LM* 140–68).

But Turner's innatist argument for the literary mind suffers from
the same problem as that for the linguistic mind: it takes the ontogenetic
situation as paradigmatic of the evolutionary or phylogenetic situation.
The argument for an innate language acquisition device (LAD) is that,
because language emerges inevitably in the normal course of child development, despite the poverty of the available stimulus, it must therefore be an instinct or innate competence, hardwired from the beginning.
In fact, I think that this argument, though mistaken, is actually *more*
plausible than Turner's hypothesis of an innate literary competence. In-
natists, like Steven Pinker and Derek Bickerton, at least recognize that
language is a species-specific trait, whose origin presents a unique challenge to evolutionary theory because there is simply no precedent for it
in the biological record and hence no possibility of generalizing across
species with similar traits. Turner, on the other hand, tends to downplay
the evolutionary anomaly of the literary mind. He obviously believes
that the literary mind is uniquely human (his second chapter is titled
"Human Meaning"). However, in tracing the origin of human literary
capacities to basic perceptual and motor functions, he opens himself to
the charge that the literary mind is in fact not uniquely human but a
universal feature of all creatures equipped with equivalent perceptual
and motor capacities. The crucial "anthropological" question Turner
avoids asking is why the presence of equivalent sensorimotor functions
in many nonhuman species has not led to an equivalent literary or aesthetic capacity.

As I will show in the fourth section of this chapter, this assumption
gets Turner into some hot water when it comes to confronting the evolutionary and anthropological implications of his argument. Now I would

like to comment on an internal difficulty that emerges in the course of his own discussion and reflects the larger anthropological issues that I wish to emphasize.

Turner, like Lakoff and Johnson, implies that what he calls "bodily" or "spatial" stories are likely primary and that more abstract stories about thought and social reality are projections from these basic sensorimotor patterns. Yet, duly cautious and empirical, he suggests that not all the evidence is in yet, so we can't be sure if it is absolutely true. For example, the claim that "abstract thought and reasoning are always grounded ... in spatial and bodily stories," although "not clearly false," is nonetheless "too extreme for the available evidence" (*LM* 51). The most we can assert, Turner concludes, is that such a claim is "plausible" (*LM* 51).

Why does Turner shy away from stating outright that abstract thought is based on the projection of direct sensorimotor experience? What kind of evidence other than that he depends on for his entire analysis—the evidence of our everyday linguistic metaphors—could persuade him that his claim is not merely plausible but true? Why the hesitation?

I think the reason for this hesitation is very significant because it demonstrates the realization that metaphor or projection is not a one-way street from simpler levels of direct, unmediated bodily experience to more complex levels of indirect, symbolically mediated experience, and this fact throws into question Turner's basic assumption that narrative projection is a continuous development from lower neurological processes to higher, more abstract ones. That is, Turner notices that, although most of our expressions do seem to project from spatial or bodily experience to more abstract concepts, projection can also work the other way around. So, for example, if my car fails to start, and I say, "It appears my car has different ideas about whether I make the reception," I am projecting onto the event of the car's not starting a story of disagreement between partners in a dialogue. Rather than projecting "upwards," so to speak, from object to mind (e.g., "My promise to make the reception is now *broken*"), I am projecting "downwards" from mind to object. I am imposing on a physical object (the car) the state of being in which it has a mind capable of ideas and, in particular, of disagreeing with other language-users.

It is important to see exactly what is at issue here. The difficulty lies not in the fact that metaphors work both ways—from body to mind and from mind to body, so to speak—but in the conclusion that, because so many of our metaphors are body- and space-oriented, that therefore metaphor *must itself be describable in terms of the same physical biological process* by which we produce associations between perceptions and motor responses. The conclusion simply does not follow, because what is really at issue is not the presence of visual and manual biases in metaphoric processing, but the origin of metaphor as such. By explaining this origin in terms of more basic sensorimotor functions, Turner interprets the presence of an inherent cognitive bias as sufficient evidence for an account of the origin of a referential process. But it is the anthropological structure and function of this referential process, not the inherent bias toward spatial and bodily reasoning, which needs to be explained.

What is so unique about the referential process of metaphor? Turner, Lakoff, and Johnson locate the uniqueness in the fact of "embodied experience," that is, of having a human body capable of interacting with the outside world. I agree that this is indeed a necessary condition of metaphor, but it is a necessary condition in the same sense that eating, sleeping and reproducing are necessary for metaphor. In other words, it doesn't really address the specific nature of the problem of metaphoric processing. What is in principle one of the strengths of the cognitivist paradigm, namely, its commitment to general scientific categories of explanation, becomes a weakness when the ambition for a general explanation is stretched too far and, in the process, erases precisely what is distinctively human about metaphoric thought.

What, then, is so unique about metaphor, narrative, and other fundamental anthropological categories? I believe that the problem of their origin is really a problem of referential processes in general, particularly, of how words or symbolic signs relate to the world. It is therefore a problem inseparable from the problem of language, which is to say, of symbolic reference generally. To tackle it, we therefore need to rethink the cognitive processes involved in acquiring and maintaining symbolic reference. Buoyed by advances in neuroscience and computer modeling, cognitive science is eager to interpret symbolic referential processes in terms of more basic neurological processes. But I think we need to be more cautious before rushing to draw parallels between symbolic functions and general sensorimotor functions. Until we have appreciated the specific problem of symbolic reference, we are ill positioned to grasp the causal relationships in the evolution of language and the brain.

III. Symbolic Reference

In this section, I will review the reasons why symbolic reference cannot be so easily assimilated to basic perceptual and motor functions. This argument will refer in some detail to Terrence Deacon's *The Symbolic Species* (1997), a wide-ranging discussion of the origin of symbolic representation by a neuroscientist and evolutionary anthropologist.[25]

First, however, a word about terminology. By "symbolic reference" or "symbolic representation" or "symbolic functions," I mean the general semiotic process of interpreting symbolic relationships. In this sense, language is of course symbolic, but so are other specifically human institutions, such as ritual, games, literature, music, and mathematics. In fact, I think that symbolic reference is the general category by which to understand other specifically human phenomena (e.g., language, art, and ritual). Insofar as metaphor (Lakoff and Johnson) and narrative (Turner) are also fundamental human categories (and I believe they are), then they too must be understood as constituted by the process of symbolic reference. The difficulty is that symbolic reference is not an easy category to define. Indeed, according to Deacon, it is an "evolutionary anomaly" that cannot be readily assimilated to presymbolic neural and cognitive precursors.[26]

For Deacon, given this "anomaly," the main problem for a general theory of human cognition lies in describing how you can get from an indexical reference system to a symbolic reference system.[27] This transition cannot be explained exclusively by neurobiology, but requires, in his view, a more global socioecological perspective. Deacon's theory is quite breathtaking in its scope and application. By summarizing the basic theoretical argument, I hope to give some idea of the significance of his anthropological research for students of literature and aesthetics.

The key lies in his model of cognition as fundamentally a process of interpreting increasingly complex layers of reference. In an illuminating application of C. S. Peirce's semiotic categories of icon, index, and symbol, Deacon describes each mode of reference as requiring a different level of cognitive response. Cognition of reference types is hierarchical in that each level implies the presence of the lower levels of reference. Thus, for example, indexical reference is not possible without first being able to recognize objects iconically.

Whereas Peirce originally defined his three categories according to a general semiotic in which icons, indices, and symbols were seen as different aspects of an *already existing* sign system,[28] Deacon in effect anthropologizes Peirce's triadic schema. He argues that iconic and in-dexical representational processes are supported by all nervous systems, irrespective of their size and complexity, but that symbolic representa-tion has evolved in only one species: our own. Deacon's use of Peirce's semiotic categories of icon, index, and symbol may strike some readers as unorthodox.[29] But I think his reinterpretation builds very construc-tively on some of Peirce's basic insights. In summarizing Deacon's basic theory, therefore, I will try to show not its faithfulness to Peirce but how it furthers the debate concerning the origin of specifically human cognitive capacities.

How does Deacon explain iconic and indexical reference? At the most elementary level, iconic reference is equivalent to stimulus gener-alization. It is the default mode of representation, when we recognize the similarity between one stimulus and another. Iconic reference is not given by the inherent similarity between two objects; it is produced by an act of cognition that takes place *before* we even understand that what we have are two distinct objects that resemble one another. "The inter-pretive step that establishes an iconic relationship," Deacon argues, "is essentially prior to this [distinction], and it is something negative, some-thing that we don't do. It is, so to speak, the act of *not* making a dis-tinction" (74). Deacon's point here, which admittedly seems extremely counter-intuitive and certainly not in line with Peirce's original schema, is that iconic reference is the most general reference type available to any creature equipped with a nervous system. In order to make predictions about the world, you need to generalize from particular cases. But in or-der to generalize, you need to have an interpretive system that produces not a distinction between discrete icons—this would assume the pos-sibility of indexical reference—but resemblance itself. Only after the act of *not* making a distinction—of noticing *only* likeness or sameness—can one decide, upon further reflection, that what one is observing is in fact an iconic relationship between two *distinct* objects. From the perspective of indexical reference, iconic reference is thus a failure to observe dif-ference. Like the failure to notice the polar bear blending perfectly into its snow-covered environment, all one sees is white on a background of more white.

Deacon's analysis of iconic reference may seem somewhat idiosyn-cratic. Isn't an icon defined by its resemblance to its object? For example, a portrait of George Bush is iconic because we recognize in the portrait features that we recognize in the real George Bush. But that's precisely the point! What inclines us to see the portrait under a primarily iconic function is the fact that so many features that we see in the real George Bush, we also see in the portrait. Naturally, we also know that the portrait isn't identical with George Bush, but our ability to notice the *difference* between the portrait and the real George Bush is not a function of iconic interpretation itself. It is instead a function of our capacity to bring into correlation *higher levels* of iconic recognition, which we can only bring into focus if capable of distinguishing between sets of icons. In admiring the subject of the portrait, for example, we do not concentrate on the wooden frame, or the dust, or the reflection of the light: all these are examples of iconic recognition that we bracket in our experience of the portrait. We recognize the similarity between this frame and other frames, this wood and other wood, this dust and other dust, this reflection and other reflections, but in appreciating the portrait, we forget about these other features, and concentrate on the likeness between the picture and George Bush.

To see how iconic reference functions at this most basic level, compare Deacon's own example of a camouflaged moth (75), whose wing coloration matches the color of the bark of a tree. A bird scanning the bark for prey will *not* see the moth if it notices *only* the resemblance between the moth and the tree. If the moth moves, or if some flaw in the moth's coloration alerts the bird to the *difference* between the bark and the moth, then the iconic interpretation is broken and the bird is forced to reassess its perception of the moth as just more bark. If the bird is alert, it may see this difference as an *index* of a moth.

This example matches our iconic interpretation of the portrait. Naturally, the latter is more complex because we are dealing with many more variables. To notice the moth, the bird needs to recognize the difference between just two categories: bark and moth. If its iconic interpretation applies to these two categories (bark and moth), then it is fine shape. If it only notices one category (bark), then it is the moth that is in fine shape. The same applies to the portrait. If our iconic interpretation is so general, or so limited, that we only notice the categories of wood, paint, and canvas, then we will see no George Bush in the portrait. If, however, we are attuned to facial recognition, as indeed humans are, then the face will appear immediately. But the fact that we also notice the wood and the canvas means, precisely, that we also know that this is not really George Bush. Our iconic recognition processes stop short of stimulating us to reach out and shake George Bush's hand. (The thrill of seeing lifelike wax figures of celebrities depends largely on the shock value of feeling as if one really were in the presence of someone famous like George Bush.)

Indexical reference builds on iconic reference. In order to pick out the moth against the background of the bark, or to notice the polar bear against its snowy background, one must notice a clue or *index* that points us toward the presence of something other than just more bark or just more snow. If one were to locate the difference between the polar bear and its white background in, for example, its black nose, then one would have an index of this difference. Instead of just seeing more snow (e.g., white, white, white, white . . .), we notice a difference (e.g., white, white, white, not-white . . .). Perhaps after some practice, one might become adept at noticing polar bears, in which case the terrain becomes not just an endless white expanse, but a varied environment with lots of different clues indicating the presence or absence of polar bears (e.g., smells, tracks, movement, startled seabirds, and so on). Indexical reference entails the ability to interpret how one stimulus can *point to* or *indicate* another based on a pattern of predictable co-occurrence between distinct stimuli, where each stimulus is in turn interpreted iconically. Deacon points out that iconic and indexical reference are similar to the more traditional categories of perceptual generalization and learned association.[30] What he wants to preserve in his notion of kinds of reference, however, is the fact that these are essentially representational strategies that increase the predictive or inferential powers of cognitively aware organisms. Icons and indices allow external physical relationships to be represented internally, which in turn allows a creature to adapt more readily to a changing environment. Iconic and indexical processes are thus indispensable features for cognitively based adaptation and evolution.

But if icons and indices are instances of an economy between internal representation and external reality, then it becomes possible for such internal representational processes to become the basis for external communication processes. And, indeed, indexical communication systems abound in nature. The dog's snarl, the peacock's tail, the rabbit's thump—all are examples of communication, where a particular stimulus is associated with a particular behavioral response: aggression in the case of the dog, mating opportunity in the case of the peacock, danger in the case of the rabbit. In fact, some indexical communication systems seem to demonstrate the same level of abstraction that linguists have traditionally reserved for language. For example, vervet monkey calls are indexical signs that have evolved to refer to specific categories of objects, for example, categories of predators, such as leopards, snakes, and eagles. Superficially, vervet alarm calls appear to be equivalent to language, because an arbitrary sign (the call) refers to an object (the particular predator). But, Deacon argues, arbitrariness is not a sufficient condition for symbolic reference. Such a viewpoint fails to grasp the crucial difference between indexical and symbolic reference.

This difference is a consequence of the multilevel hierarchy involved in the move from indexical (and iconic) to symbolic relationships. Just as indexical reference requires the ability to organize lower-level iconic relationships, so symbolic reference requires the ability to organize lower-level indexical and, ultimately, lower-level iconic relationships. But the specific difficulty in moving from index to symbol is that "the added relationship" required by symbols is "not a mere [empirical] correlation" between the sign and its object (78). It bears, rather, on the preexisting formal relationship between signs. A word does not refer directly to an object or referent. Instead, reference is mediated by the word's sense or meaning, which in turn is given by associating the word not with the object, but with other words and other meanings. When we look a word up in the dictionary, we are putting this theory into practice. We understand a new word not by actually gaining physical access to a real-world object or referent, but by associating it with others words, that is, with other meanings. As Deacon notes, the "correspondence between words and objects is a secondary relationship, subordinate to a web of associative relationships of a quite different sort, which even allows us reference to impossible things" (70).

There remains the difficulty, however, of developing a plausible hypothesis for the origin of symbolic reference given the preexisting indexical system. From an originary anthropological perspective, Deacon's interest in Peirce's semiotic categories of icon, index, and symbol focuses on the difference between the last two. In particular, the radically different cognitive strategy required by symbolic reference poses unique challenges to all nonhuman species, including our presymbolic ancestors, whose communication systems are based on indexical reference. The ubiquitous presence of the latter in the animal world suggests that symbolic representation originated as a response to a radically *different* set of selection pressures than those affecting the biological evolution of indexical systems. Only by understanding the different cognitive demands of symbolic reference, Deacon argues, can we appreciate the "evolutionary anomaly" (34) of language and why other species have failed to acquire it.[31]

Reconsider this difference. In order to be interpreted indexically, a sign must be associated either spatially or temporally with its referent. Thus, for a stimulus, such as a red light, to function as a sign and refer to an object or event, such as the dispensing of food from a chute, the stimulus must be habitually associated with the object or event. If the sign/object association is not maintained—if, for example, the red light were to go on over repeated trials without food being dispensed—then it would rapidly be forgotten. Notice that this applies also to "innate" signs, such as vervet monkey calls. If all vervet predators were removed from the monkeys' habitat, then there would be no selection pressure to maintain the indexical link between sign and object; the signs would either disappear altogether or—perhaps more likely—be adapted to another purpose for which there *was* selection pressure.

This is not the case with symbolic reference. We remember the meaning of words independently of the appearance of their worldly referents, which may never be present (as in the case of God). This is because symbolic reference is generated by the relations between words rather than by the association between an individual word and its object. Only by understanding the virtual system *first* can we then agree on its corresponding reference. As Deacon puts it, language implies a fundamental "duality of reference" (83) because it refers only by delaying or negating reference to the world in favor of reference to other words. A word (as all Saussureans know) relates primarily to other words. Reference to a nonlinguistic world is still possible, of course (symbols still depend upon lower-level indexical and iconic processes), but it is now pursued on a different basis than the kind of one-to-one associations that characterize the indexical link between the sign and its object. What distinguishes symbolic from indexical reference is the mediation of the indexical object or referent by the relationships between signs themselves.

It is at this point that a theory of the *origin* of symbolic reference runs into a paradox. If words imply a dual reference, both to other words and to nonlinguistic objects, how can a symbol system ever get off the ground in the first place? Failing other words or symbols to refer to, the only type of reference available to the first word or symbol would still be indexical. How can an indexical sign ever become a symbolic sign?

Deacon's solution to this problem appears complex because he approaches it from many angles, including a central discussion of the evolution and expansion of the prefrontal cortex in hominid evolution. But the basic theory is, I think, quite straightforward. Symbolic reference requires a shift in overall cognitive perspective. This shift occurs when a group of independently learned indexical signs are understood as bearing a relationship not merely to their co-occurring associated objects, but to one another. Perceiving the priority of the sign/sign relationships over individual sign/object relationships is the key to symbolic reference. But how is the shift in perspective produced?

To illustrate this problem, Deacon cites the language-training experiments conducted by the primatologist Sue Savage-Rumbaugh. The experiments were designed to teach two chimpanzees, Austin and Sherman, how to use a true symbolic, as well as an indexical, sign system. To do this, Deacon argues, the chimps would have to refer arbitrary symbols or "lexigrams" (as the experimenters called them) not merely to the associated objects, but to other symbols or lexigrams: the salient test for whether or not the chimps had acquired a symbolic system is whether they could learn "to use lexigrams in combinations (e.g., syntactic relationships)" (84).

In order to test whether the chimps were capable of learning this, the experimenters began with an extremely simple symbol system, involving just two "verbs" (lexigrams glossed as *give* and *pour*) and four "nouns" (lexigrams for different food or drink objects, i.e., *bananas*, *beancake*, *juice*, and *milk*). Thus, the chimps had to learn not merely the one-to-one indexical relationship between each food and drink item and its corresponding lexigram, but also the correct combination of lexigrams. For example, in order to receive juice, the chimp would have to produce the combination "pour juice"; in order to receive banana, "give banana." Sequences such as "juice banana" or "juice pour" or "pour banana" or "give banana beancake" would not be rewarded.

From the naïve chimpanzee perspective, it is not at all obvious which sequences are going to be successful: "Even with this ultra-simple symbol system of six lexigrams and a two-lexigram combinatorial grammar, the chimpanzee is faced with the possibility of sorting among 720 possible ordered sequences $(6*5*4*3*2*1)$ or 64 ordered pairs" (85).[32] Given no previous experience or knowledge of even so simple a grammar, how can the chimpanzee learn which relationships are allowed and which excluded? To solve this problem, the experimenters engaged in an elaborate training program in which the chimps were taught to distinguish between correct and incorrect sequences. In some cases, ingenious devices, such as beeping food dispensers, were introduced to get the chimps to notice when a correct sequence did not produce the desired result (e.g., the chimp requested a banana correctly, but the banana dispenser was empty—the point being to draw attention to the empty dispenser, so that the chimp could modify his request, e.g., by requesting a different food item).[33] Eventually, the chimpanzees were able to produce the correct sequences with the correct reference every time. Had they learned an elementary syntax? Had they learned that reference was a function not of indexical association, but of the relationships between the lexigrams themselves? To test for this, new food and drink objects, together with the corresponding lexigrams, were introduced into the existing system. If the chimps responded by correctly using the new lexigrams, then it could reasonably be assumed that they were using these new lexigrams as components of a symbolic system. Indeed, Austin and Sherman did use the new lexigrams appropriately, with either very few errors or none. What accounts for this remarkable rise in success? What enabled the chimpanzees to go from producing correct combinations only after hundreds or thousands of trials, to producing correct combinations with new lexigrams either immediately or with very few errors?

The answer, Deacon argues, comes from the different learning and memory strategy enabled by the possibility of combining lexigrams in an elementary syntax. Faced with the task of remembering which lexigram combinations are correlated with which features of the objective world, the chimps were presented with a choice: remember the individual correlations between each lexigram and the world (i.e., by essentially treating the lexigrams as additional stimuli to keep track of in an environment filled with competing stimuli) or, alternatively, use the lexigrams themselves as a more economical means to encode their understanding of how not merely to keep track of, but to *predict* regularities in the world. In other words, instead of being distracted by all kinds of irrelevant features of the world (e.g., the positioning of the lexigrams on the keyboard, the previous successful lexigram combination, preferences for a particular kind of food, etc.), the chimps learned that all these variables could be "offloaded" (so to speak) and in their place a systematic set of relationships between the lexigrams themselves could be substituted. These relationships constitute a set of logical rules of inclusion and exclusion, which allow only two-word combinations of a "verb" (requesting a liquid or solid) and a "noun" (naming a particular food object). When new food items are introduced, their lexigrams can be easily integrated into this system. As Deacon puts it, in shifting to a symbolic mode of interpretation, the chimps "had discovered that the relationship that a lexigram has to an object *is a function of* the relationship it has to other lexigrams, not just a function of the correlated appearance of both lexigram and object" (86).

The experiment challenges the notion that language originates by way of a (highly unlikely) genetic mutation. Unlike modern Homo sapiens, Austin and Sherman are *not* genetically predisposed to interpret perceptual or indexical relationships in terms of a more economical system involving minimal symbolic signs. In learning their elementary symbol system, they nonetheless acquired the ability to generalize not simply on the basis of perceptual experience or conditioned association, but on the basis of logical or categorical relationships between symbols or lexigrams. To be sure, the relationship between one lexigram and another is a form of association, in the sense that the chimps were trained to expect a "noun" to be paired with a "verb." But the point is that the associations between lexigrams are *a more abstract and more economical way* of encoding the indexical associations or correlations between real objects and events. The key to symbolic reference lies in the ability to project the relationships existing between easily producible symbols *onto* features of the perceptual world. As Deacon puts it:

> In the minimalistic symbol system first learned by Sherman and Austin, reference to objects is a collective function of relative position within this token-token reference system. No individual lexigram determines its own reference. Reference emerges from the hierarchic relationship *between* these two levels of indexicality, and by virtue of recognizing an abstract correspondence between the system of relationships between objects and the system of relationships between lexigrams. In a sense, it is the recognition of an iconic relationship between two systems of indices. Although indexical reference of tokens to objects is maintained in the transition to symbolic reference, it is no longer determined by or dependent on any physical correlation between token and object. (86–88)

The experiment is illuminating because it highlights the specific learning and memory difficulties presented by conceptualizing symbolic relationships. The ability to see the higher-order combinatorial regularity behind a logically related system of symbols is far from a natural or obvious step for the average chimpanzee. The major initial obstacle for the chimps was simply the bias produced by the indexical learning strategy by which the chimps learned the symbols in the first place. Given enough trials (and these often ran into the thousands), the chimps could learn the individual indexical symbol/object relationships. But the symbol/symbol relationships proved more difficult because understanding the logic behind this higher-order system of relationships required abandoning their previous indexical training. The shift to the symbolic reference strategy occurs when the chimp recognizes that the individual symbol/object references can be more economically learned and remembered when they are understood not as individual isolated associations, but as part of a systematically ordered representation of the object world encoded in the system of symbols or lexigrams.

In other words, the system of symbols is understood to function as a vastly more powerful reference system than the earlier and cumbersome process of acquiring reference to individual objects by personal acquaintance. Most of our social world is in fact dependent on symbolic categories, including institutions like money, marriage, and citizenship. As John Searle explains, these institutions are inseparable from that of language, indeed "constituted" by language, which attributes to objects a *social function* that cannot be explained on the basis of their physical or biological structure. For example, people can live together physically in a relationship that looks like marriage, but marriage alone institutes the requisite rights, duties, and obligations: these do not simply ensue from the fact of physical proximity but enter as a set of symbolic rules that we apply to it. Marriage may even exist without the partners cohabiting. All that is required is obedience to, or acceptance of, the symbolic bond.[34]

That much of our experience of the world is symbolic is not to deny that our cognitive makeup also inherits the bottom-up iconic and indexical representational strategies from our presymbolic past. Inevitably, a large part of our nervous system is dedicated to maintaining these earlier, more basic functions. But we also inherit a virtual or symbolic world—a cultural world—that involves not a bottom-up process, but a top-down one. We impose on the world categories and functions—symbolic meanings—that cannot be explained on the basis of the inherent physical and biological structure of the world and our bodies,[35] but are instead *constituted* by the process of symbolic reference.[36] It follows that a theory of symbolic culture must begin by explaining the origin of symbolic reference, which is to say, of language.

This conflict between top-down symbolic processes and bottom-up indexical and iconic ones points to a central difficulty for explanations of human cognition. The learning difficulties experienced by Austin and Sherman in their acquisition of a very rudimentary symbol system suggests not merely that chimpanzees aren't naturally equipped to learn language, but that our own cognitive evolution must have been confronted with a similar struggle—one furthermore in which we did not have the advantage of outside support from eager experimenters! It follows that cognitive science must sort out the tangled causal relations between an ontology based on the symbolic categories of language—and, I would add, culture—and those provided by neurobiology. And indeed, Deacon emphasizes this predicament:

> If we keep in mind that primate brains very much like our own have been around for tens of millions of years and that the mammal brain plan which our brain follows has probably been around for over 100 million years, it becomes evident that the logic of language is probably highly constrained to fit an ape brain logic. Though breaking up language analytically into such complementary domains as syntax and semantics, noun and verb, production and comprehension, can provide useful categories for the linguist, and breaking it up according to sensory and motor function seems easier from a global neuronal viewpoint, we should not expect that the brain's handling of language follows the logic of either of these categorical distinctions. The patterns we observe probably reflect, in a very indirect sort of way, the processing problems produced by mapping a symbolic reference system encoded in a serially presented modality onto the processing logic of an ape brain. (298)

The consequences of this dichotomy between basic sensorimotor processes and higher-order symbolic ones are significant. Failure to recognize it leads to a wrongheaded scientism, on the one hand, or to airy spirit mongering, on the other. Certainly, one can sympathize with Turner when he argues for a genuine *rapprochement* between cognitive science and literary studies. And yet his own attempt to create such a cognitive poetics reveals why such attempts will remain at best incomplete, and at worst simply misguided, if they do not absorb the central lesson that symbolic processes cannot be sufficiently explained on the basis of their underlying neural-cognitive processes. What is needed is not just a poetics inflected by cognitive science, but a cognitive anthropology.

IV. Toward a Cognitive Anthropology

In this section, I will explain why the cognitive model of representation, as elaborated by Turner and by Lakoff and Johnson, is inadequate by juxtaposing it with Deacon's idea of symbolic reference. More precisely, I will argue that it is the *evolutionary anomaly* of symbolic reference that the cognitive model overlooks in its account of representation. By assuming that such symbolic categories as narrative[37] and metaphor are selected for, just like any other biologically useful sensorimotor function, the cognitivists confuse specifically anthropological with more universal biological categories. In their enthusiasm for cognitive science, they see the origin of institutions like literature and art in the deep structures of the hominid mind. But this move from the institutional structure of social reality to the innate mechanisms of the mind seems premature at best.

The notion that the cognitive and neurological sciences can provide a sufficient account of the origin of symbolic processes depends on the mistaken assumption that symbolic reference is a genetically assimilable trait.[38] Whereas indexical signals, such as vervet monkey calls, possess the long-term referential stability that allows for genetic assimilation, so that over the course of many generations these calls become innate, symbolic reference is defined by the fundamentally open-ended nature of its reference. What characterizes the symbol is its relationship to other symbols. The sign's symbolic reference—its meaning—is thus essentially "parabolic,"[39] dependent upon the relations or "projections" within the entire network of symbols. When a new meaning is introduced into the system, it is always on the basis of the existing network of relations, from which the new meaning is "projected." But the socially constructed nature of the symbol system, that is, the fact that for a sign to be understood its meaning must be accepted by other symbol users, prohibits the genetic assimilation of symbolic reference. Meaning is essentially unstable because it depends upon a symbol-using community.

The acquisition of symbolic reference is thus not an inevitable outcome of the genotype. It is possible only on the basis of symbolic interaction with a community of symbol users. This, more than anything else, points to the central evolutionary problem of language origin: what "makes symbolic associations so difficult to learn, also makes them *impossible to assimilate genetically*" (Deacon 332). Or, as the cognitive psychologist Merlin Donald says: "Single brains simply do not invent languages or symbols, and in isolation do not appear to have the capacity to do so."[40]

In anthropological terms, this impossibility of genetic assimilation rules out a smooth and gradual transition from iconic and indexical to symbolic reference. But this is exactly what Turner assumes in his study of the literary mind. By reducing symbolic processes to cognitive processes and—ultimately—to brain processes, Turner manages to eliminate from his ontology all anthropology. In effect, Turner argues that symbolic thought is "nothing but" patterns of mapping in the brain.[41] He believes that the brain represents concepts fuzzily, that is, in more-or-less terms depending on the number and strength of the neuronal connections that are stimulated during consciousness. Instead of our concepts having clear and distinct boundaries,[42] they constantly grade into one another. Thus, just as the color red shades gradually into orange, so that we see not one red but a gradation of reds as we move along the color spectrum, so too our concepts merge together to create new concepts or "conceptual blends."

But in this Turner has confused the symbolic map with the neurological territory. No doubt, as Deacon's research demonstrates, it is implausible to expect a neat one-to-one mapping between the macrostructures of linguistic function (e.g., semantics and syntax) and the microstructures of neural processing.[43] But nor should we therefore conclude that the anthropological macrostructures of symbolic reference reduce to the cognitive microstructures of neural processing. It may well be that, in terms of neuronal processes, meaning is far from static, and no doubt word meaning is differently represented in different brains, as Deacon's research suggests. But this does not mean that at the *symbolic level* our concepts lack categorical boundaries. It all depends on how one understands the origin and function of symbolic categories.

As I have argued, symbolic categories have a specifically anthropological origin and function, irreducible to the basic categories presupposed by a cognitive science grounded in the biological functioning of the brain. From the perspective of such a cognitive science, categorization can be explained in terms of simple iconic and indexical recognition processes, which require no more than a functioning nervous system. Cognitively speaking, the capacity to differentiate perceptual experiences at the iconic level implies the ability to interpret perceptual experience indexically, categorizing sensory experience in such a manner that new experiences may be anticipated and thus acted upon. In this sense, icons function not only as icons of themselves but also as indices of more complex iconically differentiated patterns. In recognizing smoke, for example, one refers this experience not merely to past icons of smoke but to a whole sequence of iconic representations including other icons for smoke and for fire; it is the memory of this overall pattern that enables an instance of smoke to function as an index for fire. But understanding the origin and function of iconic and indexical referential processes will not help us explain the origin and function of symbolic reference. This is the error Turner makes in his attempt to explain the origin of "human meaning" in terms of the structure and function of the brain. The meaning of the symbol is a social or collective imposition that is not based on the intrinsic features of the individual brain, the sign, or the object signified.

It is important to recognize this distinction because the whole question of the origin and function of social (i.e., anthropological) categories depends upon it. If we understand social categories to originate in the individual mind, in the self's internal representation of the external environment, then we may assume that social categories are indeed merely "abstract" or "metaphoric" projections of what the individual can perceive independently of what anybody else can perceive.[44] The problem then becomes how *my* representation of a particular category can correspond to *your* representation of it. Cognitive science tends to assume that this problem is explained by the species-wide uniformity of ontogenetic development. The interaction of genetic and environmental factors so constrain us all that there can be no significant difference between the kinds of categories each individual is able to perceive and thus represent symbolically. I do not doubt that, at the perceptual level, we do indeed make more or less the same distinctions and categorizations. What I disagree with is the implication that symbolic representation emerges naturally or gradually from perceptual experience. The imposition or "projection"[45] of symbolic meaning onto directly perceivable objects or referents is a socially mediated activity, and as such it cannot be explained purely on the basis of individual cognitive processes. Without a model for the collective or social function of symbolic reference, we cannot understand the origin and evolution of human cognition.

In fact, social anthropologists have long recognized that social categories, such as kinship relations, function independently of the real biological relationships on which they are imposed.[46] Nonhuman primates can doubtless categorize immediate kin, but the imposition of a kinship system requires more than higher perceptual abilities and group living. Without language (or symbolic reference) it would be impossible to turn the ad hoc representations of the perceptual system into a rule-governed system. As many anthropologists have noted, the function of kinship systems is to *constitute* or *define* social categories in order to regulate behavior in a context that transcends mere indexical or perceptual proximity.[47] A dominant male baboon can maintain his monopoly of the females only by physically fending off other males, including his own male offspring. In the human case, the institution of the incest taboo and—derivatively—of out-group marriage accomplishes the same function, but only given the capacity for symbolic representation. Thus, in order to explain the incest taboo and the system of differences on which the kinship system rests, we must first explain the origin of language and the symbolic differences thus generated: between wife and mother, or husband and son, for example.[48] Failure to recognize this boundary can be disastrous for the individual, as Oedipus's tragedy of unknowing transgression illustrates. Knowing how this difference is instantiated in the brain does not explain its social function, which, I would argue, stands at the origin of the distinction.[49] I will return to this point in the final part of my argument.

Why does Turner make this error of conflating the social function of representation with the tendency to generalize on the basis of particular sensorimotor categories? Why does he reduce symbolic to cognitive and, ultimately, to neurological categories? Turner commits a variety of what Searle, in his critique of materialism, calls the identity error, namely, the belief that intentional (i.e., symbolically represented) states are *nothing but* neurobiological events.[50] In order to understand a particular word, it is of course necessary for its meaning to be represented in, and thus caused by, my brain. But the mere fact that neuronal processes cause our conscious experience of symbolic meaning does not mean that our experience of symbolic meaning is *identical* to these neural processes. Another way of putting this is to say that meaning is not reducible to brain processes because meaning—symbolic reference—is a collective or social reality irreducible to any individual brain state.[51] In arguing for such a reduction, Turner leaves out precisely what makes metaphoric projection—"parable"—possible: the mediation of individual experience by the collectively imposed and collectively shared sign. This is also why Deacon can declare that symbolic reference is genetically *in*assimilable. In the fundamental case of sacred or totemic prohibitions, for example, categorical interdiction of an indexically perceivable object is a symbolic imposition possible only because such an interdiction is accepted by each member of the symbol-using community. How this symbolic associa- tion is made in the brain is secondary to the public or *scenic* nature of the interdiction itself. By tracing the origin of the symbol back to the brain, and not to such a collective scene, Turner foregoes the very possibility of explaining the uniqueness of human cognition. Yet he continues to assert, quite paradoxically, that his account shows what is unique about human thought.[52]

How are we to explain this paradoxical situation in which a pu- tatively "anthropological" understanding of human cognition succeeds only by eliminating all trace of anthropology from its basic ontology? To answer this question, we need to examine a parallel "hopeful mon- ster"[53] strategy from linguistics. Linguists have long been impressed by the universality of certain features of language,[54] which allegedly correspond to universal features of the brain. The strong innatist hy- pothesis for a language organ or universal grammar is a consequence of this kind of reasoning. Turner does not believe in a language organ, but his argument for the innate existence of his basic concepts of narrative, projection, and parable is motivated by a similar projection of symbolic structures onto brain structures. In this sense, he is a victim of his own metaphor for human cognition, namely, "parable": as Turner explains, it comes from the Greek, *paraballein*, meaning "the tossing or projection of one thing alongside another" (*LM* 7). It is not that Turner is wrong about the dominance of visual and manual metaphors in our thinking. He is just wrong to see this dominance as an explanation for the origin and function of symbolic reference.

It is in fact quite unsurprising that preexisting sensorimotor patterns should be co-opted by symbolic functions. Metaphor is essentially a process of recognizing the similarity between different domains of *sym- bolically mediated* experience. For example, in perceiving the similarity between a laser beam and a slapshot by Wayne Gretzky, I might say, "Gretzky scored with a laser in the final minute." At the linguistic level, metaphor occurs as a substitution of the word *slapshot* with *laser*. Note that I cannot substitute just any word. I cannot say, "He scored with a house in the final minute." The key to metaphor, as David Lodge notes, is the bringing together of similarities with the "awareness of *difference*."[55] At the presymbolic level, we can of course make associations on the basis of perceptual similarities. As I have already explained, such associations are based on indexical and iconic reference, and they enhance the predictive powers of all cognitively aware organisms. With the origin of symbolic reference, however, the possibilities for the association of perceived similarities is vastly increased to include our generalizing from totally distinct perceptual experiences. This form of generalization is quite distinct from stimulus generalization and indexical association. As Deacon argues, it is really a form of "logical or categorical generalization" (88) because what mediates our sense of the similarity between two disparate experiences is not a perceptual association but a symbolic association between different paradigmatic (i.e., semantic) or syntagmatic (i.e., syntactic) possibilities. In metaphor, the association is paradigmatic; a word is substituted for another with similar semantic features. For example, if I say, "His lecture ignited the room," I am projecting the experience of fire onto a completely different experience, namely, a thrilling lecture. It is tempting to see this association as an example of stimulus generalization, based on the similarity between our experience of fire and of a stimulating lecture. But what fire and lectures share in common is not any physical property, but the fact that they can be referred to *symbolically*. It is the massive leap in associative possibilities enabled by symbolic reference that allows us to draw a metaphoric association between vastly different perceptual experiences.

Deacon notes that metaphor can be traced to the posterior cortical regions of the brain. This should not surprise us, he suggests, because "associations cued by attention to common perceptual features are analogous to perceptual recognition processes and so should recruit the function of the corresponding posterior cortical regions" (306). In other words, metaphor is a species of symbolic reference that relies heavily on similarity. In constructing a metaphor, we recognize a semantic or paradigmatic similarity between two different words. At the symbolic level, the capacity for recognizing common features between otherwise disparate perceptions is vastly increased, because we are now predisposed to interpret the world in terms of symbolic, rather than iconic and indexical, relationships. When Hamlet tells Polonius that a cloud looks like a camel, or a weasel, or a whale, he is putting iconic recognition processes to a highly abstracted symbolic use. Only humans could make such abstract use of iconic processes because only humans have evolved the ability to think symbolically.

Language seizes on the metaphoric possibilities offered by our presymbolic visual and manipulative biases. But from the latter's ubiquity, we should not conclude that they are themselves the source of our capacity to think symbolically. What remains unexplained in Turner's account is why prelinguistic cognitive modes need to be represented symbolically.

It should be evident that this is the same criticism I made earlier of Lakoff and Johnson (see section 2). There I suggested that the problem with their account is that they pursue the origin of metaphor solely from within the explanatory framework of ontogenetic development. Their discovery of systematic biases toward spatial and bodily metaphor in linguistic usage is understood as reflecting deep biases in psychological and cognitive development. But the developmental perspective cannot address the question of the origin of metaphor. All empirical study of our metaphoric biases already assumes the process of metaphoric substitution, which is to say, ultimately, the origin of language as symbolic reference.[56] And the simplest proof of this need for a hypothesis of anthropological origin is that language is not invented by children but inherited from adult language users.

The same critique applies to Turner. From the evolutionary and anthropological perspective, his suggestion that story, projection, and parable provide "a cognitive basis from which language can originate" (*LM* 168) merely begs the question. We cannot invoke concepts like story, projection, and parable, because these concepts are precisely what need to be explained since they are all instances of symbolic processes. Turner posits these symbolic processes as ontologically independent of symbolic reference and then derives the fact of symbolic reference from them. This is exactly what Lakoff and Johnson did to explain the origin of metaphor.[57] In each of these accounts, symbolic reference is assumed but not explained.

As I have already pointed out, Turner makes strong biological claims for his three categories of narrative, projection, and parable. These concepts, he argues, are fundamental in the sense that they evolve biologically as mental features of the brain. Hence his claim that they are selected for, just like color vision and object recognition.[58] I have argued, on the other hand, that it is impossible for narrative *as a symbolic process* to be genetically assimilated along Baldwinian lines.

But what about Turner's more basic claim that narrative is simply an adaptive feature of perceptual and motor processing? Isn't this a feature that can be genetically assimilated? My answer is that these more basic sensorimotor functions are certainly part of our biological inheritance, but then we are not talking about human narrative anymore. Instead, we are talking about basic sensorimotor functions. These are interesting in their own right, but they must not be confused with narrative or metaphor or any other symbolic process.

The distressing thing about Turner's analysis is that he oscillates, apparently without realizing it, between two versions of narrative that are entirely incompatible.[59] On the one hand, narrative is uniquely human; on the other, it is nothing but basic perceptual and motor patterning. One of his examples of a story is throwing a rock (*LM* 17). The brain's ability to process this "narrative" enables us to duck when we see someone aim to throw an object at us, because we interpret the raised arm as an *index* of the entire sequence of throwing. It is of course easy to see how such behavior is adaptive and so could lead to an innate competence for evasive action (e.g., blinking, flinching, and so on). But here is the conundrum: we duck when we see a raised arm, but so does a monkey or a bird or a dog. This is not a form of projection in the specific "literary" sense that Turner discusses in the rest of his book. It is a form of pattern completion or inference that, as Deacon explains, requires no higher complexity than indexical reference, and indexical reference is supported by all nervous systems, not just our own.

Turner evidently wants to have his cake and eat it too. If his concepts of narrative, projection, and parable are truly such elementary cognitive processes, like color vision and object recognition, then we share them with many other species. But if that is the case, then narrative—to take only his most basic concept—is not uniquely human, and his claim that cognitive science stands at the center of the human sciences must be taken with a grain of salt. In his optimism for the cognitive paradigm, Turner paradoxically erases from his discussion precisely what is human about narrative.

What, then, is to be learned from Turner's study of the literary mind? Turner's most suggestive and illuminating discussions take place when he analyzes our everyday cultural metaphors and blends. These analyses stand on their own, independently of the wider and more dubious ontological claims he makes about the origin of our literary processes in general. As I have sought to emphasize, his claim that narrative, projection and parable are independent of language—of symbolic thinking—is deeply mistaken. Given his schema, the really crucial element is projection. But what Turner means by this concept is explained, far more adequately, I think, by Deacon's theory of symbolic reference. Projection is the symbolic capacity to think in terms of symbol/symbol relationships independently of their symbol/object associations, on which, of course, together with their more basic iconic relations, they nonetheless ultimately depend. Naturally, we can project concepts independently of language; we do not have to speak out loud or even internally in order to make symbolic associations. But we cannot make these virtual associations independently of symbolic reference. When I use a map to find my way from King's Cross to Covent Garden, I am making symbolic associations, without speaking any natural language. Turner's idea of the blended space,[60] in which already existing concepts are combined to generate new meanings, is thus itself a metaphor for this symbolic world—which is to say ultimately for the origin of language in the broad anthropological sense. Symbols are indeed "nothing but" metaphors, if by metaphor we mean simply the fact that words are necessarily implicated in a network of relations with other words. In the final analysis, word-meaning is nothing but projection, because in order to refer symbolically a word must be projected onto a separate mental space where it can be thought independently of the object-world to which it nonetheless ultimately refers.

We can better appreciate Turner's analyses of language once we get past the cognitive science to the anthropological reality to which his analyses ultimately refer. The moment of specifically human cognition occurs when a particular image or story is mapped or projected from one context to a different context, as when we compare the passage of time to a flowing river, or a courageous man to a lion. As Turner implies, our concepts of the world are essentially poetic or creative because the construction of these concepts is mediated by a symbolic system that projects from a vast storehouse of symbolic associations. But the symbolic system itself is not simply an outgrowth of our more basic sensory and motor systems. Symbolic reference is a projection produced in the first place collectively; only if a group of symbol users—the minimal linguistic community—accepts the reference of the sign can symbolic projection exist. Ritual is designed to maintain the public status of individual (sacred) signs. The inflexibility of ritual is a recognition of the fact that these signs are fragile precisely because they do not possess the concrete predictability informing our direct, nonsymbolic sensorimotor experience of the world. Religious icons and stereotypically performed rituals are concrete historical indices of a world that is, in the final analysis, only available symbolically.

V. The Anthropological Origin of Symbolic Reference

Thus far, I have argued that symbolic reference is the key to understanding the difference of human from animal cognition. Theories that explain symbolic reference as evolving gradually from more basic cognitive capacities, such as perceptual association and categorization, are doomed to failure because these basic capacities are all explainable on the basis of a simpler model of representation—indexical reference—than the symbolic. From the originary perspective, the transition from index to symbol cannot be regarded as an inevitable or highly predictable consequence of ontogenetic development, for the simple reason that at the origin no such model of ontogeny can be presumed. It is rather *the origin of symbolic reference itself* that acts as the major selection pressure on the evolution of the genotype and its phenotypic effects in ontogeny. Only after a long period of brain-language coevolution can we assume the stabilization or "adaptation" of the human genotype for symbolic functions. This significantly changes the way we pose the question. Instead of asking, "What presymbolic cognitive mechanisms are adapted for symbolic functions?" we must ask, "What indispensable anthropological function does symbolic reference perform that has pushed it to its current status as a universal feature of our species?"

Let me emphasize this last point. I am saying that specifically human cognitive functions, like metaphor and narrative, are a *consequence* of the capacity for symbolic reference Simpler cognitive functions, like perceptual inference and basic categorization, must be understood as co-opted by this qualitatively different, symbolizing function. But if this is the case, how do we explain the origin of the symbolizing function? It appears that the theory must be based on a paradox: I must be claiming that symbolic reference is only explainable in terms of itself.

This is indeed my claim, and this is also the reason why we require an anthropological hypothesis for the origin of symbolic representation, instead of locating it in underlying cognitive and neural mechanisms.

As Deacon argues, symbolic reference is not something intrinsic to the brain but a peculiarity of the way humans interpret their relationship, both to one another and to the world in general (one might view the former as the minimal anthropological or ethical relation and the latter as the maximal cosmological or sacred relation). It follows that a *minimally sufficient* explanation of symbolic reference must be a functional one. And the minimal function of symbolic reference is, quite simply, symbolizing.

A less parsimonious way of putting this is to say that symbolic reference assumes intentionality: the capacity to attribute intentional mental states not only to other similar beings (e.g., other humans), but also to objects (e.g., words on the page, totems, sacred animals and objects, etc.). But in order to attribute intentionality, you need to have something to think with, that is, signs or tokens that have meaning or symbolic value attributed to them. In other words, you need to have language, a system of signs whose relationships are symbolically defined, rather than learned by indexical association. It follows that ritual (i.e., the interdiction of worldly objects though their sacralization) assumes a symbolizing function. Ritual is an elementary or primitive form of language.

Having intentional mental states entails in turn the potential to influence evolution in an unprecedented manner. Just as a dog-breeder intentionally selects for certain characteristics that will enhance the usefulness of dogs for particular tasks (e.g., hunting or sheepherding or sled pulling), so symbolic reference selects for symbolizing abilities and imposes its own selection pressures on the brain. It is for this reason that the mechanism of natural selection (i.e., the replication of "selfish" genes) cannot explain the emergence of symbolic representation. The symbolic function is instead the originating factor in a *co*evolutionary process involving human culture, on the one hand, and human biology, on the other. Within this coevolutionary process, culture can only be explained in anthropological-functional terms, geared to the use to which symbolic reference strategies are put.

Note that I am not denying that symbolic reference requires more elementary cognitive and neurological processes, which are themselves explainable as biologically evolved adaptations. Rather, I am saying that the origin of symbolic reference can only be grasped in terms of a hypothesis of its underlying function, which alone can explain how the adaptation for language (the "language instinct") got to be there in the first place. Obviously, an increasing reliance on the symbolizing function exerts a strong selection pressure on brains to *adapt to* this function. But the adaptation itself does not explain the function. Furthermore, once this coevolutionary process has been driven to stabilization—to the point where further modifications at the genetic level are no longer optimal—we are still left with the need to explain the originating process that led to this genetic adaptation. Genetic adaptation for symbolic abilities does not lead to a stasis in the overall system. On the contrary, symbolic reference contains within itself its own generative dynamic. Thus, it evolves not only in parallel to its biological and neurological substrate, but indeed far outpaces it in its representational and, consequently, in its adaptive capacities. With the origin of symbolic reference, there emerges the possibility for a new (i.e., nongenetic) kind of information transmission: the transmission of culture.

To sum up, cultural evolution is the consequence of intentional actions. The very first symbolic act must have been intentionally performed. It had a symbolic function and was performed only because it had that function. A hypothesis for the origin of symbolic representation must therefore begin with an account of its function. Since this function is specific to one species—Homo sapiens—it must also be uniquely anthropological. Thus, in order to explain the transition from index to symbol, we need a hypothesis for the anthropological function of symbolic representation.

Deacon himself—perhaps surprisingly for an empirical scientist—seems quite happy to admit the need for such a speculative "originary" hypothesis. In the third and final part of his wide-ranging argument, he answers the functional question by hypothesizing that the symbolic sign originates in response to the peculiar ecological predicament of our meat-eating and group-living ancestors. In particular, the conflict between increasing group size, required to exploit the hunting possibilities of the open savanna, and the need for groups of male hunters to ensure their paternal certainty, so that they won't support someone else's off-spring, is solved by the introduction of the symbolic bond of marriage. The crux of his argument is that the symbolic sign allows a relationship to be constructed that can function independently of the physical proximity needed for indexical sign/object associations. The symbolic bond of marriage is in effect a promise on the part of the individual vis-à-vis the entire group to sacrifice the possibility of unlimited promiscuity (which requires sheer physical dominance over competitors) for the more reciprocal or "moral" situation of a socially sanctioned marriage.[61]

This kind of "social contract" theory is of course not new. Beginning with Thomas Hobbes, philosophers have frequently speculated on the origin of social obligations from the "state of nature."[62] What distinguishes Deacon's account from thinkers like Hobbes and Jean-Jacques Rousseau,[63] however, is his attempt to situate the origin of the social contract in the origin of language. The potential for symbolic representation is immanent in the mutually contradictory pressures of increasing group size and regulating the conflict between males that such an increase inevitably leads to. We may remain skeptical of such a scenario,[64] but we must remember that this is all that can be expected of any evolutionary explanation, always formulated after the fact.

In the comparative context of evolutionary biology, however, the case of the origin of symbolic functions is unique, because the origin can only be approached from the "emic" perspective of symbol users interpreting the behavior of other (hypothetical) symbol users. There is no *outside* comparative perspective from which to measure the functional and evolutionary success of symbols. Comparison of similar traits across different species is of course the basis of evolutionary biology, but such a comparative method is insufficient for a hypothesis of the anthropological function of symbolic reference. Instead, all confirmatory evidence must be *anthropological*, that is, intrinsic to the cultural and historical record of humans since the first moment of symbol use. Competing hypotheses can only be accepted or rejected on the basis of their power to explain this cultural record more or less satisfactorily.

This is in fact no more than has traditionally been conceived for humanistic study, which begins by interpreting texts rather than the objects of unmediated experience. But in contemporary cultural anthropology, as in the humanities in general, the emic status of symbolic reference (i.e., the fact that any theory of language origin must inevitably assume the very categories it seeks to explain) has tended to produce the pessimistic view that the question of language origin is unanswerable.[65] Paradoxically, this is the same conclusion reached by impeccably empirical scientists, though for radically different reasons. The scientists have no difficulty with representation; it is rather the excessive burden posed by hypothesizing an unfalsifiable event or moment of origin that offends their idea of a legitimate scientific enterprise.

To the scientists, one need only point out that speculative hypotheses are integral to any advance in scientific understanding. As Marvin Harris has pointed out, the insistence on the primacy of data collection, to the neglect of theoretical speculation, does not lead to scientific advancement. To the pessimists in contemporary cultural theory, the idea of a positive solution to the problem of representation is less likely to be welcome, if only because global theories of cultural origin and evolution tend to be associated with the Darwinian excesses of nineteenth-century anthropology, which is in turn explained as a consequence of nationalism and imperialism.[66]

I think this dual dismissal of the origin of human linguistic and cultural capacities exposes a fundamental contradiction in the nature of anthropological research that nonetheless points us in the direction of a synthesis. This synthesis, however, is unlikely to come from the sciences, though Deacon clearly comes very close to extending a hand to humanistic inquiry in his recognition that the human brain is selected for symbolic reference, rather than the other way around.[67] His coevolutionary argument puts language and culture at the forefront of biological anthropology. What remains to be done is to understand the origin of language and culture in terms of a minimal hypothesis that can at the same time form the basis for the interpretation of historically significant works of culture and literature.

The latter is of course the bread and butter of students in the humanities. And the humanities, in contrast to the sciences, have always been receptive to empirically unfalsifiable but anthropologically suggestive ideas (witness the dominance of Freud). The success of deconstruction lies largely in its idea of representation as a deferral of the immediate possibility of falsification; symbolic reference succeeds only by deferring its relationship to the world in favor of its relationship to other signs. This is an intuitively attractive idea to the literary critic because it confirms our experience of reading fictional texts. But the notion of deferral, if it is to be more than the source of a philosophical critique of logocentrism, must be grounded in the anthropological reality that is our capacity for language. And this capacity, I have argued, is not a function of the brain, but of the relationship between brains, signs, and the world. The capacity to interpret the sign symbolically is indeed the condition of human cognition. It remains only to minimize this assumption by providing a plausible context for the origin of the symbolic function.

There are, however, some specific constraints on a hypothesis of origin, beyond its plausibility and explanatory power for the interpretation of particular cultural and literary texts. In particular, the hypothesis must explain how the first "originary" sign was not a mere index but a symbol. It must explain, in short, the "paradox" of representing worldly objects via fictional or narrative signs.[68] The first symbol had to be understood already as a *metaphor* or *narrative projection* of its object, hence as qualitatively distinct from any previously given indexical sign of the object. The referent of the first sign would be an instance of what Durkheim called the sacred.[69] Henceforth the central object is understood only via the collective imposition of a metaphor designating its sacrality. This essentially negative or interdictive relationship makes the symbolic relationship between sign and object impossible to grasp indexically.

Is fiction or narrative really a consequence of ethical or religious interdiction? Is our remarkable facility with symbols a consequence of the deferral of sensorimotor or indexical response? Is the origin of symbolic reference essentially a process of negation, which is to say, of nascent irony when we represent the opposite of what can be indexically inferred? From the perspective of iconic and indexical reference, the major obstacle to learning symbols is simply their counter-intuitiveness. Why indeed try to indicate one thing by demonstrating its opposite? What explains the emergence of this type of reference?

Surveying the empirical evidence, Deacon argues that the dramatic expansion of the prefrontal cortex evident in the hominid fossil record from (roughly) late *Australopithecus* to archaic Homo sapiens is a result of selection for symbolic reference. The key to the prefrontal cortex, he argues, is that it functions as a mediator between direct sensory and motor functions of the brain. In particular, the prefrontal cortex is active in inhibiting "the tendency to act on simple correlative stimulus relationships," thereby increasing the ability to sample "alternative higher order sequential or hierarchic associations" (265). The expansion of this particular area of the brain in human evolution suggests selection for the peculiar memory and learning requirements of symbolic thought.

Experiments with chimpanzees and other nonhuman primates have illustrated the general significance of the prefrontal cortex for overriding or inhibiting salient stimulus/stimulus and stimulus/response relationships in order to generate higher-order indexical associations. In one experiment cited by Deacon, food was placed in multiple wells while a monkey watched. The monkey was then allowed to retrieve the food.[70] In the normal course of things, the monkey won't sample the same well twice. Once the food is removed, it moves on to the next well. But

prefrontally damaged monkeys fail to sample efficiently; they persever-
ate, returning to the same well repeatedly, even after the food has been
retrieved.

Deacon suggests such experiments indicate the role of the prefrontal
cortex in generating higher-order indexical associations. In the case of
the perseverating monkey, prefrontal damage prevents the animal from
overriding the first rewarding stimulus in order to sample another well.
It is as if the monkey cannot divorce the original stimulus (the well)
from the motor response (the act of sampling the well). In the normal
case, the original stimulus is of course remembered, but precisely the
original context is now understood as indicating the *absence* of food. The
ability to negate the original indexical relationship is, Deacon suggests,
a crucial function of the prefrontal cortex.

These experiments give us some hints about the problem confronting
a species that makes the leap from indexical to symbolic representation.
The ability to work with highly abstract associations independently of
immediately salient stimuli is the distinctive mark of symbolic thought.
(Think, for example, of the ability to read a novel in a busy airport, or to
rehearse in one's mind the main points of a lecture while driving a car,
or to picture the perfect swan dive at the top of the five-meter diving
platform.) The ease with which we do these things makes it difficult for
us to grasp the challenge it presents to other species. But this is precisely
the challenge that confronted our remote ancestors who originally made
this leap from index to symbol. What peculiar circumstances could have
led to such an event?

One particular experiment cited by Deacon vividly illustrates the
paradoxical conditions necessary for symbolic reference to get off the
ground. In the first stage of the experiment, chimpanzees were required
to choose between two unequal piles of candy. Not surprisingly, they
always chose the larger pile. The experiment was then complicated when
the selected pile was given not to the chimpanzee who chose it, but to
another chimpanzee. Despite repeated trials, the chimps seemed unable to learn that the smaller pile should be selected in order to get the
larger pile. In each trial, the chimpanzee watched in obvious frustra-
tion and disappointment as the larger pile it had selected was given to
another. Deacon speculates that what makes the problem so difficult for
the chimpanzee is the salience of the immediate stimulus. The chimp is
unable to override this stimulus and conceptualize its opposite: choos-
ing the smaller pile in order to get the larger. As Deacon puts it, this

solution is counterintuitive for the chimp, because it "is overshadowed by the very powerful influence of its mutually exclusive and otherwise obvious alternative" (414). The difficulty lies in the paradox of selecting the lesser object in order to obtain the greater one.

Evidently, this type of problem is not habitually encountered by chimpanzees in their daily life. Yet, if Deacon is right, this kind of pragmatic paradox is a regular feature of human interaction. Deacon argues that it is the peculiar learning bias granted by an expanded prefrontal cortex that makes such tasks both easy and natural for humans. But, he adds, the expanded prefrontal cortex is itself a consequence—not a cause—of the origin of symbolic reference. What circumstances could have led to the latter?

We see in these experiments an indirect example of the kind of "pragmatic paradox" that Eric Gans proposes as the basis of symbolic representation.[71] The term "pragmatic paradox" is actually due to Paul Watzlawick, Janet Beavin, and Don Jackson, who have explored the pragmatic or behavioral consequences of paradox in communication, especially in pathological communicative situations that lead to schizophrenia.[72] They are themselves elaborating on Gregory Bateson's notion of the "double bind," namely, the failure of a "victim" or schizophrenic patient to respond normally to a paradoxical statement from a caregiver or "mother," owing to the victim's inability to distinguish between the difference in logical types or levels of abstraction in the meaning of the caregiver's statement.[73] Because the child fears rejection, it is unable to draw the mother's attention to the paradoxical nature of her statement and instead feels compelled to respond as if there were no paradox. This, Bateson argues, often leads to highly aberrant metaphoric interpretations and eventually, in extreme cases, to schizophrenia. For our present discussion, what is significant about Bateson's double bind is that it locates the source of schizophrenia in a feature that, far from being abnormal, is actually very common to human communicative situations. Watzlawick et al. multiply examples of pragmatic paradox, including commonplace injunctions like "Enjoy yourself!" or "Be spontaneous!"[74]

Like Bateson and Watzlawick, Gans sees pragmatic paradox as endemic to human communication, a basic feature of language. His interest in it, however, is not primarily psychiatric or psychological. Like Deacon, he argues that such paradoxes reveal a great deal about the evolutionary anomaly of language. In elaborating a hypothesis for language origin, we need to take into account both the anomalous nature of language compared to other animal communication systems and the paradoxical structure of symbolic reference itself.

Gans relates the two by hypothesizing that symbolic reference emerges as a response to the pragmatic paradoxes engendered by presymbolic mimesis. Refining René Girard's theory of mimesis, Gans argues that imitation, which is the condition of all socially learned behavior, inevitably leads to conflict over scarce objects (such as food).[75] When B imitates A in order to appropriate object X, the situation produces conflict because A is no longer simply a model for B but an obstacle. As ethologists have noted,[76] mimetic conflict, which is potentially debilitating to the social order, is stabilized by the evolution of a pecking order; B defers to A's higher rank, leaving the object for the latter's possession. But, Gans points out, greater mimetic propensity makes this solution increasingly unstable. When B proceeds to imitate A by refusing to leave the scene of mimetic attraction, this creates a dangerous and inherently conflictive situation, which Gans describes as a "pragmatic paradox" (*SP* 20), because what serves to increase the object's attraction also increases the danger of conflict. At a certain point, the mimetic symmetry of the situation undermines the asymmetry inherent to the pecking-order solution in which B defers to A, or B overthrows A and assumes the alpha position. Instead, both A and B serve as mediators for one another: B imitates A and A imitates B. In this situation of mutual mimetic reinforcement of the other's desire for the object, neither A nor B can appropriate the object independently of the mediating and potentially dangerous presence of the other. But, equally, the high level of mimeticism prevents either individual from simply abandoning the scene.

This intolerable situation of pragmatic paradox is resolved when both A and B accept the other's abortive gesture of appropriation as no longer a straightforward index of the object's availability, that is, as a sign to be imitated in an unselfconscious strategy of object appropriation, but rather as a higher-order sign that negates the first-order indexical relation between sign and object. This higher-order sign refers only by negating the previous positive, indexical reference to the object. It is thus not truly an index at all. Its mode of reference is rather *paradoxical* because it succeeds only insofar as it undermines the salience of the self-evident connection between gesture and object. The originary sign thus signifies by *negating* each individual's prior indexical attachment to the object. The consequence is a dynamic oscillation between sign and referent, in which the sign oscillates between the dual modes of index and symbol. As an index, the sign indicates the presence of the object, but this concrete reference to the object is immediately punctured by the realization that the sign is equally a response to the other's symmetrically produced sign. The individual abandons the original indexical conception of the sign and returns to a nascent symbolic understanding, which, as Deacon persuasively shows, functions not by referring directly to the object, but by mediating this reference to the object through other signs. The pertinence of Gans's hypothesis is that it allows us to understand that the origin of this new sign/sign relation is none other than the mimetic relation between subject and rival, which is to say, ultimately, the relation between the individual and the entire sign-using community. Durkheim had already understood that the origin of religion lies in the projection of the social relation onto totemic objects, but he could give no further account of projection as a function of the symbolic sign.

The originary sign thus solves the problem of maintaining a highly salient stimulus in view while simultaneously refusing to act on this same stimulus. This is precisely the problem that Boysen's chimpanzees in the candy experiment could not solve (i.e., the problem of being presented with a pile of candy that could only be appropriated by negating the normal response pattern). In the experiment, the chimp fails not simply to defer immediate gratification but to *project* the salience of the primary indexical relation onto a parallel symbolic reality, in which reference is constituted not by physical or worldly co-occurrence, but by the relationships between symbols. As Deacon implies and Gans explicitly hypothesizes, the originary model for the projection of an indexical sign to a symbolic sign is negation. In negating the priority of the indexical relation, the sign refers to its object only by paradoxically representing its opposite. The symbolic sign is thus fundamentally ironic; it points to its object only to reject it. In effect, the sign says "Here is the object, but you cannot have it."

The paradoxical structure of symbolic reference is similar, but not identical, to that of play, as Bateson has analyzed it.[77] In Bateson's account, what separates play fighting from real fighting is the frame of reference: the participants in the former are distinctively self-conscious about their movements. Bateson is keen to see in this transition to "metacommunication" (i.e., from signals to an awareness that "signals are signals") a major evolutionary step that implies not only "language ... but also all the complexities of empathy, identification, projection and so on" (179). Implied in Bateson's analysis of play, and of paradoxical communicative structures in general, is the transition from indexical to symbolic reference. In light of Deacon's neurological and primatological research, however, it seems doubtful that Bateson's casual observations of monkeys playing in the zoo will bear the weight of his claim that they already demonstrate the paradoxical structure of symbolic reference. After all, even genuine fights for dominance are highly "ritualized" or stereotyped affairs that depend largely on the proficiency of the signaler to communicate his strength without actually having to come to blows. Only with a hypothesis for the emergence of symbolic reference can we begin to analyze the paradoxical structure inherent to such human practices as play, ritual, irony, and art.

Let us take the case of irony.[78] The standard definition of irony is saying the opposite of what one really means: a "figure of speech in which the intended meaning is the opposite of that expressed by the words used" (OED). What the standard definition captures is the fact that irony functions as a negation of a preexisting meaning. But this negation is not accomplished simply by adding *not* to a previous statement, as with logical negation. Rather, ironic negation functions by reframing or recontextualizing the existing sense of the phrase or sentence. The meaning is not simply canceled. It is situated in a new (ironic) context, so that a tension is generated between what is said and what is really the case.

But this tension between meaning and reality, far from being a mere figure of speech, is in fact the sine qua non of symbolic reference. As we have seen, symbolic reference emerges as the negation of its independent indexical constituents, which nonetheless provide the basis for interpreting the sign symbolically. Rather than respond on the basis of a previously given perceptual and motor pattern, the subject of pragmatic paradox responds by accepting the indexical sign *as a sign of itself.* It is this paradoxical attention to the *form* of the sign-in-itself that undermines the naturalness inherent to the indexical response, which interprets the sign/object relation spatiotemporally as a relation of part to whole or part to part. This relation is something that is most often directly perceived, as in the classic example of smoke (the sign) indicating fire (the object). Even in the case of "arbitrary" alarm calls, such as those produced by vervet monkeys, the interpretation of the relationship between sign (the alarm call) and object (the predator) is still dependent upon the assimilation of the arbitrary structure of the sign/object relation to the indexical associations of direct perceptual experience.

In the situation of pragmatic paradox, on the other hand, the subject's attention is drawn away from the object itself toward the object's mediation by the indexical sign. The index becomes a meta-index, that is, a sign that thematizes its relation to the object, a relation now understood to be a consequence not simply of predictable co-occurrence, but of the meaning or "being" granted to the object by the co-participants in the symbol-using community. What is specifically ironic in the symbolic relationship is the sign's irreconcilable difference from the indexical mode of interpretation. The sign is linked to its object not naturally, but conventionally: in the former, sign and object co-exist in a "horizontal" spatiotemporal relationship; in the latter, the sign is pursued as a response not to the object, but to the other's sign. Thus, once the sign is divorced irrevocably from its indexical object, its "meaning" can itself become the object of a new ironic meaning. The arbitrariness or "verticality" (*SP* 14) of the signifier is a corollary of this fact. When the child imitates its parent who utters the word "cat" while pointing to a real cat, the child learns the meaning of the sign ostensively. But once the meaning of the word has been learned it can equally be applied to other cats. In learning the word "cat," the child does not seek to pursue the ostensive referent; it learns to *name* the cat by imitating the word produced by the parent. In the ontogeny of language acquisition, the conflict of appropriative mimesis (Girard) is wholly eliminated. What the child imitates is not the nonlinguistic gesture toward the object, which leads to conflict, but the signification *of* the object. Unlike the object it designates, the word may be easily reproduced and thus universally shared. In the symbolic configuration that defines human communication, the imitation of the sign can be successfully pursued precisely because the goal of imitation is no longer the appropriation of the object but rather a self-conscious thematization of it.[79]

It would, however, be a gross oversimplification to see this as a case of ontogeny recapitulating phylogeny. The child's language acquisition is biased from the start thanks to hundreds of thousands—perhaps even millions—of years of brain-language coevolution. It has therefore become all but "natural" for the child to imitate gestures of meaning rather than of appropriation, symbols rather than indices. But, in phylogenetic terms, we cannot assume the "naturalness" or "givenness" of this easy transition. This is the major conclusion reached by Deacon, on independent empirical grounds, in his study of primate brain evolution.[80] In presenting a minimal originary hypothesis for language origin, Gans accepts the necessity of this conclusion. The transition from index to symbol, from "natural" to "conventional" signification[81] cannot be discerned empirically, through stages of increasingly complex indexical and iconic reference strategies. But nor should it be left as a metaphysical conundrum that can only be interpreted in terms of an irreconcilable ontological dualism (e.g., idealism vs. materialism, conventional vs. natural meaning, nature vs. culture, etc.). Rather, the difference should be minimized in terms of a hypothesis of origin. According to Gans's hypothesis, the pragmatic paradox precipitated by the presymbolic mimetic relationship between subject and model is resolved when each individual learns to pursue the sign not as an index, but as a conventional sign. It goes without saying that this conventional relationship can always be undermined or deconstructed by pointing out the ironic dependence of the sign on its indexical constituents.[82]

Irony defines the mode of attention paradigmatic of symbolic interpretation because it demands that we continually seek to counter the reduction of a symbol to an index. What tempts us toward irony is the feeling that our interlocutor knows how we will respond based on what we can both perceive to be the case. If I say, "What a gorgeous day for a walk!" in the face of torrential rain, I am speaking ironically because the rain is an index that both I and my interlocutor associate with the unpleasant experiences of getting wet, being cold, and so on. My words are not an index of what is really the case, but of what I would like to be the case. In short, I project onto the real situation of rain an imaginary situation in which it is sunny. In referring to the imaginary situation, I compensate my resentment toward the real situation of a torrential downpour. We are attuned to the aesthetics of irony because it captures the fundamental incompatibility between the symbolic world we desire and the indexical world in which we live. Whether we are commenting ironically on the weather or appreciating the ironies of Greek tragedy, the same fundamental structure operates. In each case we are displacing an unpleasant indexical experience onto a symbolic world in which that experience becomes an occasion for pleasurable irony.[83]

From our external, historically privileged perspective, it is perhaps too easy to understand the original projection from index to symbol as an act of ironic negation of indexical relations. From the vantage point of modern symbol users, we immediately grasp the utility of substituting a symbolic object for the real one and account for this utility by pointing to the greater referential economy permitted by language in the long run. But at the moment of origin, no such perspective is possible. To the original participants, the inaccessibility of the central object cannot be grasped in terms of a "theory of projection." Symbolic projection is then rather understood as a revelatory event, upon which the very survival of the community depends. According to Gans, this provides the originary model of the sacred; it captures the fact that sacrality is not in the first place a naive fantasy produced by overimaginative minds—which must in fact be the conclusion of Turner's cognitive model were it ever applied to the sacred. Rather, the sacred stands at the origin of projection. In projecting the deferring function of the sign onto the central object, the community interprets the object as the cause of this deferral. The object is no longer an index of an appetitive need, but a symbol or fig- ure representing the collective interdiction of all such needs. And the most powerful collective symbol is the divine being or god who alone is capable of withstanding the multiple and conflicting desires of the surrounding community.

This model of "originary projection" also explains the fundamen- tal distinction between true symbolic narrative and the mere indexi- cal association of contiguous events. Narrative implies a symbolically constructed agent or self (which is, in the first place, a god or divine agent, not a human—the latter rather being modeled on the former). The ability simply to perceive and remember sequences of contiguous events, however, entails no additional effort to understand this sequence as produced by an agent or self different from the perceiving subject.[84]

Ritual and myth commemorate the origin of symbolic reference by attributing the deferring function of representation not just to the sign, but to an entire numinous ontology of the sacred. From our perspective, this is a category error, an expansion or projection of the symbolic world to the natural world. But this original "alienated" mode of symbolic experience is not something that can be eliminated once and for all. It can only be *minimized* by recognizing its proper place in anthropological and historical explanation.

If today we understand the conflict-deferring function of ritual and myth as the minimal anthropological origin of the symbolic sign, then to the original participants no such self-understanding is pos- sible, because no such level of historical self-reflection is available at the very first moment of history. Our ability to formulate a hypothesis of cultural-symbolic origin is a condition of our historical distance from this origin. In taking this entire history for granted, the cognitive model of representation reduces what is only accessible through concrete anthropological and historical analysis to an ontology of the brain and its neurological connections. This is of course consistent with the scientific and metaphysical ideal since René Descartes. But, as Deacon's work makes clear, it is not consistent with a more subtle account of the coevolution of language and the brain. And the simplest demonstration of this truth, I have argued, is the fact that language—symbolic reference—is a specifically human mode of representation, qualitatively distinct from the indexical systems that preceded it.

What are the practical consequences of my analysis for literary study? I am not saying that we can ignore cognitivism. On the contrary, I think that this kind of cross-disciplinary research is exciting and necessary. At the same time, this research needs to be more fully aware of some of the traditional philosophical problems involved in any account of the origin of representation. More precisely, I do not think it is possible in our "postmetaphysical" era to assume that symbolic representation can be traced so easily to internal ideas or perceptions, in a way fundamentally no different than John Locke's. No doubt, with modern developments in evolutionary biology and developmental psychology, cognitivism is far better equipped to grasp the essential uniformity of human experience. Unlike Locke, who famously used the metaphor of the mind as a sheet of "white paper,"[85] biology does not need to rely on pure metaphor for an explanation of the mind as a product of evolution (if it did, then biology would be a poetics rather than a science). But when it comes to the problem of the origin of symbolic representation, the cognitivist model is no better off than Locke's notion of the *tabula rasa*. And this is ultimately because the mind, whether as white paper or as a biologically evolved adaptive system, cannot construct symbols without the anthropological context of the originary *scene* of representation.

Instead of taking the presence of such a scene for granted, I believe we need to confront the problem of representation head on. The originary hypothesis explains the origin of symbolic representation not as a *consequence* of biological evolution or the struggle for reproductive fitness, but indeed as a new system that coevolves with biology. The general semiotic approach I advocate requires that we trace and explain the shift from an indexical to a symbolic representational system. Both

Deacon and Gans, upon whom I have relied for much of this argument, understand the problem of human origin to be a problem about the origin of symbolic reference. But I don't want to give the impression that they have said the last word on representation. Far from it. The single most important point I wanted to make is this: If we want to explain the origin of what we take to be universal human categories, for example, metaphor and narrative, then we are going to have to bite the bullet and explain what the anthropological function of these categories is. But in order to do that, we need to take seriously the fact that symbolic representation is irreducible to the causal mechanisms of biological functions. Instead, positively speaking, we need to recognize that the only explanations available to us lie in the functioning of the historical institutions of human culture itself. This does not mean that we have to renounce the search for a unified explanation. On the contrary, the whole point of the originary hypothesis is to minimize our explanation of culture, and all of its many forms, by presenting a minimal anthropological context from which they can be more generally understood. To put it as pithily as possible: the answer to biological reductionism is not cultural idealism, but anthropological minimalism.

Chapter 2

Imitation and Human Ontogeny:
Michael Tomasello and the Scene of Joint Attention

René Girard's mimetic theory has sometimes been criticized for being unrealistic in its implications for human ontogeny.[1] More precisely, it can be argued that mimetic rivalry, if it is really as fundamental as Girard maintains, would be far more evident among young children, who are universally recognized to be "imitation machines." If children learn by imitation, why are they not constantly fighting among themselves, as Girard's theory predicts? We all know the proverbial story of the children in the nursery who reach for the same toy despite the fact that there are many other toys in the room. But has anybody actually tested for mimetic rivalry among children? And what age group are we talking about? Do prelinguistic infants compete mimetically? When do children "ironize" centers of attention, like Hamlet at his uncle's court, or Tom Sawyer whitewashing his aunt's fence?

In what follows, I take a closer look at the role of imitation in human ontogeny. Much of what I say relies on Michael Tomasello's account of human ontogeny. Tomasello is a well known comparative psychologist at the Max Planck Institute in Leipzig, and he has done a great deal of empirical work on children and nonhuman primates such as chimpanzees. My remarks will draw mainly on his account of imitation and cultural learning in *The Cultural Origins of Human Cognition* (Cambridge, MA: Harvard University Press, 1999). In this book, Tomasello provides a fascinating picture of how children, beginning at about nine months of age, acquire higher cognitive functions, including eventually language, mathematics, and music. Tomasello's main interest, however, is not in the later period of cultural development, when children acquire advanced and culturally variable skills like long division or algebra. Rather, he is interested in what is universal in childhood development. His particular focus is therefore on the period just prior to the child's first birthday, when the child begins to engage with adults in what he calls "scenes of joint attention." Students of generative anthropology may be surprised to learn that Tomasello's theory of cognitive development is very close in spirit to Eric Gans's reflections on the elementary linguistic forms (the ostensive and imperative).[2] What Tomasello calls the *joint attentional scene* is the ontogenetic analogue of what Gans calls the *originary ostensive scene.*

Tomasello's Anthropology

Tomasello begins by asking why it is that, despite our close genetic relationship to chimpanzees, we are nonetheless so different from them. Unlike chimpanzee societies, human societies are complex, and they make use of complex symbolic and material artifacts. Tomasello argues that we cannot explain this difference in purely biological terms because "there simply has not been enough time for normal processes of biological evolution involving genetic variation and natural selection to have created, one by one, each of the cognitive skills necessary for modern humans to invent and maintain complex tool-use industries and technologies, complex forms of symbolic communication and representation, and complex social organizations and institutions" (2). Tomasello believes there is "only one possible solution" (4). This solution involves reducing the multiple differences between humans and chimps to one essential difference. Unlike chimps or other animals, humans are able to build on culture *cumulatively.*

In arguing for a fundamental constitutive difference between humans and chimpanzees, Tomasello separates himself from most primatologists and evolutionary biologists, who tend to define human culture in continuity with animal examples of what the science writer Richard Dawkins calls "the extended phenotype." For example, birdsong can be regarded as a particularly ingenious way for transmitting bird genes. Young birds learn mating songs by imitating their parents; they do not emit them naturally or spontaneously. Likewise, chimpanzees can be said to acquire culture by imitating the tool-making and tool-using skills of their parents. Tomasello argues that such definitions of culture fail to grasp the key to specifically human culture, which is the ability to build upon culture recursively. Tomasello calls this the "ratchet effect" (37). What he means by this is that human cultural artifacts are not simply passed down unchanged from generation to generation, like the songs of a particular bird species, or the tools of the chimpanzee. They are intentionally modified by the users themselves. More specifically and more interestingly, Tomasello argues that humans participate in a collective attentional scene, the history of which stretches back to the very first scene of collective human attention. Chimps make termiting sticks as they have always made termiting sticks, but the human capacity for symbolic representation has, for better or worse, enabled the spear to evolve from pointed stick to nuclear warhead.

The skeptic may counter that this is always the case with evolution. Things tend to get more complex, as competition forces organisms and cultures to specialize into particular environmental and cultural niches. But Tomasello's point is not just that human culture is more complex, but that this complexity is built into the process of cultural transmission. Among humans, culture is modified at a rate that transcends, by several orders of magnitude, the mechanisms available to biological evolution. The rapid pace of human cultural evolution suggests that we are dealing with qualitatively different mechanisms of evolutionary change. Since humans differ very little from other primates in terms of their biology, the difference must lie in the particular mechanism used by humans to transmit culture. For Tomasello, our capacity to transmit and modify culture intersubjectively—that is, within the shared space or *scene* of collective attention—is what separates us from other social animals, including most notably our closest living genetic relative, the chimpanzee.

Though one can disagree with Tomasello on the particulars of his theory—and I will look at some of those particulars in a moment—it seems hard to deny his general point that human culture is fundamentally different from animal culture. Yet the astonishing fact is that Tomasello's position among scientists is anomalous. Why is this the case? Why do the vast majority of scientists appear so eager to deny or ignore the obvious differences between humans and nonhuman animals when it comes to symbolic phenomena such as culture and language? If I were forced to explain this curious fact, I would put it down to our natural inclination to identify with others. We can't help but explain nonhuman behavior in human terms because that is how we interpret our own behavior. Humans have an irresistible urge to anthropomorphize the world, and this urge spreads to other animals who appear to behave like us in certain respects.

I realize that this explanation is rather counterintuitive. Surely we can expect the scientists, of all people, to be more objective. But I'm afraid I can't think of a better explanation. For a long time, we believed the whole cosmos operated in terms of human beliefs and desires. We seem to have gotten away from seeing our preoccupations mirrored in the rocks, trees, and stars. But it seems as though a residual element of this "cosmological anthropology" remains when we turn to animals, and in particular to our closest primate relative, the chimpanzee.

So what are we to do? Well, one thing we can do is listen to people like Tomasello. When it comes to comparing human societies with non-human primate societies, I think we have no better guide. His extensive knowledge of the literature in primatology, his own empirical research on chimpanzees and children, and above all his theoretical sophistication, make him an ideal guide for navigating the controversial subject of human origins.

Of Chimps and Children

Based on his empirical experiments with children and chimpanzees, Tomasello argues that children go through a "nine-month revolution." This is when they adopt a cognitive perspective on the world unknown to chimps or other animals as they begin identifying with the intentions and attentions of others. Before nine months, children interact with adults dyadically, for example, by imitating facial expressions, or participating in "proto-conversations" or turn-taking rituals (e.g., peek-a-boo games). Students of Girard's mimetic theory may wish to see this pre-nine-month phase as the "Girardian" stage of human ontogeny, when infants imitate adults directly without paying attention to the world outside the model. At around nine months, however, children begin to follow the attention of adults in order to attend to external objects. This is the basis of pointing gestures. Children begin to understand that adults are beings like themselves who have goals and plans toward objects ("intentions"), and they begin to identify with those intentions by following the gaze of adults and predicting the adult's behavior on the basis of their perception of both the adult and the adult's relationship toward external objects. Tomasello calls this the "scene of joint attention," and he believes it to be the fundamental basis for specifically human forms of imitation and cultural transmission. We might call this the "Gansian" phase of human ontogeny, the discovery by the child that it is a participant in the general scene of human culture.

To get a flavor of Tomasello's argument here, consider his analysis of the widely cited example of "culture" among a group of Japanese macaques. In the 1950s an individual named Imo was observed to wash her potatoes before eating them. Gradually the habit spread, first to Imo's closest relatives, then among the other group members. After two years, about forty percent of the troop was observed to be industriously washing potatoes. The scientists interpreted this as an example of humanlike cultural transmission, because the group's members appeared to be *imitating* Imo's invention of potato washing.

As it turns out, however, potato washing is not quite the cultural revolution in food preparation the scientists thought they had discovered. Other individuals in other troops quite separate from Imo's have since been observed to do the same thing. Unsurprisingly, the displeasure of chewing on sand and grit appears to be something we share in common with monkeys, who frequently can be seen to engage in the perfectly natural practice of brushing the sand off their food before chewing it. The potato washing habit is therefore better explained as an *extension* of this natural brushing behavior. Given exposure to water *and* sandy potatoes, sooner or later the monkey will discover that washing the potato with water is a more effective sand-removing technique than simply brushing it. But the real clincher for Tomasello is the fact that the rate at which the habit of potato washing spread within Imo's troop remained constant throughout the two-year observation period. If individuals really were imitating the behavior of their fellow macaques rather than relying on individual trial and error, one would expect the rate of transmission to increase dramatically as the number of potato washers increased. But this was not the case. Tomasello's conclusion is that the macaques were not so much imitating Imo's behavior as being led by her to favorable circumstances in which each individual could *discover for itself* the elegant beauty of potato washing. The fact that Imo's closest relatives adopted the habit first is consistent with this hypothesis. As they foraged with Imo, they were the most likely members to be in the same vicinity of water and sandy potatoes. They therefore were also the first to discover, one by one and by individual trial and error, the handy trick of potato washing.

Tomasello calls this type of social learning *emulative* rather than imitative. The difference is that in emulative learning the disciple focuses not on the model's particular behavior but on the objects with which the model is interacting. Chimpanzees, for instance, are very good at observing other chimpanzees interact with objects, but they do not then imitate the other's behavior with respect to the objects involved. Rather, they are led to interact with the objects and discover for themselves the *natural affordances* of the particular objects attended to. For example, a young chimp may observe its mother crack a nut with a stone. It will then pick up a stone and discover that the stone makes a pretty good hammer. What the chimp has learned is not a particular behavior (the mother's technique of nut cracking), but a fact about stones, and more precisely, a fact about the impact of stones on nuts. This is something that is learned by the chimp in its interaction with the stone and the nut, not by imitating its mother's gesture toward the nut or stone. The chimp does not oscillate its attention between mother and the objects involved, in a conscious effort to reproduce her particular gesture. It therefore has not learned a new behavior by imitation. Hammering is something the chimp can do individually, given the natural affordances of the objects involved. Provided with a stone and a nut, and given the general primate capacity for grasping objects (Thank God for the opposable thumb!), the chimp discovers how to crack a nut. The behavior is emulative rather than imitative because, as Tomasello puts it, the chimp "focuses on the environmental events involved—the changes of state in the environment that the other produced—not on a conspecific's behavior or behavioral strategy" (29).

In order to test his theory that chimpanzee learning is emulative rather than imitative, Tomasello devised a series of ingenious experiments testing both two-year-old children and chimpanzees. The experiments involved getting the subjects to imitate the behavior of a model. Tomasello describes how the children almost always insisted on imitating the behavior of the model, no matter how bizarre or inefficient it was. For example, if the model switched on a light by using her head, so would the children. Or if the model used a tool in an extremely inefficient fashion to reach an object, the children would use the tool in the same inefficient manner, despite the fact that the natural affordances of the objects presented a much easier way to do the same task. The chimps, on the other hand, simply experimented with the objects no matter which way had been demonstrated to them beforehand. Evidently, the children were imitating the model whereas the chimps were attempting to emulate the outcome of the experiment independently of the model's particular behavior. Whereas the children were focused on the model's *behavior toward the goal*, the chimps were focused on the outcome of the experiment. The difference is important because it explains why chimpanzees have such great difficulty learning to use symbols. The ability to separate behavior from outcome is necessary before the model's gesture toward the object can be transformed into a genuine symbol that designates or "means" the object. What Tomasello's experiments strongly suggest is that children, but not chimps, are predisposed to focus on the model's *behavioral stance toward the object*. They are entering into the model's particular intentional stance toward the object.

Joint Attention

Key to Tomasello's ideas about language acquisition among children is his hypothesis concerning the joint attentional scene. Before nine months, children interact with the world much as other primates interact with the world. That is, they are aware of the objects around them and of other individuals interacting with those objects, but they never enter into the other's intentionality toward those objects. If a pre-nine-month-old child is playing with an object and an adult walks into the room and says, "Look, let's play with this!" while holding out a toy car, the child may reach out and grab the car and start sucking on it, or manipulating it, or whatever, but it pays no attention to the adult's intentions toward the toy. It pays attention either to the toy or to the adult, but not to the relationship between adult and toy. In other words, the child does not think to itself, "Oh, mommy wants to show me this new toy," or even, "This person wants to show me this thing." On the contrary, if Tomasello is right, it does not even "think" at all, at least not in the way an adult thinks, which according to Tomasello is an internalized version of the kind of joint attentional scenes children first experience at nine months. Thus, in grabbing the toy the pre-nine-month-old child does not look from mommy to toy and back to mommy again. The toy is simply another object to interact with, but it receives no further significance beyond the child's own interest in it. Tomasello's argument is that chimps never really go beyond this "egocentric" stage of understanding objects, which is why primatologists never observe chimps pointing in the wild. That is, they do not distinguish between my intention toward objects and your intention toward objects, so there is no point in trying to get you to pay attention to my attention toward the object. As far as chimps and pre-nine-month-old children are concerned, there is only the point of view of the self, into which all other perspectives are innocently absorbed.

At around nine months of age, however, children begin to engage in what Tomasello calls *joint attentional scenes*. Initially, this begins with simple checking on the attention of an adult in relation to an outside object, but it quickly evolves into gaze following, when the child looks from adult to where the adult is looking, and to acts of pointing, when the child tries to direct the attention of an adult to some external object. What Tomasello is keen to stress in this ontogenetic "revolution" is the fact that the scene is fundamentally triadic in structure: "Joint attentional scenes are social interactions in which the child and the adult are jointly attending to that third thing, for some reasonably extended length of time" (97). The child's attention shifts between the adult and the object to which both adult and child are attending. In this collective sharing of attention toward a central object, Tomasello sees the roots of symbolic culture, including language, symbolic play, and ritual.

Joint attentional scenes, however, are not examples of language, at least not language in the sense usually intended by philosophers or linguists.[3] They are rather the minimal condition of language. On the other hand, nor are they simply perceptual events of the kind that nonhuman primates and other animals engage in. All animals, including of course all humans, perceive the world around them and are able, on the basis of those perceptions, to form sensorimotor representations that allow them to anticipate events in the world, including the actions of other conspecifics. However, these anticipations are still perceptually based, in the sense that they are individually learned image schemas or sensorimotor representations. To borrow a usage from the evolutionary anthropologist Terrence Deacon, these perceptual and sensorimotor representations are *indexical*. They are based on the capacity of all animals to form categories of perceptual events, including categories of communicative events, such as the widely publicized example of vervet monkey distress calls.[4]

The scene of joint attention is quite different. Indeed, Tomasello claims that it bridges the gap between perceptual representation (which we share with all animals) and language (which only we possess). What differentiates the joint attentional scene from language in the narrow sense employed by linguists is the fact that language "abstracts" from the scene to include only its most portable aspect, which is the symbol or word itself. On the other hand, what differentiates the joint attentional scene from perceptual events is that it includes "only a subset of the child's perceptual world" (97). That is, the joint attentional scene focuses the child's attention on a central object, against which all other perceptual objects and events become background or "periphery."

Let me emphasize this difference between perceptual events and the joint attentional scene. Animals can of course focus their attention on discrete objects or events in the world, as when a cat tracks the movements of a mouse, or a chimp warily eyes the presence of a male rival. In the joint attentional scene, however, the child is not merely paying attention to the object, but to *someone else's attention toward the same object*. In other words, the child grasps that the significance of the object is mediated by the attention of the other. It is this capacity to separate the other's intention—his or her internally represented goal—from the perceptual reality of the object that distinguishes the joint attentional scene from otherwise superficially similar perceptual scenes. The child learns that the adult's intention to the object is distinct from its own intention toward the same object. Moreover, in making this distinction between self and other, it lays the foundation for participating in an intentional relation that is truly collective or intersubjective, because in recognizing the difference between the other's intentionality toward the object and the object itself, the child learns to take a perspective on the object distinct from its own. The child is now imitating a particular intentionality toward the object that is transposable to other scenes in which the object may appear. Tomasello calls this "role reversal imitation" (105) because it implies that the child is able to grasp that an adult's intentional stance toward an object is something that can be adopted by the child itself. This is something we do all the time—indeed, whenever we use language. For example, suppose you tell me that the peculiar thing on your dining room table is a "grazza." Later, when my wife walks in the room and makes a face while staring at the peculiar object on the table, I turn to her and say, "Oh, that's a grazza." I have not merely imitated the word, I have also reproduced your intentional stance toward it. That is, I have recreated the joint attentional scene by adopting your perspective, and this time I have reversed the roles because I am now instructing someone else, as you had instructed me before.

A skeptic might object that these joint scenes of attention are not so very different from the attentional scenes other animals engage in. Animals are not rigidly tied to the same perceptual construal of a particular object. A tree may represent a number of different things. Depending on the context, it may represent an escape route, a nesting site, or the location of food. But Tomasello's point is not that perceptual scenes are inflexible but that they are always tied to the natural affordances of the objects and that these affordances are discoverable by the individual's dyadic interaction with the object. At no point does the chimp seek confirmation *from another conspecific* in order to see that the tree is a nesting site or an escape route or source of food. It can discover these things for itself. Furthermore, it is impossible for the tree to represent all these things *at the same time*. The chimp does not choose between different representations of the tree that it can hold in its mind simultaneously. Rather, the representation of the tree remains a function of the chimp's particular goal, which is either to eat, escape, or sleep. As Tomasello says, "the animal is attending to different affordances of the environment depending on its goal" (126).

In the case of symbolic attention, however, the goal is not defined by the practical affordances of the environment, but by the attentions of both individuals in the attentional scene. When a child points to a tree, the goal is to secure the adult's attention to the same object. And this is, in the end, what language does. It secures the other's attention toward some external object or, in the case of declarative sentences, some external idea or "signified." When it comes to specifically human cognitive functions, what is primary, as Emile Durkheim saw, is the *social relation*. It is the latter that mediates our more basic indexical perceptual and sensorimotor functions. The latter are basic functions that we share with all other animals. It is the mediation of these functions by the joint attentional scene that distinguishes human from animal cognition.

In a manner reminiscent of Deacon's theory of symbolic reference, Tomasello argues that language emerges as a negation—or, in Hegelian terms, a transcendence—of more basic perceptual and sensorimotor representations. In order to construe an object in symbolic terms one must impose an intersubjective relation onto a perceptual relation. That is, one must enter into a joint attentional scene that can define the object "arbitrarily" in terms of each participant's shared attention to the object. This creates an intersubjectively shared "space"—a period of deferral, if you like—between the two participants in which the object is "centralized" as the shared focus of attention. Rather than seeing the object as a function of my individual biological needs (e.g., as a place of rest, escape, or food), I see it as a function of your attention, which—as students of mimetic theory well know—may be in conflict with my own pragmatic designs on the object. Gans, following Durkheim and Girard, suggests that the originary act of symbolic designation is an act of *sacralization*. The designation of the object as sacred is not something that can be understood on the basis of the natural affordances of the object. On the contrary, it is an arbitrary imposition, in the sense that its "functionality" is given by the intersubjective relation itself. The object is now attended to as a function of the symbol used to designate it. As Tomasello points out, this is the basis for the perspectival nature of symbols. Language is used in order to get someone to attend to the world in a certain way. In designating an object symbolically, I first have to decide what symbol to use. For example, I could call a tree, *that tree, the oak, the tree in my backyard, the monstrosity that blocks my sunlight,* or any number of things. But how I choose to construe it is, in the end, always a function of how I think I can best get you to attend to it with me. That is, I choose between different symbols by simultaneously monitoring your attention to the object. This is in fact how children acquire language and this is also what we mean by imitation in the specifically human context. Symbols are "attention getters." They are the tried and tested means passed down from previous generations of language users for participating in joint attentional scenes. "In imitatively learning a linguistic symbol from other persons," Tomasello says, "I internalize not only their communicative intention (their intention to get me to share their attention) but also the specific perspective they have taken. As I use this symbol with other persons, I monitor their attentional deployment as a function of the symbols I produce as well, and so I have at my disposal both (a) the two real foci of self and communicative partner and (b) the other possible foci symbolized in other linguistic symbols that might potentially be used in this situation" (128). As this passage implies, Tomasello's theory is aimed at explaining the ontogenetic pathways of the child's entrance into the "mimetic triangle" of human culture.

Objects as Symbols

One thing I would like to emphasize in Tomasello's account of human ontogeny is his view that the child's symbolic interpretation of intentional objects follows, rather than precedes, the child's acquisition of ostensive words in scenes of joint attention. At first, this might seem rather counterintuitive. We tend to think of words as horribly abstract whereas objects, even symbolic objects, are tangible and concrete. At least you can manipulate a toy car, even if it is "only" a representation, a model of the real thing. The word *car*, on the other hand, is by comparison a very abstract thing, little more than a puff of air or, in the case of writing, black dots on the page or computer screen.

But that is precisely the point. In order for the child to move from concrete perceptual and sensorimotor representations to abstract symbols, it needs to override all those perceptual and sensorimotor associations it has learned in the first nine months of its life. But this is a very hard thing to do if your raw material consists of graspable objects with all kinds of preexisting intentional and natural affordances. An interesting discovery of Tomasello's experiments was that it is very hard for children under two to intentionally interpret a cup as a hat, or a pencil as a hammer, for example, by putting the cup on their heads, or hammering with the pencil. These symbolic interpretations are difficult for the child because the objects already possess clear cut intentional affordances. The cup is for drinking, the pencil for drawing. These more basic perceptual and sensorimotor representations tend to override the child's relatively undeveloped capacity for symbolic association and metaphoric thinking.

In a particularly poignant experiment, Tomasello demonstrates how hard it is for children under two to interpret nonarbitrary objects in purely symbolic terms. Children aged eighteen to thirty-five months were asked to give the experimenter an object. In the first stage of the experiment, the experimenter simply asked for the object by name. All the children responded appropriately. In the second phase, the experimenter asked for the object by holding up a toy replica of the object (e.g., holding up a toy hammer in order to get the real hammer). Interestingly, the children under twenty-six months had extreme difficulty with this task. They reacted instead by reaching for the toy held up by the experimenter. Children over twenty-six months, however, had no difficulty interpreting the toy object symbolically as a request for the object represented. Tomasello suggests that the reason the task is so difficult is "that the younger children engaged with the toy object as a sensorimotor object," and that this engagement prevented them from interpreting the object as a symbol of *something else*, namely, the real object the experimenter was requesting (86). This is an interesting finding because it suggests that symbolic iconicity, far from being a natural stepping stone toward language, is in fact something children grasp only once they have already mastered ostensive words (e.g., "Juice!" "Dog!" "Tree!" etc.). I interpret this as additional evidence that, phylogenetically speaking, we have no choice but to interpret the origin of language and culture as a radical break from preexisting animal forms of culture and communication. There is no shortcut from perceptually based modes of iconicity and indexicality to genuine symbols. The unbounded human capacity for metaphor and other forms of symbolic analogy begins with the "vertical" separation between the central object and the intersubjectively shared sign. The aborted gesture of appropriation that defers the indexical relation between subject and object is the "humble" beginning of humanity—the "little bang," as Gans puts it.[5] The key ingredient of the originary scene is the minimal symbolic sign.

Human Phylogeny and the Joint Attentional Scene

Before I conclude, I would like to make a small criticism of Tomasello's account of human phylogeny. In general, I agree with most of what he says on this topic. I agree that evolutionary biologists, anthropologists, and psychologists have, by and large, neglected the "cultural" factor in human evolution. Instead, there has been too much emphasis on the genetic or biological side of things. Tomasello rightly disputes the simplification of this issue into an inflexible dichotomy between biology and culture. As he points out, the dichotomy doesn't really exist. What "exists" are different ideas about history. There is phylogenetic time, which is the perspective of biological or genetic evolution. There is historical time, which is the perspective of human beings reflecting on their relationship to past culture and in particular to past ideas that other human beings have had about themselves and the world around them. And, finally, there is ontogenetic time, where biology and history each play an indispensable role in the formation of the human individual. Tomasello thinks that evolutionists have favored looking at human evolution in phylogenetic or biological terms because it just seems easier and more elegant. It is much simpler to posit a genetic event as the cause of something because genetic events are more manageable than cultural events, which tend to be rather messy and imprecise affairs. Hence the temptation to see human cognition in terms of a number of discrete "modules" that are genetically wired to produce different "types" or "categories" of cognition. So, following this line of argument, there must be separate cognitive modules for perceiving objects, for knowing persons, for recognizing number, for acquiring language, and so on and so on. Obviously, this sort of thinking is not very rigorous and it is easy to see how it can quickly get out of hand. Do we need a module for chess? What about the God gene?

Tomasello rightly cuts through the confusion implicit in this kind of thinking. His expertise on human ontogeny allows him to see that the cultural side of the story is really much more important than the typical evolutionist admits. This is what is so valuable about Tomasello's account. He sees the importance of culture—the mediation of the child's attention by the joint attentional scene—in changing the biological pathways of the child's cognitive development, as it goes from perceiving the world much like other primates do, to seeing it in terms that only humans do. However, I have to point out that Tomasello doesn't always follow his own advice. In his concluding section, after he criticizes the modular theorists for their ad hoc practice of explaining human cognition in terms of multiple discrete genetic events, he goes on to propose a genetic event of his own:

> My attempt is to find a single biological adaptation with leverage, and thus I have alighted upon the hypothesis that human beings evolved a new way of identifying with and understanding conspecifics as intentional beings. We do not know the ecological pressures that might have favored such an adaptation, and we can hypothesize any number of adaptive advantages it might have conferred. My own view is that any one of many adaptive scenarios might have led to the same evolutionary outcome for human social cognition, because if an individual understands conspecifics as intentional beings for whatever reason—whether for purposes of cooperation or competition or social learning or whatever—this understanding will not then evaporate when that individual interacts with conspecifics in other circumstances. (204–5)

It's too bad Tomasello doesn't follow his own advice. Here he gets it exactly backwards. Understanding other conspecifics as intentional beings like oneself is not a "genetic event" because there is no conceivable reason why, genetically speaking, such an event should occur, as he himself admits. Or, to put the same point differently, there are so many reasons why the capacity to identify with others is beneficial *from the perspective of those who already have it* that the number of plausible originary scenarios is limitless. But the real issue is not the infinite number of scenarios we can imagine for causing individuals to identify with one another. It is the presence of the scene of identification itself, which takes place, as Tomasello elegantly shows, in the joint attentional scene between parent and child. It is the joint attentional scene that must be explained, not the "genetic" ability to identify with others. The "selection pressure" to see other beings like oneself is given by the structure of the (joint attentional) scene itself. The mimetic "pressure" to maintain attention on a central object *that is also the center attention of the other* leads the subject to begin to identify with the other's internal representation of the object, and vice versa. Tomasello's detailed observations of young children provide empirical confirmation of this hypothesis. Where Tomasello trips up is when he translates his theory of human ontogeny into a hypothesis for a single genetic event in human phylogeny. But the joint attentional scene is irreducible to a genetic event. The origin of humanity is the first scene of joint attention, the minimal mimetic triangle of the originary hypothesis.

Conclusion

I began this essay by asking why it is that Girard's mimetic theory has so little to say about human ontogeny despite the fact that children are "imitation machines." I now wish to propose an answer. The reason is that Girard's theory does not distinguish systematically between two kinds of imitation, imitation of a model and imitation of an object. For Girard, imitation is always ultimately imitation of someone else. This is why he associates the mimetic crisis with the loss of difference between subject and object. In a mimetic crisis, the rivals becomes so obsessed with each other that they no longer grasp that what they are designating is something external to both of them, the central object of the joint attentional scene. Girard's idea of imitation is almost wholly based on this idea of dyadic imitation.

What Tomasello's account suggests, however, is that dyadic imitation is a necessary ontogenetic step toward gaining access to the intentions of the other. This is a far more constructive notion of imitation. In paying attention to the behavior of the other, I am not merely imitating the other, but entering into the other's perspective on the world. As Tomasello suggests, I am identifying with the other. But this identification would not be possible without the presence of a third element, which is the object to which we are both paying attention. In *Signs of Paradox*, Gans emphasizes the necessity of including the object as an indispensable third element in the mimetic relation, despite the fact that this seems to contradict Girard's original idea of the mimetic crisis:

> Why should the intensification of mimesis lead the subject away from the other's behavior toward the object to which it is directed? This movement reflects an internalization of the

model's motivation, the self's closer assimilation to the other's own reality. The more closely I imitate my model's goal-direct-ed action, the more I share the goal of this action, which is not located in the action itself but precisely in the external object. . . . Whence the apparent paradox that as imitation becomes more intense, it prefigures the triangular structure of human representation, focusing less on the model's behavior and more on the object to which it is directed.[6]

Tomasello's account of human ontogeny confirms Gans's theory of imi-tation. The child learns to imitate not merely the external action of the other, but the other's internal goal as well. The joint attentional scene is the basis for the child's acquisition of wholly abstract objects, such as the ideas or "signifieds" of declarative language.

In proposing that mimetic rivalry dissolves the mimetic triangle between self, other, and object, Girard reverses the passage from nature to culture, or, in Tomasello's ontogenetic terms, from the infant who interprets the world much like other primates do, to the child who inter-prets the world symbolically in terms of the joint attentional scene. But this reversal is not really a reversal of the originary passage from nature to culture. It is a historical renewal of it. In the case of children, this historical renewal is experienced ontologically, in the sense that their identity as individuals is dependent upon their cognitive acquisition of culture, as they begin to participate in scenes of joint attention and in-ternalize the mimetic configuration between self, other, and center of attention.

One can agree with Girard that too close a focus of attention on the other can lead to forms of mimetic rivalry that may become counterpro-ductive. But Tomasello's research suggests that imitation is in fact a far more flexible phenomenon than Girard acknowledges. The child's iden-tification with someone else is possible only once the child can engage in scenes of joint attention. But entry into the latter is also the source of an immense cultural productivity that can turn mimetic rivalry into any number of more "peaceful" solutions. Indeed, the conflict between self and other—for example, in the scenes of sibling rivalry examined by Girard in his analyses of literary and religious texts—frequently provides the motivation for constantly renewing the joint attentional scene, for instance, in an extended dialogue in which the interlocutors attempt to see the other's point of view and vice versa. Tomasello cites research that young children who have siblings are more likely to identify with other points of view, because they have learned from an early age to engage in joint attentional scenes in which their desires have been in conflict with someone else's. The joint attentional scene provides the opening to ultimately limitless forms of negotiation and deferral as participants seek to engage each other in their shared and—thanks to their status as co-equals in the scene—sharable perspectives on the world. The generativity of this scene is the core of Tomasello's theory. His reflections on the ontogeny of this scene, as children are encouraged to participate in it by their parents, is a powerful example of originary thinking in the social and cognitive sciences.

PART II

THE END OF LITERATURE

Chapter 3

The Critic as Ethnographer

The discipline of literature is no longer restricted to literature. Literature still forms a large part of what we study in English and Modern Language departments, but our interest in the interpretation of classic works by authors like Shakespeare, Goethe, and Proust has now been extended to embrace all kinds of other texts, including texts that do not appear to be literary at all, for example, oral testimonies, rituals, advertisements, pop music, and clothing.

But in what sense are these nonliterary objects "texts"? They are texts because they invite interpretation. But what is interpretation? Interpretation is the symbolic process whereby we translate the significance of one thing by seeing it in terms of another. For example, to those who worship it, the totem at the center of the rite is not just a piece of wood (that is, an object to be described in terms of its intrinsic physical and chemical structure); it is also a *symbol* of the deity who inhabits the wood as a living presence. The surest indication of the reality of this presence is the fact that the totem commands continued sacrifice from its worshippers, whose very lives are consequently understood to depend on it. In the act of sacrifice, the totem is interpreted to refer to the deity. This form of *symbolic* reference is not to be confused with more basic referential processes, such as stimulus generalization. The latter is a form of *indexical* reference (for example, inferring the presence of weevils inside the totem on the basis of seeing the kind of small holes weevils bore), and it is widely used by many other animals, for instance, in the alarm-call systems of vervet monkeys.[1] Animals do not interpret signs symbolically, in terms of their linguistic, aesthetic, or sacred significance. They interpret them indexically, in terms of cognitive processes that remain unmediated by the collective act of symbolic signification.[2]

This irreducible anthropological fact explains the current preoccupation in literary studies with culture as an object of general symbolic interpretation. For if humanity is defined as the culture-using animal, and if culture is defined as that object which invites symbolic interpretation, then it follows that literary studies stands at the center of an

nded on these assumptions. For who is better trained
critic in the exercise of searching for symbolic signifi-
g beyond the literal surface to see the deeper, more *sacred*
th?

, for example, the following remark by Stephen Greenblatt, ⎯ ⎯flects on the significance of his encounter, early in his career, with Clifford Geertz's *Interpretation of Cultures*: "Geertz's account
of the project of social science rebounded with force upon literary critics
like me in the mid-1970s: it made sense of something I was already
doing, returning my own professional skills to me as more important,
more vital and illuminating, than I had myself grasped."[3] Notice how
Greenblatt interprets Geertz's influence on literary critics like himself.
It is not that Geertz teaches him something new, but that Geertz draws
out the hitherto unrecognized significance of what he "was already doing." Before he read Geertz, Greenblatt (we may surmise) felt uneasy
about spending his time writing about texts that make no ontological
claims about the extratextual world. What indeed *is* the point of literary
criticism? Geertz provides Greenblatt with an edifying anthropological
answer. The point of reading literature is to discover the deeper significance of culture. And since culture is synonymous with humanity, as
Geertz maintains, literary criticism is a privileged way of doing anthropology. When you read literature, you are learning something "more
important" about what it means to be human.

Does this mean Greenblatt really wants to do anthropology rather
than literary criticism? I think it is indeed instructive to read Greenblatt's work as an abortive attempt to found a kind of *literary* anthropology. I say "abortive" because Greenblatt's contact with anthropology
remains in the end only tentative. This is not simply because he relies
almost exclusively on Geertz for his idea of anthropology. It is rather
because he fails to recognize the full anthropological implications of his
own idea of a "poetics" of culture.[4]

What Greenblatt takes from Geertz is not in the end a theory of
culture, but rather an analogy—or, better, a *model*—for how to think
and write about the texts in his own field of literary criticism. Geertz's
writing, in its style and manner of argument, serves as the model for
Greenblatt to imitate, just as the talented disciple learns by imitating
the acknowledged master. But the secret to a good imitation, which is to
say, one that is genuinely culturally productive, is to imitate *with a difference*. Like a good metaphor or analogy, the point is not perfect identity

— *Emulation, not imitation*

(A = A), but identity-in-difference or resemblance (A is like B). If the resemblance is too great, the analogy will be dismissed as unoriginal ("Greenblatt is just a pale imitation of Geertz"). If the resemblance is too weak, the analogy will be lost altogether, and the result will be, again, dismissal ("Greenblatt completely misrepresents Geertz, and, therefore, as a faithful Geertzian, I dismiss him"). Of course, the jury is still out (and will be for some time) on the long-term historical significance of Greenblatt (and, for that matter, of Geertz too), but over the recent short term Greenblatt's influence on literary studies is not in question.

Let me venture an altogether unremarkable hypothesis for Greenblatt's recent "short-term" success. Greenblatt has an uncanny ability to take ideas that are "in the air" and turn them to a practical use that is directly accessible to his more immediate academic audience. His use of Geertz is a good example. What Greenblatt takes from Geertz, what he "imitates," is the idea that literary criticism, like anthropology, is an ethnography of the cultural other. What makes his imitation different (and readily appreciable to literary critics) is the fact that Greenblatt applies his ethnography, not to those few premodern cultures still to be found on the farthest margins of the "developing" world, but to what is conceived to be the premodern element in the high culture of the West itself. Greenblatt's imitation is thus truly a *literary* form of ethnography because its very idea of ethnography is demonstrated to be internal to the literary texts themselves.

But what accounts for Greenblatt's timeliness? What makes his writings on cultural otherness so appealing at the present time, to the extent that he has become himself a much-admired model, imitated and emulated (and envied) by so many others? A full answer to such a question would no doubt require a consideration of multiple historical factors, but I believe underlying them all is a more readily grasped *desire*. What motivates Greenblatt in his aesthetic criticism is the same thing that motivated the original writers of nineteenth-century anthropology, namely, a deep fascination and curiosity for cultures radically different from our own.

But here we encounter a crucial historical difference. Compared to the early anthropologists, the anthropological writer today seems to be at a distinct disadvantage. The "classic" ethnographer wrote at a time when it was still possible to observe, in distant pockets of the known world, tribal cultures relatively untouched by Western ideas and institutions. In contrast, the contemporary ethnographer has no tribe to study, at least no tribe that has not been influenced by the spread of Western culture through its chief instrument of dissemination, the modern exchange system.

With no cultural other to encounter in the contemporary world (that is, no culture sufficiently different to shock the Western observer into recognizing the coherence of his own), the gaze naturally turns inward to the history of the very culture anthropology had originally hoped to turn its back on. But this inward turn, as Greenblatt's work at times poignantly demonstrates, is tinged with a sadness and nostalgia that is a reminder of the lost hopes of the old romantic anthropology. There are, to be sure, no longer any illusions about being able to observe the originary "elementary forms" of culture in some as-yet-undiscovered primitive tribe. Instead, the search for such an origin is henceforth shadowed by the realization that the origin is "always already" a representation, which is to say that culture is by definition removed from its historical origin, that historical self-consciousness is the condition of being human, whether you are from the West or not. But with this realization, the anthropological writer turns from the world of the present to the world of the past and, in particular, to those texts that seem to preserve some trace of the sacred, of which the modern world appears so obnoxiously bereft. Classic texts are reread for signs of the experience of sacrality, and the historical archive itself is opened to the search for strangeness, for the alterity that will show us *in fictional form* something of the original mystery of a world still enchanted by the sacred. What was for so long a rite of passage for the professional anthropologist, namely, the firsthand observation of a nonliterate tribal culture, has been translated into a "rite of passage" for the professional literary critic: the archival encounter with the textual otherness of discrete "historical cultures" or "aesthetic periods." Henceforth the critic's understanding of the canonical aesthetic work is mediated by those texts produced on the margins of the cultural period in which the aesthetic work originally emerged.

The new historicism is thus truly an "ethnography of the text," its fieldwork conducted in the historical archive, which is carefully combed for instances of unfamiliarity and strangeness (for example, pamphlets on long-since-forgotten religious debates, transcripts from court cases, manuals on witch hunting, and so on). The hope is that, by juxtaposing in loose analogic fashion these unfamiliar documents dredged up from the past with the familiar texts of the aesthetic tradition, the latter may be renewed for appreciation by the "happy few"—that handful of critics (mostly other professors and their willing graduate students) who have both the leisure and temperament to follow the literary ethnographer into the miscellany of the historical archive. The point is not to "reduce" the aesthetic text to the status of a historical document (a criticism too easily made by more traditionally minded scholars), but on the contrary to defend and preserve the aesthetic text as an object distinct from those ephemeral cultural products offered for mass consumption by the modern exchange system. For by insisting on the necessary historicity of the aesthetic text, the critic distinguishes his authentic "historicist" reading from those inauthentic ones recycled for popular consumption. In this manner, the popular reading of the text is defamiliarized and negated, and in its place is substituted the unfamiliar one of the critic.[5] But the underlying intention of the historicist reading has been clear all along. The real aim is to shock us with the experience of cultural otherness. For perhaps in our shock we may catch a glimpse of the originary (sacred) difference that the early anthropologists had set out to find when they left behind the familiar shores of their own (desacralized) culture.

As I have implied in these remarks, there is a religious aspect to the ethnographic search for otherness. But it is religious in the paradoxical sense that the search for otherness is permanently haunted by the absence of religion, by the self-consciousness that the traditional ritual structures of a communal culture, rather than being universal and self-evident, are local and particular. The quest for cultural difference, which is to say, the romantic anthropology that arose in response to the "scientific" anthropology of the Enlightenment, can emerge only in a culture where religion itself is no longer a dominant force.

Hence, for example, the current interest among critics in the notion of "performativity," which is a combination of the pragmatics of speech-act theory (J. L. Austin, John Searle) with the romantic anthropology of the cultural other (Johann Gottfried Herder).[6] Implicit in the idea of the text as embedded in the particular occasion of its original performance is the desire to return the lifeless words on the page to an imagined, more vital ritual context, one in which the immediate experience of collective belonging prevails over the loneliness and alienation that is the historical condition of the modern reader's relationship to the past.[7] But because the desire for collective membership is by definition denied to those who interpret a ritual *as an aesthetic text*, the aesthetic experience of alienation becomes unavoidable. Instead of being returned to the collective context of the ritually integrated community, the reader is forced to remain an aesthetic outsider, like the anthropologist observing the rites of some exotic tribe. This alienating experience of the otherness of history leads to the assumption, subsequently taken to be axiomatic, that only a sufficiently "historicized" (that is, "ethnographic") form of literary scholarship is able to show us the true (that is, unfamiliar) meaning of the text—which is to say, its essential cultural difference.

And yet ethnography, whether directed at the contemporary other or the historical other, is still a part of anthropology in the broad sense.[8] If Greenblatt tends to ignore this fact, Geertz certainly does not. Indeed, *The Interpretation of Cultures* (which Greenblatt cites as having had such an enormous influence on him) is explicitly concerned with elaborating a general theory of culture. So why does Greenblatt choose to ignore this aspect of Geertz's writings? Surely the theory deserves to be carefully scrutinized before we decide to put the ideas to practical use?

I think the reason for Greenblatt's delicate sidestepping of the theory has to do with a variety of factors, the most prominent of which is that Greenblatt's interest in Geertz extends only as far as it enables him to justify his own disciplinary interest in the culture of a particular aesthetic period.[9] Yet it would be both misleading and unfair to suggest that this theoretical shortcoming is somehow unique to Greenblatt. For the same shortcoming characterizes the discipline as a whole, which for all its talk of culture is less interested in exploring the anthropology implicit in this concept than in using the word as a convenient label for any object the critic deems fit to interpret.[10]

There is no question that the idea of culture has become ubiquitous in literary criticism. But the curious thing is that it has done so with very little fundamental reflection on what culture actually is—whether, for example, it is optional or not, and why it should be preferred to the category it has by now largely replaced and upon which the discipline of English was built in the first place, namely, literature. What exactly is the difference between literature and culture? And how can we explain this extraordinary gravitation toward the concept of culture among today's critics of literature?

Culture and the Market

There is no doubt that the old *high* culture, once singled out for special treatment by critics like Matthew Arnold, T. S. Eliot, and F. R. Leavis, is dying—if it is not indeed already completely dead. But as the old high culture dies, popular culture—the "culture of the people"—emerges to fill the void. But the impetus behind popular culture is not the same as the impetus behind high culture. It is not motivated by the same desire to attain, by long and arduous study, a place in "the great tradition" of Western literature, but by the far more pragmatic need to satisfy the desire of the individual *consumer.*

I think the same economic impetus lies behind the current use of the concept of culture in the universities. It is evident, for example, in the creation of fields like cultural studies: programs concerned exclusively with the popular culture of the present, which is to say, the culture of the marketplace. As our lives become increasingly suffused with the ephemeral products of the market, the idea of culture hurries to keep pace, desperate not to lose out on such a rich profusion of material and symbolic wealth. The old division between sacred and profane, which, as Durkheim saw, subordinated economic to ritual exchange, has been reversed: culture is now everywhere *because* the market is everywhere, which is the same thing as saying that culture is nowhere. The centralizing function of culture—implicit in the old metaphor of a literary "high" culture—has been "decentered." Modern critics like T. S. Eliot and F. R. Leavis believed high culture to be essential to the spiritual survival of the community, and they fought hard in their essays (and, in Eliot's case, in his poetry too) to defend it and to oppose what they took to be the corrosive effect of the economic exchange system on human relationships. But their criticism was already the sign of the old high culture's demise, which was the effect—and not the cause—of the rise of the market and of the increasingly global consumer culture it trades in. But when culture becomes decentered, which is to say, desacralized, it also becomes an object for systematic theoretical reflection.

It is in this broad historical sense that we should begin to understand the current fascination among literary critics for anthropology and the concept of culture. Greenblatt's interest in Geertz is thus only a local instance of this broader picture. Indeed, I would submit that the "long" wave of theory in literary studies, from New Criticism through structuralism and deconstruction, to new historicism, cultural studies, and beyond, constitutes a single ongoing attempt to come to grips with the problem of, in Eric Gans's phrase, "the end of culture."[11]

Yet few critics have been tempted by Gans's further suggestion that the central problem of modernity—the problem of the end of culture—is best approached not from the (impossible) perspective of a projected "end of history," but from its minimal hypothetical point of origin.[12] Instead, theory in the humanities remains in a state of permanent paralysis, caught in a kind of interdisciplinary no-man's-land: on the one hand, forbidding itself the luxury of the "grand narrative" out of a superstitious fear of committing the teleological sin of nineteenth-century evolutionary anthropology and, on the other, discontented with the ad hoc synchronic empiricism of the social sciences.

So where does the critic go? Greenblatt, as we have seen, goes to Geertz. But Greenblatt's appropriation of Geertz is not really theoretical.[13] What inspires Greenblatt in his reading of ethnography is the romantic desire to "go native," to get inside the culture of the anthropological other. This is the real point behind the new historicist anecdote. Like the fetish or relic of an exotic ritual, it signifies the critic's professional credentials as the uniquely qualified interpreter of the cultural other. Who else would have noticed so much significance in such an insignificant detail?

But I think we can do better. And I think we can do better by reading Geertz *theoretically*. This will enable us to see how, even in the case of an avowed "culturalist" (that is, someone who defines anthropology as the "interpretation of cultures"), the paradox of understanding how "culture" emerges from "nature" all too quickly results in the unconscious expulsion of culture altogether. That this expulsion is also the defining condition of the scientific explanation of culture merely underscores the fact that Geertz's interpretive approach has not yet adequately synthesized the form of his philosophical presuppositions with their intended anthropological content. For despite his conviction that it is the *symbolic form* of culture that lies behind its immense historical productivity, Geertz is unable to translate this claim into a truly originary definition of the human. Geertz's anthropology thus remains bound by the same metaphysical limitations that also motivate the scientific and philosophical traditions' denial of literary anthropology's right to exist. The fact that Geertz is usually derided by more hardnosed, scientifically minded anthropologists as an obscurantist because of his interpretive or humanistic strategy is no argument against this point.[14] On the contrary, it merely demonstrates the extent to which the modern discipline of anthropology, whether narrowly empirical or broadly humanistic, remains obstinately attached to this same metaphysical tradition. Yet it is precisely for this reason that the literary critics are better positioned than their colleagues in the social sciences to appreciate the fact that symbolic or interpretive anthropology—in a word, a *literary* anthropology—begins not with an empirically testable hypothesis of origin, but with a minimally conceived heuristic fiction or "originary hypothesis" that is tested not by what precedes it empirically, but by what follows from its minimal anthropological assumptions. But before we can explore these epistemological points further, we must understand the inadequacy of those answers implicit in the empirical approach.

Ethnography and the Evolution of Culture

How does Geertz explain the origin of culture? Geertz proposes that culture functions as a "set of control mechanisms ... for governing behavior."[15] The implication is that culture continues a process that is inherent in the natural biological process of evolution. In this sense, culture is understood to be an extension (albeit a remarkable and unprecedented one) of the means whereby complex chemical structures evolve the means to reproduce themselves—to become, that is, more complex biochemical forms. For the origin of life may itself be described as the origin of a mechanism for self-replication. The genetic "code" is the means whereby physical and chemical matter discovers how to replicate itself, where this replication is regulated by the process of natural selection. The difference between a DNA molecule and the proteins it encodes (not to mention the actual organisms, like amoebas and elephants, that ultimately evolve by natural selection) is a difference in complexity of structure. Rocks and water are relatively "stable" structures because they maintain themselves by the physical and chemical forces of atomic and molecular attraction alone. Compared to rocks and water, amoebas and elephants are breathtakingly complex. So how do they manage to "survive" the tendency for energy to disperse itself over simpler structures? The answer is that they do not. Amoebas and elephants (like all living things) die. But not before passing themselves on, so to speak, through their genes, so that new amoebas and elephants can come to exist and then die. Expressed from the viewpoint of the genes, rather than the self-contained unit of the organism, the function of things like amoebas or elephants is to increase the chances for the genes to replicate themselves. These phenotypes are, as Richard Dawkins puts it, "vehicles" by which strings of DNA, in the context of natural selection, manage to regulate their own reproduction.[16]

This is the struggle for life told from the point of view of its most basic ingredient: the gene. But what does human evolution look like told from the point of view not of biology but of humans seeking to understand themselves as cultural beings? This is the specifically *anthropological* question that Geertz at least implicitly poses by attempting to address the problem of the origin of culture. But the curious thing about Geertz's answer is that he remains of two minds about it. On the one hand, he wants to follow his anthropological instincts and interpret culture as the *defining difference* in studying human evolution; on the other, he downplays this difference and instead explains culture as an extension of general biological evolutionary processes. These two contradictory tendencies form the unconscious subtext to *The Interpretation of Cultures*.

Consider first Geertz's biological claim for the origin of culture. Geertz argues that culture is causally necessary to complete the underlying biology of humans. Without culture, humanity would be, he says, an unfinished genetic "monster."[17] In a memorable phrase, Geertz calls humanity the "unfinished animal" because of its extraordinary dependence on extragenetic factors (46). Whereas the "behavior patterns of lower animals are . . . given to them with their physical structure," for "man, what are innately given are extremely general response capacities" (45–46).

But to what extent is this really a causal argument for the origin of culture? Geertz bases his conclusion on the fact that genetically and anatomically *modern* humans require culture to complete the ontogenetic process. For example, linguists have long recognized the presence of a so-called "critical period," from birth to around age twelve, when the child requires contact with other (adult) language users in order to become itself a competent speaker and therefore a participating member in the culture. But this already assumes the genetic completion of the phylogenetic formation of modern Homo sapiens, that is, a prolonged evolutionary period in which symbolic culture and genes coevolved to become, in terms of ontogeny, mutually dependent upon one another. The question still remains as to what motivated the initial origin of the "extragenetic, outside-the-skin control mechanisms" (44). And it is this initial point of cultural origin that Geertz assumes, uncritically, to be a predictable consequence of more general evolutionary processes.

The larger issue here is the presence within the modern discipline of anthropology of a conflict between scientific and humanistic models of explanation. When Geertz discusses human evolution, he draws on the dominant scientific paradigm, the biological theory of evolution. This theory, which is all but undisputed in what Thomas Kuhn would call the "normal" science of biology, explains the origin of culture not as a sudden "big bang," but as a gradually emerging trait with clearly recognizable evolutionary precursors. Taking this scientific approach, the evolutionary precursors of human culture—its "elementary forms," so to speak—are to be inferred not merely from an examination of the fossil record but, more concretely, from observations of the living "protoculture" of such closely related primates as chimpanzees. Examples of protoculture among chimpanzees would include things like their call system, tool use, grooming, and group hunting.[18]

On the other hand, when Geertz turns to contemporary or historical examples of human culture, the biological theory of evolution recedes abruptly into the background, and Geertz instead relies on his own (highly cultivated) anthropological intuitions in order to explain the phenomena he observes. For example, in the context of a discussion of Balinese ritual, Geertz begins with an intuitively persuasive definition of religion that enables him to pinpoint what is distinctive about ritual as compared to what he calls the scientific, the aesthetic, and the commonsensical "perspectives" by which people grasp the world around them (110–11). Significantly, it is also in this context that Geertz asserts the originary necessity of symbols for explaining the function of cultural institutions like religion and art. The question is: what enables Geertz to assume the originary significance of symbols (for example, when he discusses particular cultural institutions like Balinese ritual), but to ignore this same significance when he discusses human evolution more generally? Or, to put it slightly differently, what enables him to assert, on the one hand, that symbols are unique to human cognition (and therefore to the concept of culture) and, on the other, to deny this same anthropological difference?

The inconsistency has to do with the different epistemological contexts for Geertz's discussion of culture. Approached from the direction of biology rather than anthropology, culture is to be interpreted as simply another species-wide "trait," like bipedalism and binocular vision. In this context, culture is explained as one would explain any other biological trait, that is, by comparing it to similar traits observed in other species and then explaining its existence as a product of either homologous or convergent evolution. When, on the other hand, culture is approached from the perspective of anthropology, it is no longer considered to be simply one trait among others. On the contrary, it is taken to *constitute* our very understanding of what it means to be human: the origin of culture is the origin of anthropology. This is ultimately what leads Geertz to define, somewhat cumbersomely, symbolic representation as the "intertransposability of models for and models of," and then to assert that this capacity for symbolic transposition is the "distinctive characteristic of our mentality" compared to animal cognition (94). In other words, specifically human culture has the unique double-sided ability to refer to an already existing reality *and* to shape reality to itself: the former is an example of a "model *of* reality"; the latter, a "model *for* reality" (93).

Why Interpretation?

This indispensable link between the presence of symbolic culture and the need for human self-understanding—that is, for anthropology—is what makes it both possible and necessary for Geertz to rely on his intuitive, nonempirical understanding of culture when he engages in the anthropological task of the "interpretation of cultures." Now for the student of religion, it is certainly not atypical or controversial to work in this intuitive and illustrative fashion. Indeed, this has been the preferred method of comparative religion at least since the days of James Frazer and the Cambridge ritualists. It is, furthermore, no mere coincidence that students of literature work similarly when they propose a "theory" that will then be confirmed by their interpretation of a selection of literary texts. In both cases, it is never altogether clear how the theory is to be distinguished from the confirmation of the theory in the interpretation of particular texts; on the contrary, one is frequently tempted to conclude that the interpretation is itself an instance of the theory.

But why should cultural anthropology and literary studies be unable to separate the presentation of their constitutive theories from the testing of those same theories? Why is it the case that when one interprets a particular cultural work one is, as is frequently pointed out by those who disagree with the interpretation, always already being "theoretical"? Or, to put the same question slightly differently, why are the most heated debates in the humanities always centered on the desire to expose someone else's ideology, which is to say, the unexpressed theoretical presuppositions that are understood to be *unconsciously determining* the interpreter's discourse?

These questions get to the heart of the debate about the epistemological status of interpretation. The implication is that the fundamental categories assumed by cultural analysis do not exist independently of their representation. To define one's fundamental concepts or categories of analysis is also to identify the constitutive elements of one's theory because the interpretation that follows from the theory has no other ontological guarantee than the existence of the definition itself. This does not mean that every interpretation is also therefore a "theory," at least not in the sense that one normally understands this term. What distinguishes a theory from the broader category of interpretation is an epistemological and methodological principle: the theory functions as a *more minimal*—and therefore more easily sharable—interpretation of its object. It functions not merely to reproduce a preexisting historically specific interpretation of the cultural object, but to identify the minimal cultural categories necessary for the interpretation of the object to exist in the first place. It is, in short, the basis of a minimal anthropology. The first moment of any interpretive anthropology begins with the analysis of the originary categories that constitute its definition of the human.

An analogy from sports may help to illustrate the point. In soccer, the winning team is whoever scores the most goals in a given period of time. But what is a goal? The definition of a goal is when the ball crosses the goal line. But notice the peculiar thing about this definition. There is nothing inherent in the actual physical objects involved that enables us to explain the causal origin of the definition. There is nothing intrinsic to the structure of the ball, or the goal line, or indeed to the players involved, that determines the fact that when the ball crosses the goal line it counts as a score of one point.[19] Interpreting the event as a goal requires understanding the definition because the definition constitutes its object. It is only because all those involved in the game (the players, the referee, the spectators) grasp this definition that they also understand the game.

Now imagine the arrival of an anthropologist from Mars who wishes to analyze the behavior of a group of humans kicking an inflated spherical object around an open space. He observes that the behavior of the players (as well as the spectators) centers on the ball. He also observes the extraordinary ecstasy of one half of the players and the dejection of the other half when the ball crosses the goal line at one end of the field. He might even write an account of this behavior in his journal, so he can share his observations with his colleagues back on Mars.

Has our Martian visitor truly understood soccer? He has seen the agony of defeat, the glory of victory, the wild cheers of the crowd, but has he really understood what is going on? Is he able to define to his Martian colleagues what soccer is?

Consider the problem from the point of view of the Martian. What categories does he possess by which to interpret the game? Suppose that our Martian is also an accomplished scientist. He has studied all kinds of life forms throughout the universe, including humans. He has a good understanding of human physiology and is well-versed in Darwin's theory of evolution by natural selection. So he goes to work interpreting soccer in terms of these biological categories. What does he see? He sees that playing soccer is good exercise: it increases overall muscle power and aerobic fitness; it enhances motor skills (especially of the feet and legs); and it coordinates the actions of the individual with those of the group. He concludes that soccer functions as a form of "play," that is, as a rehearsal for the real-life struggle for survival, which will select only the fittest individuals. Our Martian observer is pleased at his discovery. It is now clear to him why soccer—and other sports like it—are played by humans the world over: soccer enhances the individual's reproductive fitness. And why not interpret soccer in these functional biological terms?

Because that is not how *we* interpret soccer. Soccer is not just a form of exercise to increase muscle tone and aerobic fitness, or to attract mates, or to increase social intelligence. It is also a game, and as a game it includes a set of symbolic rules that constitute our way of interpreting what happens on the soccer field. And herein lies the key to our Martian's truly understanding the function of soccer: he must be able to grasp what he observes in terms of symbolic rules, which means minimally being able to define what counts as a goal. To be able to represent what soccer is, both to himself and to his fellow anthropologists on Mars, he would have to be able to grasp the constitutive symbolic categories of soccer. He would, in effect, have to be able to write a version of the rule-book of soccer in his journal. If he cannot do that, then he has not understood the game.

But notice what is assumed by this example. It assumes a desire on the part of the Martian to *enter into dialogue* with humans. For how could he possibly even begin to understand concepts like goal, game, player, defeat, or victory without also being a language user like us? But why should our Martian be capable of representing the world symbolically as we do? Without this capacity, there is simply no way for the Martian to grasp the conceptual structure of soccer and hence no way for him to define its constitutive categories, such as the definition of a goal.

Symbolic Anthropology

Now reconsider Geertz's definition of culture as a system of symbols that both regulates and constitutes human behavior. The regulative function of culture is implicit in Geertz's notion of culture as a model *for* patterning human behavior. A religious rite regulates human action; it tells us *what* to do in *this* particular situation. The constitutive function, on the other hand, is implicit in Geertz's idea that the process of symbolization is responsible for creating the social reality of religion in the first place. In an important sense, the religious rite constitutes a reality that is quite separate from the world of everyday perception. This is the "model of" aspect of the rite. The rite does not just tell us what to do, it also functions as a model *of* the world.

But this world is not the same thing as the world of sensuous perception. It is not the world of rocks, trees, and cats—what J. L. Austin called the "medium-sized dry goods" of common perceptual experience. It is rather the social reality that is constituted by the very performance of the rite. For example, in undergoing the sacrament of marriage, two hitherto unmarried individuals are incorporated into the institution of marriage. But the rite of marriage exists only because it is itself part of a total social reality, which includes things like the church and its hierarchy of priests, as well as the church-goers, both married and unmarried, who make up its membership. A rite exists as part of a total institutional reality, and as such it functions as a representation of the world into which each individual—through its various rites of passage—is incorporated.[20]

But here we seem to arrive at an impasse overlooked by Geertz. For how do we test the truth of religious representations? If religion indeed functions as a model *of* the world, as Geertz maintains, then this implies a difference between the model and the object it describes. Surely the model deserves to be tested by judging its ability to measure up to the object it also purports to represent? Ought we not to submit the religious model—if indeed it is a "model"—to the same standards of empirical falsifiability as we do any other scientific model?

To ask this question is to assume that there is ultimately no difference between religious and scientific representations of the world. Geertz sometimes talks as though this is the case. For instance, he refers to the example of a scientific theory of hydraulics used in the construction of a dam and argues that the theory is both a model "of" reality and a model "for" reality: it is a model *of* reality because it seeks to explain the real physical relationships existing between the water and the dam; it is a model *for* reality because on the basis of the symbolic model, one can then manipulate reality to build nonsymbolic things; for example, one could build a real dam. Geertz then goes on to say that "for psychological and social systems, and for cultural models that we would not ordinarily refer to as 'theories,' but rather as 'doctrines,' 'melodies,' or 'rites,' the case is in no way different" (93).

But this last statement is simply not true. Culture is not the same thing as a scientific theory. Rites are not "models" in the same sense that a theory of hydraulics is a model. A scientific model is tested quite differently from a cultural "model." Science aims to explain the intrinsic structure of the world. The latter is not held to be dependent upon the formulation of the model for its existence. The fundamental entities that a scientific theory aims to *discover* are not understood to be coterminous with the model used to explain them. What makes one scientific model ultimately preferable to another is the fact that a model is judged not merely against another model, but against the objective standard provided by a preexisting nonsymbolic reality. This is what we mean when we say that a model is empirically testable. It is empirically testable because it strives to give an account of a world that exists outside the medium of symbolic representation. Of course, the model must inevitably make use of symbols, but the latter are conceived to be "transparent" to their objects. For the scientist, symbols function as a useful means for accessing a reality that exists outside the mediating function of language itself. This does not mean that we must therefore naively believe that the model is *the same thing* as the reality it seeks to describe. How could it be, since representation implies the very division between the symbol and its object that makes scientific modeling possible in the first place? Precisely the model's utility as a scientific explanation is a condition of the assumption that it refers to a reality that is ontologically separate from it.

But the same is not the case for cultural representations. Culture does not aim to explain the intrinsic causal structure of the physical and biological world. In an important sense, a cultural "model" (for example, a religious rite) constitutes the world to which it also refers. The rite isn't a blueprint for the physical structure of the world. It is rather a blueprint for *human action*. Its "truth" is tested by its pragmatic value as a model for how to think and behave as a member of a community, where membership in this community is ultimately given by the constitutive function of symbolization itself.

The trouble with Geertz's theory of interpretation is that, as in the case of the interpretive theories of Nietzsche and his postmodern disciples, he does not recognize this distinction between scientific explanation and cultural interpretation. Geertz assumes there is no difference between a cultural performance and a scientific theory. Both are equally "models of" and "models for" because both are equally dependent upon the use of symbols. But this is to ignore a basic difference in how symbols function in each case.

Word and World

One way to grasp the difference is to see it in terms of the notion of "direction of fit" between symbol and object, word and world.[21] A scientific model uses symbols (usually iconic models or drawings, rather than words in the narrow linguistic sense) to construct an accurate representation of the world, where this world (that is, the fundamental ontology assumed by physics, chemistry, and biology) is assumed to exist outside the constitutive categories of the symbols themselves. Its direction of fit is thus world → word: it manipulates symbols to fit, as closely as possible, the nonsymbolic structure of the world. A cultural "model," on the other hand, uses symbols to construct ex nihilo, so to speak, a social reality that exists *on top of* the brute physical reality described by physics, chemistry, and biology. Its direction of fit is thus both word → world and world → word: it seeks to make the world conform to the word, but it also assumes the existence of the world designated by the word. In performing a rite, for example, the participants seek to recreate their shared experience of a world that is, in the final analysis, only available as a rite: that is, as part of a social reality that is constituted by the very symbolic categories also used to refer to it. The rite is both a performance and a representation, both a "model for" and a "model of." It constitutes the category (the sacred) that it also seeks to represent as an independently existing object. This constitutive or "performative" element of symbolic representation holds for all specifically anthropological categories, for example, the sacred, the aesthetic, the ethical, the moral, desire, linguistic and economic exchange, and so on: in short, precisely those categories assumed by culture and treated as objects of inquiry in the humanities. Without the symbols, there would be no possibility of, for example, religious experience because the very category of the sacred depends upon the symbols that are used both to constitute it and to make it accessible. Compare this cultural "model" of representation to a scientific theory of hydraulics. The physics and chemistry of the flow patterns of water do not owe their existence to the theory. Water would continue to flow in conformity to the physics and chemistry of water, whether or not a scientific model existed to explain these patterns.

In the normal course of things, we take the constitutive function of symbols completely for granted. When I buy a cup of coffee, I do not consciously think about the fact that my giving someone else money in exchange for the coffee constitutes the abstract exchange value of the coffee. Rather, I immediately grasp the situation as bound by the institutional status of coffee shops, money, customers, owners, employees, and so on, and my exchange of money for coffee takes place in the context of this immediately graspable social reality. But it is precisely the ease with which we interpret the brute physical phenomena of the world in terms of their symbolically mediated institutional functions that makes it so easy to forget that the possibility of interpreting the world in this symbolic fashion is an extremely remarkable and, from an evolutionary standpoint, quite unprecedented phenomenon.

But here is the central paradox: there is no way you can get just *a little bit* of symbolic culture. One often hears that chimpanzees and other nonhuman primates have "protoculture," meaning they have "a little bit" of culture but not as much as we do. But this is the wrong way to look at the origin of culture. Culture is not collection of things that we can add to and subtract from, like a pile of stones. Social behavior is either symbolic (and therefore an instance of culture, in the sense used by Geertz), or it is not symbolic (and therefore not cultural). There is no halfway point. You are either interpreting the world symbolically, that is, in terms of the symbolic imposition of value on the brute physical reality of the world, or you are interpreting the world in terms of more basic perceptual-cognitive functions. This is why accounts that seek to dilute the definition of culture in terms of the elementary or unconscious "protoculture" of chimpanzees or other nonhuman animals (including ancestral prehumans) are ultimately mistaking the symbolic function of culture for some *other* nonsymbolic function, for example, a more basic biological function, like reproductive fitness.

The Text as Origin

We have already seen, in the example of the Martian anthropologist, what is wrong with this kind of reductionist approach, but it is worth repeating the essential point, this time by focusing on what is specifically "anthropological" about the problem of human origin. From the scientific perspective, human origin is understood to be a strictly empirical problem. The solution is not to invent a story—a "text"—that explains why humans are the way they are, but to examine the available empirical evidence, including that of both our hominid ancestors (whose living patterns are to be inferred from fossil remains) and our closest living primate relatives, in particular, chimpanzees and bonobos. This evidence is then to be interpreted not in the context of personally invented theories, definitions, or speculations, but in the context of the currently reigning paradigm in the life sciences, which is the biological theory of evolution.

I do not wish to dispute the explanatory power of this approach. On the contrary, its achievements in the life sciences are undeniable. In the social sciences, on the other hand, it is far from clear whether scientific method can eclipse the traditional discovery procedure of textual interpretation, which continues to be the tacitly accepted "method" in the interpretive text-based disciplines that constitute the central core of the humanities. This was most aggressively apparent during the heyday of deconstruction, which attempted to show that the ad hoc empirical methods of the social sciences ultimately depended upon the textual methods of the literary scholar. Today the lessons of deconstruction have not simply been forgotten. On the contrary, they have been assimilated to the point of a commonplace. The real inheritors of deconstruction are those literary scholars, like Greenblatt, who have turned Jacques Derrida's and Paul de Man's scrupulous attention to the blind spots and aporias of the canonical texts of the literary and philosophical traditions to nothing less than all culture. Not just Shakespeare and Hegel, but economic, juridical, governmental, and other assorted "cultural" objects that record the otherwise mundane interactions of everyday social life, are now up for grabs. All are "texts" to be interpreted for their ironies and paradoxes, using the methods of literary analysis. No document or cultural artifact is too insignificant to find its way into the web of semiotic significance spun by the new historicist. Indeed, the more apparently insignificant the cultural object, the more gratifying it becomes to demonstrate its hitherto unrealized cultural-aesthetic significance.

The interdisciplinary success of periodic literary offenses like deconstruction and new historicism seems obvious to me. It has nothing to do with the superior merits of one or other of the particular theories that continually jostle for attention in the small but vocal marketplace of academic literary criticism. Rather, it has to do with the basic definition of the human implicit in the very discipline of literature. For if literary critics can agree on one thing, it is that what takes primacy in the study of culture is the necessity of textual interpretation. Translated into a definition of the human, this premise becomes the basis of a literary anthropology or, as Greenblatt likes to put it, a cultural poetics. The human is a text to be interpreted, not because there is "nothing outside the text" but because without the text there is no humanity. To the biologist or physicist (as for any natural scientist), it is certainly absurd to claim there is nothing outside the text. But to those concerned centrally with the study of the human (that is, those in the humanities and the "anthropological" social sciences), it is literally quite true that without the mediating presence of the originary scene of symbolic representation— "textuality," if one likes—there is no humanity and therefore no object of study.

It should therefore be unsurprising that the anthropologist most widely known for his symbolic or interpretive approach to culture should also be the most congenial figurehead for literary critics in search of broader disciplinary legitimacy. For what could be more breathtaking than to discover, as Greenblatt did in the 1970s, that at the heart and soul of the human sciences, in the discipline of anthropology itself, lay a method that had been practiced by literary and biblical scholars long before the first anthropologists arrived on the scene.

Does this mean that literary criticism and cultural anthropology are ultimately concerned with the same thing? Is Greenblatt really an anthropologist? Is Geertz really a literary critic? Is it possible that the difference between literary criticism and anthropology is ultimately dependent upon an underlying unity that has been obscured by the modern university's tendency to fragment anthropological knowledge into ad hoc areas of specialization?

My inclination is to answer this last question in the affirmative. I think that there is a great deal more to Greenblatt's use of Geertz than mere superficial borrowing of another discipline's concepts for reasons of prestige. The trouble is that Greenblatt himself fails to pursue this convergence to its ultimate anthropological source, thereby leaving himself open to the charge, unfair or not, that his appropriation is indeed superficial. In reading Geertz, Greenblatt recognizes something familiar to his literary sensibilities: namely, that anthropology, like literary criticism, is constituted by the act of interpretation. But this moment of cross-disciplinary recognition is all too brief because it fails to ask the next logical question: what is (the origin of) interpretation? In the heady excitement of discovering that another discipline shares a similar "method," it is forgotten that this similarity of method is a consequence of the similarity of the object.

This object is humanity itself. In anthropology, this fact is no doubt more obvious than in literary criticism, which deals with texts rather than with real people. But once we realize that texts are produced by humans alone and that the "exotic" non-Western cultures studied by classic ethnography are the products of humans essentially (that is, biologically) no different from ourselves, then we arrive at the conclusion that at the origin of both interpretive anthropology and literary criticism lies the assumption that the human is most succinctly defined as the creature which represents itself by its culture, which is to say, by its "texts."

But once we make representation the center of an anthropology, isn't this just to invite the radical relativism of poststructuralist theory? For if humanity knows itself only through its representations, then it becomes impossible to locate an origin that is not always already a representation. In attempting to trace a representation back to its supposed origin, the anthropologist or literary critic is engaged in a supposedly hopeless task because every origin turns out to be another representation. At no point in this "hermeneutic" circle can we definitively establish the priority of one representation over another. Nor, needless to say, can we hope to extricate ourselves from the circle altogether. The anthropologist who studies another society's representations is not thereby excluded from (the prejudices of) his own. On the contrary, contemporary cultural anthropology has hammered this point home more forcefully than any other. But after the routine accusations of ethnocentrism have died down, we are still left with the fact that the discipline of anthropology, ethnocentric or not, begins with the critical attempt by humans to understand themselves. That the need for this self-under-standing was prompted by the discovery of cultures vastly different from those of Western Europe is not an argument against anthropology. On the contrary, it is a demonstration of its critical coming of age: that the anthropology implicit in the West's own self-understanding could not assume the historical inevitability of its own culture. Anthropology had to historicize itself, which meant comparing the texts of its own tradi-tion with those to be found in the traditions of others and then sorting out the historical differences and similarities. That these other traditions were, more often than not, also oral traditions merely demonstrated the necessity that the anthropologist had to travel to witness the occasion of their performance in order to record them for (later) theoretical reflec-tion. In an oral culture, there are no lending libraries that allow one the convenience of armchair study.

Ethnography Revisited

Geertz, like the literary critics who champion his work, is aware that the human is defined most significantly by its use of symbolic cul-ture and, furthermore, that the interpretive methods of cultural anthro-pology are constituted by this definition. However, unlike the literary critics (who take this assumption more or less for granted), Geertz also seeks to justify the interpretive definition of the human empirically, that is, by giving a "scientific" account of human evolution that explains the origin of what he calls the "extragenetic, outside-the-skin control mech-anisms" that constitute the human animal (44).

Why does Geertz do this? Is an empirical account of human origins a necessary prerequisite for the development of an anthropology? Geertz obviously thinks that it is, for why else would he venture to give such an account? But it is important to realize that Geertz's empirical account of human evolution, though not substantively incorrect, bears no neces-sary logical relationship to his fundamental premise that the human is defined by its use of symbolic representation. All the empirical evidence Geertz cites to confirm his definition of the human stands outside the definition itself. You could grant Geertz every single empirical claim he makes, and you still would not have to grant him the further claim that the human is defined by symbolic interpretation. The latter stands prior to any possible empirical claim. It stands at the origin of the hu-man itself.

To see the difference between the logical and empirical status of the claim that humanity is constituted by its use of symbolic culture, consider once more Geertz's account of the origin of culture. Geertz argues that humans (or protohumans, for when could we properly speak of humans?) increasingly came to rely on nongenetic control mechanisms. This created a feedback loop between brain and culture. Over the course of hundreds of thousands, perhaps even millions, of years, this in turn led to an increasingly plastic brain—that is, a brain that depended less on hardwired control mechanisms and more on external "cultural" forms of control.

There are a number of points I wish to make about this account of human evolution. The first is that it is entirely circular. All that Geertz is saying is that, biologically, humans came to depend on cultural specialization because culture was necessary for biologically unspecialized humans. The reference to coevolution between (internal) genes and (external) culture should not blind us to the circularity of the argument. For what is *not* explained is precisely how cultural control mechanisms became sufficiently externalized to become subsequently an indispensable element in human biological evolution. Instead, this process of externalization is accepted as self-evident. Implicit in the empirical description is the very definition of symbolic culture Geertz seeks to establish. The account functions not as an empirical explanation, but as an inference based on a preexisting conceptual definition that, as we have already seen, is assumed by the disciplines of both cultural anthropology and literary criticism.

The second point is related to the first, and it responds to a possible methodological objection. What is wrong with Geertz's beginning with a conceptual definition of the human and then seeking to test this empirically? Is this not simply good scientific method? I agree that this is good scientific method if one's definition of science is that a definition or hypothesis must be empirically falsifiable. But Geertz's definition of culture is not empirically falsifiable. The particular cultural examples Geertz cites (for instance, when he discusses Balinese ritual) are not empirical tests at all, but rather illustrations that lend plausibility to his definition of symbolic culture. In themselves these particular analyses do not serve to falsify the definition. On the contrary, they are illustrations of the definition at work because the possibility of seeing them this way depends upon accepting the definition in the first place. The same applies to Geertz's account of human evolution. The account is plausible, but it does not establish his definition of human culture empirically. In fact, if anything, it tends to do the opposite. By turning to the biological theory of evolution, Geertz risks undermining the anthropological claim he wishes to establish, namely, that humanity is defined by its biologically unprecedented use of symbolic culture.

This leads me to my third and final point. Geertz's account of human evolution actually displaces the anthropological claim he wants to make for the *difference* between cultural interpretation and scientific explanation. This is because Geertz ignores the fact that, evolutionarily speaking, the origin of symbolic interpretation must be regarded as anomalous, not typical.[22] Geertz talks about the development of symbolic culture as though it were an entirely natural and predictable occurrence. But the fact of the matter is that there is no other species on earth that has evolved symbolic culture. We just have to examine the unfortunate situation of our closest living relative, the chimpanzee, to grasp the magnitude of this anomaly. Thanks to our capacity for symbolic culture—and hence to religion, art, science, and technology—we have adapted to every corner and climate of the globe. Meanwhile, the chimpanzee has been confined to marginal habitats in the rainforests of central and western Africa (habitats which are every day becoming more marginal, thanks to rapid deforestation by humans). The question that Geertz avoids asking is why chimpanzees, who are obviously a highly intelligent species, and who use rudimentary "tools," live in groups, and apparently engage in coordinated hunts and intergroup raiding parties,[23] have nonetheless failed to evolve a system of symbolic communication. Surely, from the point of view of comparative biology upon which evolutionary theory is based, it is aberrant in the extreme to treat the marginal case (language) as representative of other systems of communication? By judging our case as typical, rather than as anomalous, we are forced to regard our nonhuman primate cousins as failures—a species who came close but did not quite make it to our capacity for symbolic cognition.

It may be objected that I am missing Geertz's point here and thus unfairly accusing him of something he does not say. Geertz does not talk about chimpanzees at all. So how can I criticize him for failing to notice the difference between chimpanzees and humans? I can criticize him for this failure because what I am concerned with is not the fact that Geertz ignores chimpanzees in his discussion of human evolution, but that his view of the origin of culture as an unproblematic occurrence ignores the fact that no other species has evolved it.

To put the point differently, the empirical problem of discovering facts about the origin of human culture cannot ultimately be separated from the theoretical problem of representing those facts in an over-all narrative about the origin of human culture. It is no doubt com-forting to believe that a sufficiently critical and skeptical mindset—in a word, a sufficiently *scientific* mindset—will be enough to safeguard against the countervailing desire to clothe the scant empirical remains in a more satisfying, more completely realized aesthetic narrative. But it is ultimately the latter, not the former, that responds to our *narra-tive desire*. Scientific accounts of human origin are of course not pure myths; their narratives of human development are inferences based on the available empirical data. But because these accounts are also narra-tives that fulfill a basic human desire for something other than the bare facts alone are capable of revealing, it is not always easy to separate the desire to tell a good story from the evidence that constrains the tell-ing of that story.[24] No doubt this helps to explain the disproportional market share that automatically goes to scientific, rather than purely philosophical or anthropological, popularizers of the latest thinking on human self-knowledge. Scientists and their general reading public are by and large untroubled by the theoretical problem of the origin of hu-man representation. On the contrary, armed with the latest facts they appear ever closer to solving the problem of precisely when and how language and symbolic culture originated. The speed with which these accounts need to be revised as more evidence is discovered just shows how these accounts are motivated by empirical rather than theoretical considerations. But the problem of producing a more accurate picture of human evolution is not just an empirical problem. It is a *theoretical* problem about how we choose to define the human in the first place.

The Regulative and Constitutive Functions of Culture

Let us return for a moment to Geertz's definition of culture as a nongenetic control mechanism that functions both as a regulation of an already existing reality and a constitution of a new reality. In what sense does culture both regulate behavior and constitute it? The differ-ence implies the duality of symbolic reference. In the performance of a culturally significant act there are two directions of reference: there is an "external" reference to past cultural performances, which are being com-memorated or represented by the present performance; and there is an "internal" reference to the current performance, in the sense that something new is being produced. The performance is both representational in the classical Aristotelian sense (a "model of") and performative in the sense of the speech-act theorists (a "model for"). As J. L. Austin was fond of pointing out, when the minister says, "I hereby pronounce you husband and wife," he is referring both to past contexts (past marriage ceremonies) and to the present context (the current marriage, which did not exist before the speech act was produced).[25] As the central figure in the ordinary-language approach to philosophy, Austin's attention to the performative dimension of language marked a welcome relief from philosophy's longtime obsession with systems of reference based exclusively on the declarative sentence. Because the sentence can be separated from the scene of its performance in a way that "ostensive" ritual expressions (like those analyzed by Austin) cannot, it is easy to forget that the possibility of logical truth, based on the correspondence between a sentence or proposition and the state of affairs it refers to, depends upon a more elementary linguistic form (the ostensive), in which truth is produced by the context of the utterance itself.[26] When the child says, "Kitty!" while pointing to a coyote, the utterance is not false, for the purpose of the utterance was not to designate the object as a member of the semantic category "cat," but to draw someone else's attention (perhaps an inattentive mother) to the presence of the coyote.[27] The response elicited by the mother would not be, "No, that's not a kitty, that's a coyote," but rather an urgent cry to warn the child away from the offending animal. The child's utterance is "felicitous" precisely because its semantic function is so impoverished. There is no occasion for ambiguity because the object appears within the same scene as the utterance of the word.

If the production of symbolic reference were restricted in this fashion to the physical proximity between the word and its object, human language would never have evolved beyond the indexical communication systems used by many other animals. This unignorable fact should alert us to the absurdity of the notion that symbolic reference evolved "naturally" from animal signal systems. And yet this is precisely the standard textbook explanation in evolutionary anthropology. Geertz is only reproducing this standard view when he claims that human culture emerged gradually, increasingly shaping the human brain to adapt to the artificial environment made possible by culture. But what is neglected in this definition of culture as a control mechanism is precisely the wherewithal to produce the artificial "cultural" environment in the first place.

The problem can be put more sharply when we adopt Geertz's own terminology of "model of" and "model for." If the genetic code functions as the exemplary case of the "model for," in the sense that the genotype is the "model for" the phenotype, then culture models behavior not by storing its models in the genotype, but by storing its models *virtually* in the collective memory that we call symbolic culture. Of the two halves of the model-for/model-of dichotomy, the real difficulty lies in explaining the origin of the model-of side of the definition. For implicit in the notion of a set of signs functioning as a virtual model *of* something else (as a map stands to the territory it represents) are the twin features of arbitrariness and displacement that set symbolic reference apart from all other reference systems in the animal and biological world.

How Did Symbols Originate?

Whence came our capacity to think abstractly in terms of symbols? How are we to account for the "transcendence," or, in Geertz's scheme, the "externalization," of the sign on the basis of the "immanence," or "internalization," of genetic control mechanisms? The notion of the sign as a model *of* something else is only possible once the symbolic world of signs (which finds its psychological correlate in the separate "mental space" of internal reflection) has been separated from the world of things. Between the function of the sign as a symbolic model *of* something nonsymbolic, and its real-world application as a model *for* doing something, lies a space that cannot be simply erased by hopeful appeals to the dialectic between the genotype and its increasingly externalized phenotype. Culture and language are not phenotypic traits precisely because they cannot be genetically assimilated.[28] In order to explain their function, therefore, we cannot resort to the standard biological categories of explanation.

The problem may be put in terms of the opposition between the interpretive and scientific conceptions of human origin. Geertz knows that an interpretive anthropology properly begins with a definition of culture that makes clear the anthropologist's aims, methods, and assumptions. But he also knows that the definition is itself an interpretive act and therefore implicated in the very process it seeks to explain, which is the production of culture. This does not mean that the definition is simply equivalent to the "emic," or internal, perspective of the culture observed by the anthropologist. The definition is the anthropologist's, not the informant's (which is not to say that the informant may not later choose to adopt the anthropologist's perspective). But it is nonetheless true that the anthropologist's method of discovery is to move back and forth between the "etic" perspective of his theory and the "emic" perspective of the cultures he interprets by way of that definition.

Is this the best that the interpretive anthropologist can do? For, if it is, how are we to test the truth of the anthropologist's definition of culture? By what standard are we to judge the merits of the anthropologist's interpretation over the interpretations provided by those he studies? On the one hand, the claim is being made that the anthropologist's perspective, given by his definition, provides the privileged perspective for understanding a particular culture. On the other, the claim is that the definition is an extrapolation of what is already implicit in the cultures under observation. So why should we privilege the anthropologist's perspective at all? Why not privilege that of the people he observes? After all, their perspective is closer to the originary source of culture, is it not? Should it therefore not also be a truer, more faithful expression of the "essence" of culture?

Geertz is well aware of this paradox. And he normally embraces it by moving quite easily between the twin perspectives of generalizing theorist (of the underlying concept of culture) and local historical and ethnographic observer (of multiple and different cultures). But inevitably at some point in this endless hermeneutic circle between etic definition (of the concept of culture) and emic participation (in a particular culture), it is tempting to put an end to all the interpretive instability. Geertz does this when he explains culture not by interpreting the concept, but by inferring its presence on the basis of nonconceptual empirical evidence. But in reducing the categories of cultural interpretation to those of biological explanation, Geertz eliminates, in one stroke, the fundamental interpretive crux of all culture, namely, the paradox between representation and performance, "model of" and "model for." Culture—and therefore the human itself—depends upon this paradox for its existence. Any anthropology that eliminates this paradox also eliminates the possibility of its own historical formulation. The solution is not to eliminate the paradox, but to include it as a constitutive element of one's anthropology. I will return to this point later.

The lesson to be learned is that it is impossible to derive the anthropological concept of culture from the scientific categories assumed by the biological theory of evolution. We may choose to infer the presence of culture from the empirical evidence (for example, from anatomical changes, such as bipedalism, increased relative skull size, reduced incisors, decreased sexual dimorphism, increased manual dexterity, and so on). We may even interpret the discovery of sharp-edged flints as evidence of tool use and therefore of symbolic thought because the flints appear to have been intentionally flaked according to an abstract and repeatable design. But the only indisputable evidence of symbolic culture is when we unhesitatingly attribute to an object a symbolic function—as, for example, when we stand before the cave paintings in Lascaux. We have no idea what particular cultural function these paintings performed (were they perhaps part of a hunting ceremony?). But we nonetheless interpret them immediately as aesthetic objects—that is, as demonstrating a formal interest in the appearance of the representation itself. These are not merely models for, but models of. They possess the same formal relationship to their content as that presupposed by the art objects of our own and other contemporary and historical cultures.

But notice where we have now arrived. In pointing toward the exemplary symbolic function of art, we are drawing the same conclusion we noticed in Greenblatt's appropriation of Geertz: that art and (in particular) literature have a central role to play in anthropology. So what is it about art and literature that makes them such exemplary objects for criticism, which is to say, for cultural interpretation? Why is the criticism of culture to be modeled on the analysis of the aesthetic object?

Mimetic and Aesthetic Paradox

The reader will by now be unsurprised to hear that the answer to this question depends on an originary analysis of the structure of the symbolic sign. Such an analysis, however, is not without its obstacles, the most significant of which is simply the obstacle of the philosophical and aesthetic tradition itself. For well over two millennia, the category of representation has been dominated by the Aristotelian definition of mimesis as an artful imitation of its object. This definition is accepted uncritically by Geertz, as well as by Greenblatt, who explicitly associates his literary anthropology (as the designation "poetics of culture" makes unambiguously clear) with the kind of formal analysis of structure first conducted by Aristotle in his *Poetics*. In order to be able to mount a challenge to this all-but-impregnable tradition, we must therefore make a clean break with the traditional Aristotelian categories. Such "clean breaks" in intellectual history are of course very rare, and we should not be surprised by the lack of support they get at the time of their inception. The more original the idea (that is, the more clean the break), the less likely it is to be noticed, and the more built-in resistance there will be to its adoption as an alternative paradigm for thinking about the traditional problems. But if a new idea really is an improvement over its precursors (and not just another crackpot theory from the lunatic fringe), then it will eventually prove itself in the marketplace of ideas. I believe René Girard's groundbreaking studies of mimesis are beginning to show us the chinks in the armor of the traditional "metaphysical" understanding of representation.[29] Girard's theory remains highly controversial. But it is the mark of new and powerful ideas that they inspire such controversy because they inevitably go against the grain of established opinion.[30] We are far from having appreciated the full implications of Girard's theory. In what follows, I wish to make a few suggestions about the relevance of his analysis of mimesis for understanding the "anthropological" turn in literary studies today. In so doing, I will inevitably be contributing to the wider debate about literary knowledge and its relationship to the social and biological sciences.

How does Girard understand mimesis? Girard reinterprets the Aristotelian definition of this category by drawing attention to the conflict implicit in all imitation. In effect, Girard shows that the Aristotelian notion of mimesis as objective (dramatic and tragic) form is grounded in the conflict that is also the explicit content of high literature and, in particular, of the Greek tragedy Aristotle took as the paradigm for his theory of catharsis. Girard's anthropology is thus explicitly "literary" in the sense that it insists on the wisdom of the content of great works of literature. But because this insistence is made on the basis of a translation of literary content into the self-consciously theoretical terms of an anthropological hypothesis, one cannot simultaneously accuse Girard of pursuing a merely "empty" formalism. On the contrary, what irks many a literary formalist is precisely Girard's insistence that the content of literary form, far from being "arbitrary," is in fact interpretable in terms of an anthropological hypothesis of origin.

But why exactly is imitation conflictive? We can answer this question by taking as our point of departure Geertz's notion of symbolic modeling. As Geertz's model-for/model-of terminology suggests, "models for" exist throughout the animal kingdom. The simplest example of a "model for" is when one individual imitates another: the latter functions as the *model for* the former. Given the greater efficiency of imitation as a mechanism for the transmission of valuable (that is, adaptive) behaviors, we can assume that it would be increasingly selected for among species where group living had evolved as viable evolutionary strategy.[31] But what this straightforward conclusion neglects is that there are negative as well as positive consequences to imitation. The most obvious negative consequence is increased competition and rivalry among conspecifics. Imitation is fine when what is imitated is the model's behavior alone. By imitating the alpha male, I may learn a good mate-attracting strategy, or an effective hunting technique. But it is in the nature of imitation to imitate not just behaviors but the direction of behavior toward objects that satisfy real appetitive needs. The alpha male's attention to females or to food attracts my attention to these objects too. The major problem for imitative social behaviors thus becomes one of controlling the conflict that imitated attention to external objects inevitably produces. This is usually done through pecking-order hierarchies. Given our sense of moral reciprocity, it is tempting to see these hierarchies as unpleasant impositions on a world of otherwise unconstrained "free" individuals. Nothing could be further from the truth. Animal hierarchies are implicit in the very structure of imitation. The evolution of a pecking order is a development that expands the possibilities of imitation as a mechanism for the transmission of innovative behaviors. Rather than regard the animal pecking order as an unnecessary repression of the individual's "free" behavior, we should understand it as an optimization of imitative possibilities within the context of the group as a whole. Since imitation increases rivalry among individual group members, it will tend to destabilize the group. The solution to the destabilizing effect of imitative rivalry is the pecking order which functionalizes the asymmetrical relationship already implicit in the mimetic subject's relationship to the other model-mediator. I may learn a valuable behavior by imitating you, but at a certain point in the mimetic process, your behavior will also become an obstacle to me, for example, when it leads to our convergence on the same object. Disputes over objects such as mates or food are settled by one-on-one fights that do not so much upset the hierarchy as reconfigure it, for instance, by my winning a fight for the alpha position. Such incessant jockeying for position in the social hierarchy has been fascinatingly documented by studies of nonhuman primates such as chimpanzees.[32]

It is at this point that we can identify the "missing link" in Geertz's deanthropologized concept of culture. What is missing in Geertz's idea of symbolic modeling is an appreciation for the "pragmatic paradox" implicit in all modeling behavior, human or otherwise, but which only becomes explicit or *represented* in the human case when the mimetic paradox latent within the structure of imitation itself becomes manifest in the pragmatic form of a collective "mimetic crisis," the formal solution to which is the originary symbolic sign.[33]

What is a pragmatic paradox, and how is it related to the Girardian mimetic crisis? At the simplest level, imitation implies the cognitive capacity to treat analogous beings as "models for" behavior. This capacity need not be terribly advanced. We often associate imitation with highly intelligent species, such as chimpanzees. The synonymy between the words "imitate" and "ape" points to this association. But even insects are capable of imitating one another, for example, when they swarm toward a food source. The important point is that imitation allows for the transmission of information from one individual to another independently of the genetic system. Each individual functions as a "model for" the behavior of another.

But let us take this argument a step further. If imitation functions as an extragenetic control mechanism for the transmission of behavior between individuals in a group, at what point in this relationship does the behavior of the model become not merely a "model for" me to imitate, but a "model of" something independent of both the model's behavior and mine? At what point in the imitative process do I become aware of the fact that I am not merely imitating others' actions, but imitating their actions as a *representation* of an object separate from the behavior itself, which is to say, as a formally closed gesture that *re*-presents the object to the other? The shift in mimetic attention depends on our capacity to interpret each other's behavior not merely as an instrumental action toward achieving an immediate goal, but as a collectively produced symbol that designates the object as prohibited, even if only for a moment, to immediate appropriation. This space of symbolic deferral constitutes the twin moments of the aesthetic and sacred functions of the originary sign: on the one hand, the aesthetic moment focuses our attention on the formal closure of the sign itself, thereby allowing us to profit from its minimal linguistic deferring function; on the other, the sacred moment leads us from the sign to the object, which is subsequently interpreted, in an inaugural act of sacralization, to be the divine origin of linguistic deferral.

The difference between simple imitative modeling and genuine symbolic modeling thus occurs when I interpret the model as a participant in the symbolic act of sacred designation. I imitate the other as a sign of the object's inaccessibility, of its sacrality. In conceiving the other-model's gesture toward the object as a representation, I convert my own gesture in conformity to his as a sign that makes the object "present" to us both on a *different scene* from that of immediate perception. This "other scene" is simultaneously subjective and objective, private and public: the object is publicly designated as sacred and therefore as prohibited to the community as a whole, but this very act of collective interdiction establishes within each individual a corresponding subjective "aesthetic scene" in which the external object may be possessed "fictionally," that is, in the individual's private "literary" imagination. Presence on this internal imaginary scene implies not just the previously given perception of the object as satisfying to individual appetite, but the henceforth unavoidable fact that imaginary presence—symbolic meaning—is a consequence of the other's intentional participation in the designation of the object. The status of the object as intentionally significant is a consequence of its being mediated by the other's sign. The object now stands opposed to both of us. Publicly, the object is "sacred" because it appears capable of withstanding the desires of both subject and model. Privately, however, each individual imagines himself the sole possessor of the object. In the latter "aesthetic" scene, desire is fulfilled in imagination because it is deferred in reality. The private aesthetic scene compensates for the subject's necessary experience of separation from the sacred in the collective context.

The resulting "mimetic triangle," in which subject and model are situated equidistant from the central object, defines the fundamental center-periphery structure of the originary scene of representation. The scene is constituted around a sacred center, which stands opposed to the individuals on the periphery. But because the individuals on the periphery are also the ultimate source of the collective sign, the sacred center does not exist without its human periphery. The center is thus a locus of sacred meaning, the originary source of all historical forms of cultural significance. Culture is the history of the reproduction of the center-periphery configuration of the originary scene, first in ritual (in which a central sacred figure stands opposed to its profane worshippers), then in aesthetic works (in which the form of the artwork guarantees the deferred or narrative presence of its imagined content).

But what in this originary scenario motivates the inaugural separation between sign and object? When do both subject and other model-mediator become aware that they are imitating not merely a model *for* accessing reality but a symbolic model *of* a cultural reality that is also constituted by the production of the sign? What turns the gesture of appropriation *toward* an object into a symbolic designation *of* it?

Let us retrace the stages of mimesis so far. It is in the nature of imitation to lead the individual to the appropriation of external objects, such as food. But imitation leads to conflict when both hands converge on the same object. At this point, imitative behavior is blocked by the incompatibility between the imitation of the model and the appropriation of the object. This is the occasion for what Eric Gans calls a "pragmatic paradox": the subject imitates the model-mediator, but this imitation leads to the convergence of both subject and model-mediator upon the same object.[34] The intrusion of the model-mediator into the subject's awareness of the presence of the object feeds back into the subject's consciousness of the mediated status of the object: the subject sees that the model "intends" the object. The same pattern applies to the model-mediator. As imitation draws both subject and model together toward the same object, they increasingly mediate each other's attention to the object. The shift from imitation ("model for") to representation ("model of") occurs when each rival's "aborted gesture of appropriation" is understood by both individuals as no longer a movement to be unselfconsciously imitated, but as an intentionally and collectively produced sign indicating the presence of the object to the other. This latter sign is not to be confused with the indexical signs used by other animals—for example, the submissive gesture of a subordinate to the alpha. On the contrary, the production of symbolic reference requires that both rivals maintain their "equality" with respect to the centrally designated object. There is no question of submission to an other-rival here. If we may speak of submission in this context, it is the submission of both subject and other-rival to the central object, which consequently becomes a sacred object.[35] The need to defer mimetic conflict thus becomes the occasion for reproducing, first in sacrificial ritual, then in literary and other aesthetic forms, the underlying center-periphery structure of the originary scene of symbolic representation. But the condition of the symbolic designation of the central object remains the reciprocity implied by the "equal" exchange of signs among the reciprocal "models" on the periphery.

Originary Anthropology

Why must we bother to formulate such an originary hypothesis? What makes it any better than the standard definition of humanity as simply that animal which uses culture? The answer to this question lies in the fact that every definition of humanity unavoidably assumes the paradoxical structure of the originary scene of representation, even when it seeks to expel this paradox from its definition. For we must not forget that the formulation of the hypothesis was itself a response to the inadequacy of the idea that humanity is definable, in fiat metaphysical terms, as the culture-using animal. In the most general sense, the priority of the originary hypothesis over other theories of representation lies not in the actual details of its particular formulation, but in the fact that it is formulated at all; the status of the hypothesis as self-consciously originary and hypothetical has priority over any decision we make with respect to the internal details of the hypothesis itself. Once we have decided on a particular formulation, however, we must take responsibility for it. The hypothesis defines not just our particular interest in this or that cultural work, but also the anthropology by which we are able to situate the historical significance of the work more broadly. Originary thinking forces us to make a decision about what is historically significant and, moreover, to do so in terms that are not simply left to individual intuition but are rigorously traceable to the terms of our anthropology, which is to say, to our definition of the human implicit in the formulation of the hypothesis.

The hypothesis thus allows us to minimize the central paradox that any theory of culture inevitably encounters. In its minimal originary form, this paradox is simply the paradox of representation. Scientific and logical models of representation seek to expel all paradox from their definition. It is rather those explicitly cultural "models"—that is, the religious and aesthetic institutions that have, until recently, always stood at the ethical center of human social organization—that turn paradox into their greatest ally, because it is culture that itself originated in symbolic-mimetic paradox. Culture is both a representation and a performance, a "model of" and a "model for." Scientific definitions of the human ignore this paradox as a matter of course. From a purely scientific vantage point, attributing an exceptional status to human origin seems like false hubris. But from an anthropological viewpoint, we have no choice but to consider human origin as exceptional because the very fact that we are self-conscious of this origin, in a way that other species are not, compels us to seek an explanation for it. Whether the explanation for human origin be conceived in the form of a myth, a science, or a literary anthropology, all are equally attempts to respond to the fundamental mimetic paradox that led to the origin of the cultural scene of symbolic representation. Only humans are self-conscious of themselves as historical beings because only humans have evolved the paradoxical ability to represent their own origin.

Literature and the End of Culture

What are the practical consequences of my analysis for literary study today? If I am right in my argument, there is a great deal of significance to the current interest in culture among literary critics. But this interest remains only "unconsciously" anthropological: the bigger epistemological questions that motivate the idea of a literary anthropology remain peripheral rather than central to theoretical debate in the discipline. As literary studies continues to expand its disciplinary borders to embrace all manner of objects as grist for its interpretive mill, it becomes increasingly imperative to grasp the originary anthropological categories that lie behind this expansion. The idea of culture as a general interpretive system is everywhere invoked, but there is very little dialogue on the underlying anthropological context implied by this definition. Instead, the analysis of literature continues to take for granted what is implicit in its very interpretive procedure. There is, for example, still a rather narrow preoccupation with the idea of discrete aesthetic "cultures" from different historical periods ("the Renaissance," "the romantic," "the modernist," and so on), without any fundamental reflection on why the interpretation of literature should be restricted to a particular historical period rather than applied to a wider anthropological-historical context. The widespread skepticism in the humanities that is routinely directed toward universal scientific explanations of culture (for instance, in sociobiology, evolutionary psychology, the cultural materialism of Marvin Harris, and so on) is no doubt well-founded, but unless this skepticism is also made the constructive object of a specifically anthropological approach to culture, it becomes impossible to respond to these scientific explanations other than purely negatively. Yet the function of the theorist in the humanities is not merely to play the negative role of the radical skeptic (the natural sciences having in any case proved themselves immune to the critiques of the theorists). The true potential of theory in aesthetic and cultural criticism lies in the elaboration of an independent research strategy that eschews the narrow empiricism of the social sciences, yet without also throwing out the theoretical baby with the empirical bathwater by then proceeding to deny the very possibility of anthropology itself.

This denial is implicit in Greenblatt's idea of a literary "enthnography," which refuses to see culture as anything other than a local manifestation of a particular historical-aesthetic period. Despite his frequent references to Geertz, Greenblatt has little interest in debating the fundamental anthropological premises that underpin *The Interpretation of Cultures*. My argument has been, on the other hand, that we must not lose sight of these broader theoretical questions because they define the very anthropology we use as a tool to analyze culture. Even the denial of anthropology, as in the case of Greenblatt and his disciples,[36] is itself to take a theoretical position, which in turn functions as the master strategy that enables the particular critic's interpretation of the concrete problems of literary and cultural history.

Geertz's work is instructive because it quite explicitly attempts to ground his interpretive strategy in a general theory of culture. But, as we have seen, his approach remains incomplete, largely because he is unable to translate his "metaphysical" definition of symbolic culture into a minimal anthropology. Thus, when he attempts to ground his definition of symbolic culture in a theory of origin he ends up, paradoxically, expelling culture from his very definition. No doubt anthropology's long-standing desire to emulate the natural sciences makes it proportionally more difficult for its individual practitioners to grasp the essentially hypothetical and symbolic, which is to say, *fictional*, status of its founding categories. It is rather the ever-marginal literary critics—namely, those whose work remains relatively untouched by the empiricism of scientific method and by the lucrative funding and prestige attached to the notion of genuine scientific research—who are also therefore better positioned to grasp the full anthropological significance of the idea that humanity is defined by its use of symbolic culture. But to draw out this anthropological significance, literary studies must become aware of its central role in formulating the hypothetical and minimal cultural *scene* of human origin. This minimal "originary scene" is based not on the empirical evidence pursued by sciences like paleoanthropology and primatology, but on the "literary" evidence of the historical and cultural tradition itself.

That the specifically Western tradition of a literary high culture has an important role to play in formulating such an anthropology is not to be dismissed, in knee-jerk fashion, as a narrow ethnocentric prejudice. On the contrary, to discern the anthropology implicit in the works of this tradition is to recognize that, like high culture itself, a literary anthropology is concerned not merely with the ephemeral consumer products of the present, but with the enduring works of the past. Certainly, this is, at the very least, implicit in Greenblatt's insistence that Shakespeare is the privileged site for his reflections on culture as "the circulation of social energy." But in order for these "Shakespearean negotiations" to become the basis for a genuine literary anthropology, critics like Greenblatt will have to bite the bullet and pursue their ambivalent relation to high culture to its more minimal theoretical and anthropological source.

Ultimately, the minimal faith of any anthropology is simply a faith in the general project of human representation. This is but another way of formulating the problem of human origin. Humans originated when the reality of mimetic crisis became too destructive to remain unrepresented: "too destructive" in the sense that failure to surmount it would lead to the extinction of the species. The deferral of this crisis via the originary sign is the first moment in the never-ending historical project of representing—and therefore attempting to understand—this originary crisis. To reject this minimal faith in representation is to reject, in nihilistic fashion, humanity itself. But nihilism is not a realistic alternative to anthropology, if only because the resentment of the nihilist depends upon the same cultural resources that it also wishes to destroy.

Chapter 4

The Culture of Criticism

I

The peculiarity of culture is that you know it only by doing it. You know what culture *is* only by knowing what it is *for*. In this sense, culture is roughly like a tool, its form or shape—its definition—derived from its function. A hammer is used for driving nails, and its particular shape is well suited to this task. But if I have no hammer, I could (in a pinch) use a stone. The stone would become my hammer, its structure temporarily determined by my perspective—that is, by my knowledge of what hammers are for.

This analogy between tools and culture has prompted some to argue that tools are a kind of *elementary culture*. Clifford Geertz, for example, suggests that the originary form of culture can be found in the "proto-cultural" activity of early humans.[1] What is protoculture? Protoculture is culture without symbolic thought, and it includes such socially mediated or imitatively learned activities as hunting and toolmaking. Does this mean that lions, which hunt in groups, have protoculture? How about chimpanzees? They hunt in groups and use tools. Do they therefore have protoculture?

Consider the argument for chimpanzees as users of culture. In her pioneering studies of wild chimpanzees, Jane Goodall notes how they modify branches to make termiting sticks.[2] They tear a branch from a tree, strip away its leaves, and poke the stick deep into a termite mound. When the stick is withdrawn, they eat the termites that have gathered on it. Jane Goodall emphasizes the creativity of this task, which seems to rival our own much-vaunted creativity. Would not a man left naked and hungry in the jungle make a termiting stick in exactly this fashion? Goodall goes on to point to another, more significant feature of chimpanzee tool use. A young chimpanzee watching his mother at the termite mound attempts to imitate her, but he selects a stick that is too short and manipulates it "clumsily and incompetently."[3]

The point is not just that the task is complex, but that it must be learned, first by observing the mother, then by imitating her action, then

by repeating the whole task until the chimp becomes an expert at selecting, constructing, and using termiting sticks. Surely we must agree
with the primatologist that this is an example of culture. The appetite
for termites is instinctive, inherent to the biology of the chimp, which
like all animals experiences hunger that must be satisfied. But the particular technique selected by the chimp for satisfying his hunger is not
instinctive but learned by imitation. It is an unambiguous instance of the
primatologist's definition of culture as "the non-genetic transmission of
habits."[4]

From this assumption others quickly follow. For if we grant that the
object exists only by virtue of those who intentionally see and use it as
this kind of object, then we are committed to the idea that the object
varies depending on the group using it. We can assume, for example,
that different chimpanzee groups will develop distinctive "styles" of termiting, as they imitate different individuals who have hit on different
techniques for eating termites. Each group develops a different "culture"
of termiting. Perhaps one group favors green sticks, whereas another
favors brown. Perhaps one group strips the bark off its sticks, whereas
another prefers to leave the bark intact. And perhaps yet another, less innovative group has failed to develop the termiting stick at all! Will it not
be necessary to divide the theory and analysis of each particular culture
of different chimpanzee groups into separate disciplines? For if chimpanzees use culture, there is no such thing as a univocal chimpanzee
culture, only the interpretation of multiple and different chimpanzee
cultures.

This last remark is intentionally absurd. We do not have disciplines
organized along the lines of a theory of different chimpanzee cultures,
because we do not recognize culture as a property of chimpanzees at
all.[5] It is no mere prejudice to observe that chimpanzees, for all their
ingenuity, are not using culture. This is not because chimps lack the
intelligence to produce culture. That would be to interpret them unfairly
in terms of something they have no need for and therefore cannot be
judged as lacking. Rather, it is because the concept of culture is meaningful only to those who are capable of grasping it as a concept in the
first place. And chimpanzees do not need the concept because they have
no need of the language by which to express it.[6]

Why then do we insist on saying they have culture? The desire to im-
pute culture to the chimpanzee is our desire, not the chimpanzee's. We
want to see ourselves reflected in these comically humanlike creatures.

We want to bring them, whether they want to or not, into our world. We can see this tendency in the way we treat our pets. We interpret the cat's indifference as proud haughtiness, or the dog's unhesitating obedience as loyal friendship. It requires a considerable critical effort to step outside this kind of "anthropological phenomenology" to avoid imputing to the gestures of these animals a significance that only we are able to see.

But why shouldn't we engage in this kind of anthropological phenomenology? Why shouldn't we interpret the world in terms of categories that we alone use—for example, categories like love and resentment, or morality and the sacred? The answer is that we cannot abandon these categories without abandoning humanity itself. These categories constitute the symbolically mediated world through and by which we live. They are the "veil of appearances" that transforms the natural world described by science into a world that is humanly livable.

This fundamental difference between the anthropological world of appearances and the physical and biological world described by science is the generative basis of any anthropology that takes the human capacity for symbolic representation seriously. Scientific explanation depends on the assumption that it is indeed possible to lift oneself out of the world told from our point of view. Science looks for causes that are intrinsic to the structure of the world. Why did Joe get sick? Because he consumed meat infected with a harmful strain of the bacteria *Escherichia coli*. By attributing Joe's sickness to E coli bacteria, we identify a cause that exists independently of our way of interpreting the world as imbued with meaning, and we explain Joe's sickness by referring to this cause. The cause inheres in the physical and biological relationship existing between E coli and Joe's gut, whereas symbolic meaning exists only among those who interpret the world symbolically according to concepts like revenge or justice. It is for this reason that we do not hold the E coli in Joe's gut responsible for his sickness. For the concept of responsibility implies moral judgment, the deeply held belief (so deep that it is also an emotion) that we are answerable for our actions. If I had knowingly planted E coli in Joe's hamburger, then I, not the E coli, would be responsible and therefore answerable for causing Joe's sickness. But notice how the idea of a cause has now been transformed from the realm of the natural to become implicated in a web of meaning that does not so much explain the event in terms of physical and biological causes as judge it under a collection of concepts. Imagine that Joe takes a turn for the worse and dies, and that Sally now accuses me of murder. I admit to having intentionally put E coli in Joe's hamburger, and the judge asks, Why? Neither he, nor Sally, nor the jury will be satisfied with a purely scientific explanation of how the E coli infection caused Joe's death. They want to know what motivated me to introduce E coli into Joe's hamburger. And the cause of my actions is predicated on concepts, not on a scientific account of the causal structure of the world. Perhaps I explain my actions as motivated by my resentment of Joe, who had become the intolerable object of Sally's affections.

We arrive at the following conclusion that has important consequences for understanding the difference between scientific and anthropological explanation. Scientific theory presupposes a stable ontological and epistemological difference between subject and object. The astronomer may be limited by the power of his telescope, just as the biologist is by the power of her microscope, but that doesn't mean the existence of the objects they observe depends upon the instruments through which they observe them. On the contrary, the objectivity of their representation of these objects (for example, in a theory of the structure of Mars, or a theory of the structure of the cell) is dependent on the fact that their representations, which may yet be wholly theoretical and speculative, are nonetheless empirically testable and therefore ultimately falsifiable, even if the possibility of empirical testing must await the advance of the science itself (as Charles Darwin's theory of evolution was tested, first by Gregor Mendel's experiments with peas, and then by the discovery of DNA).

But culture is not an object like the stars or DNA. There is a self-referentiality to cultural explanation that makes it impossible for the inquirer simply to propose a theory and then submit it, like the scientist, to an arena where it is objectively tested. This is not because scientists are "objective" whereas cultural theorists are merely "subjective." The scientific arena is objective not because scientists are peculiarly free of all personal agendas, but because for a hypothesis to be empirically testable it must refer to objects that exist independently of the particular thoughts and beliefs of those responsible for formulating and testing the hypothesis. What is being tested is not only the scientist's belief about the hypothesis, but ultimately the hypothesis's reference to an independently existing reality.[7]

Or think of it this way: if culture is only knowable while one is doing it, then what is to distinguish a theory of culture from the testing of that theory? The theory is presented as an objective representation of its object (culture); but if the object is available only while one is doing the theory, then the theory can be "tested" only by reproducing the theory. Theory and object collapse into each other. Theory is both subject and object. It is the product of the theorist, but it is also an object of study. The science of anthropology is inseparable from the art of cultural criticism, or as it is most often referred to today, from *theory*.

II

This movement away from the "scientific" object toward the subject's prior construction of the object is the characteristic mode of theory as it is understood today in the humanities. Consider the critical method known as deconstruction. How do we judge it? Not by submitting its central claims to a procedure of empirical testing. Rather, it is judged by reproducing the style and argument of the writing of its master exponent, Jacques Derrida. Derrida serves as the model for reproducing the theory of deconstruction.

No doubt this is why literary critics so often explain, or, as Harold Bloom more provocatively puts it, repress the origin of their theories by referring to—or, à la Freud, agonistically displacing—their personal encounter with, and imitation of, previous master critics. "Poetry," Bloom writes, "is not a struggle against repression but is itself a kind of repression ... In relation to the precursor, the latecomer poet compels himself to a fresh repression at once moral and instinctual."[8] It is unlikely that Terry Eagleton was thinking of Harold Bloom when he wrote, in the preface to his widely read account of literary theory, "hostility to theory usually means an opposition to other people's theories and an oblivion of one's own. One purpose of this book is to lift that repression and allow us to remember." But he has it about right when he remarks that "criticism ... for Bloom is just as much a form of poetry as poems are implicit literary criticism of other poems, and whether a critical reading 'succeeds' is in the end not at all a question of its truth-value but of the rhetorical force of the critic himself."[9]

Or recall what Stephen Greenblatt said about his encounter with Clifford Geertz's writings in the 1970s: "Geertz's account of the project of social science rebounded with force upon literary critics like me in the mid-1970s: it made sense of something I was already doing, returning my own professional skills to me as more important, more vital and illuminating, than I had myself grasped."[10] As I noted in the previous chapter, it is not that Geertz teaches Greenblatt something new. Geertz shows Greenblatt the significance of what he "was already doing." In demonstrating the preeminence of interpretation in the social sciences, Geertz reassures Greenblatt that literature too can be dignified with the appellation "social science." But this is no mere empirical science. It is a science that is theory-savvy, because it understands that the objects to be analyzed are socially constructed and therefore that the barrier between theory and object breaks down. What we have are not empirical models of the world, but pragmatic models for doing criticism. Criticism becomes an end in itself, its prestige linked not so much to the communication and empirical testing of ideas, but to the personalities responsible for promoting ideas that are always already constructed. Derrida, Bloom, Eagleton, Geertz, and Greenblatt are celebrities in the culture of theories of culture.

But this fact should not surprise us if culture is indeed defined by how it is done. For what we should then expect of a theory of culture is not a model *of* the way the world actually is (a scientific theory), but a model *for* how to participate in culture (a discipleship). To be a critic in the humanities entails mastering a set of concepts and categories that are not intrinsic to the object but intrinsic to the master/disciple relationship itself. Grasping the meaning of the discipline's underlying master concepts entails familiarizing oneself with their use in the particular "interpretive community" one has chosen to enter (literature, anthropology, philosophy, etc.). Indeed, one does not so much choose the discipline as get chosen by it.

The awareness that humanistic inquiry is "institutional" rather than "natural" has led to any number of polemics against a mythical old-guard that, so we are told, mistakenly believed in nature rather than culture. In 1983 Eagleton could still thrill us with polemical statements like this one: "the idea that there are 'non-political' forms of criticism is simply a myth which furthers certain political uses of literature all the more effectively."[11] But such statements do not so much diagnose the problem as reproduce it, by sacrificing over and again the mythical father. Other commentators have more shrewdly observed that what seems to structure the practice of academic criticism is the desire for institutional membership itself.[12] Hence the bewildering proliferation within the discipline of an abstruse and recondite jargon, or the stubborn refusal to define terms clearly or argue systematically. Such tactics are deliberately alienating and mystifying, because what is thereby demonstrated is not a commitment to accepted standards of definition and argument, but a much narrower commitment to the terms of the group. This explains literary theory's ambivalent power over its disciples. It attracts only by simultaneously repelling. It promises membership into a select group that is distinguished from the merely ordinary by the difficulty of its prose, the abstruseness of its constitutive categories, and its oppositional stance toward the political and cultural status quo. The need for institutional belonging emerges as the primary function of critical practice in the humanities.

Such, at least, is the argument of Mark Bauerlein, who ends his brilliantly deadpan analysis of the discipline with the following comment:

> Current usage shows that criticism is not about knowledge of objects, but about the politics of inquiry, which includes the political status of the inquirer. Literary study is no longer literary analysis. It is now an occasion for institutional certification. Those who use terms in the right way display their intellectual discernment, their cultural interest, their political sensitivity, and their moral regard, which is to say, their eligibility for entering today's academic order. Critical terms are tokens of belonging.[13]

There is a certain plausibility to this argument, particularly when one recognizes that the elementary function of culture, as Durkheim saw, is to establish group solidarity through the repeated performance of the group's rituals of membership. Entry into the discipline of literary criticism requires something like a rite of passage, one that is difficult to make sense of if you are not involved in the practice that gives the group its unity. Indeed, to the outsider these practices will be irritating precisely because their apparent uselessness (What is the point of literary theory?) is belied by the extreme seriousness with which they are undertaken. This paradox only exacerbates the outsider's desire for membership, which in turn reproduces the experience of membership to those on the inside who notice in the discomfort of the would-be disciple a confirmation of their own desirability and superiority. In this context, critical terms indeed function, as Bauerlein suggests, "as tokens of belonging."[14]

Yet rather than explore this point further, Bauerlein abruptly ends on it. This is regrettable, because it implies that the unconscious

mimeticism of criticism is all but inevitable. Bauerlein is certainly justi-
fied in his criticisms of the discipline, but he offers no theory to replace
those he criticizes. Instead he suggests (somewhat disingenuously) that
his glossary of critical terms is intended to clarify, rather than critique,
the institutional function of those terms.[15] In this larger sense, there is
nothing ultimately to distinguish Bauerlein's critique from the critiques
he critiques. For all take their central task as the critique of someone
else. But at what point in this endless exercise of exposing the other's
assumptions do we begin the more constructive task of identifying those
minimal assumptions that are necessary for dialogue to take place at all?
This is something Bauerlein shies from answering. Having convincingly
diagnosed the brutality of the murder of literature and literary criticism
in his "autopsy," there is little for Bauerlein to do except sharpen his
scalpel and eagerly await another victim's arrival in the morgue.

I do not wish to imply that Bauerlein's criticisms are somehow in-
valid simply because they exploit the very thing he abhors. On the contrary, cleaning the pigpen means getting your hands dirty. Taken individually, Bauerlein's analyses of the anti-methodological usage of critical
terms in the discipline are unimpeachable. But the fundamental question Bauerlein leaves unanswered is why literary method should remain
tied to literature other than for purely methodological reasons. Despite
his generally sound criticisms of the state of the discipline, Bauerlein
nonetheless shares with those he criticizes an assumption that itself remains unjustified. This assumption concerns the use of literature as the
privileged vehicle for theoretical reflection. Even those who denounce
literature as an ideological mask of the center's power over the victimized periphery contribute to this privileging. For in exposing the ideological function of literature, they still insist that we must attend to the
literary text as the privileged interpretive object in order to discover how
power is secretly being manipulated. The difference is that Bauerlein
believes he can justify this attention on methodological and pragmatic
grounds alone. Since literature is a matter of institutional definition,
then any discipline that bases itself on that definition must stick to it for
pragmatic reasons, otherwise systematic inquiry becomes impossible.
What Bauerlein objects to is not the fact that literature is institutionally
defined, but the avowedly anti-methodological character of criticism itself. But is the choice to study literature a purely methodological choice?
This is a question that needs to be considered if we are to understand the
function of criticism today.

So let us consider it. As Bauerlein's analysis of criticism's paradoxical strategy of being methodically anti-methodological suggests, criticism in the "small world" of academia fulfills an important function that rarely gets noticed by those who otherwise accuse it of elitism and willful obscurantism. This function, however, though it shares something in common with religion, is not truly religious. Nor is it scientific. The central function of criticism is neither to sacralize the object nor to explain it. Rather, it is to engage the reader in an experience that is best described as aesthetic in structure. To read the work of one of the celebrity critics in the humanities—for example, a work by Stephen Greenblatt—is to be engaged in an experience that has more in common with reading high literature than with reading history, sociology, or economics (or any other social, let alone natural, science). For what separates a work of criticism from science, on the one hand, and religion, on the other, is the fact that, like literature, criticism makes no ontological claims about the nature of the world it represents. Science assumes the necessity of making such claims. Indeed its constitutive theories are formulated in such a manner that they can be tested empirically for their truth. For Karl Popper, this is how one distinguishes science from pseudo-sciences like psychoanalysis.[16] Scientific theories are falsifiable because they are judged not just on their own terms for coherence and parsimony, but also by their ability to explain a world that exists independently of the theory.[17] Religion also makes reality claims, but these are not presented as hypothetical. They are, rather, the foundation for a world that is held to be transcendent with respect to the world of experience.

In contrast to both science and religion, criticism neither commands a collectively experienced belief in the sacred, nor submits its central claims to a well-defined procedure in which they are empirically tested. Instead, the truth of its assertions is guaranteed by the *desire of the reader alone*, who accepts them as provisionally true—that is, true for the duration of the analysis but normally no longer than that. Once you have finished reading an author like Geertz or Greenblatt, you are left with the impression of having been treated to a tour de force in cultural interpretation, but you are rarely left with a clear grasp of the motivating categories and concepts behind the analysis, of the overall coherence of the argument. It is the style that impresses.[18] If the analysis is sufficiently persuasive, as many have held Freud's to be, it may be granted the prestige and status of a theory, which is simply to say that the critical analysis has become widespread enough to be elevated to the level of a collectively held doctrine that functions as the mimetic basis for readers to discover *for themselves* patterns of hitherto unrecognized cultural significance. Criticism becomes theory when it can successfully take the place of literature itself.

But notice what is implied in this movement from criticism to theory. For a critical analysis to attain the status of theory implies a reversal of the traditional hierarchy between criticism and literature. A work of (mere) criticism becomes a work of (prestigious) theory when it successfully manages to overshadow the literary and sacred texts it interprets. Traditionally, criticism is an exercise in refining the reading public's aesthetic judgment. The point is not to outdo the originality of the poet. It is to contribute to his greatness by providing further commentary on his creations, as in Samuel Johnson's preface to his edition of Shakespeare. The cultural significance of the poetry itself is taken for granted. The shift from criticism to theory undermines and then reverses this hierarchy. First it destroys the assumption that there is such a thing as high culture and good taste. Then it resurrects it, this time in favor of the critic by implying that if there is any remaining significance to be found in the works of high culture, the critic alone is able to demonstrate this. But note the latent contradiction in this movement from criticism to theory. Criticism unproblematically assumes the aesthetic significance of the works it interprets. Theory denies this significance, but only by seeking to appropriate aesthetic significance for itself!

We arrive at what is perhaps a surprising conclusion. Theory is the last remaining holdout of what used to be called high culture. Hopelessly unable to compete with consumer culture on its own terms in the marketplace, theory is limited almost exclusively to the sanctuary provided for it by the university.[19] This is not, however, to be taken as a sign of theory's intellectual impotence. On the contrary, it is an indication of its secret superiority, which is not for the many but for the privileged few. For what theory strives to give its readers is a position in the cultural vanguard. This is aesthetic modernism with a vengeance. And like aesthetic modernism, it seeks to capitalize on, and ultimately outdo, the aesthetic experience of reading Homer, Shakespeare, or Proust.[20]

Greenblatt all but admits to a version of literary modernism when he explains how reading Geertz helped him renew what was for him a stagnating discipline. What impressed him most, he writes in his 1997 essay "The Touch of the Real," was less Geertz's emphasis on literary analysis than the fact that Geertz had expanded literary analysis from canonical aesthetic works to noncanonical ethnographic texts: "The specific force of Geertz's work for New Historicism resided in the expansion of these [literary-critical] terms to a much broader and less familiar range of texts than literary critics had permitted themselves to analyze."[21] Following Geertz's lead, Greenblatt would seek to defamiliarize our experience of the canonical aesthetic work by juxtaposing it with culturally marginal texts, the point being "to surprise and to baffle" the reader who might otherwise "assume a comfortable place in a preexisting analysis" (15). Thus renewed, criticism "could venture out to unfamiliar cultural texts, and these texts—often marginal, odd, fragmentary, unexpected, and crude—in turn could begin to interact in interesting ways with the intimately familiar works of the literary canon" (20). In a particularly revealing remark, Greenblatt suggests that anthropology and literature both entail "a sustained practice of 'estrangement,'" an aesthetic device the "Russian formalists" first applied to "literature" (26). Like the modernists and romantics before him, Greenblatt hopes to renew the high-cultural project by scandalizing us with the centralization of the hitherto marginal figures of the cultural periphery.

Does this mean that literary criticism is reducible to a contest for power or "cultural capital" among competing charismatic personalities? Is criticism to be understood as the way we unconsciously legitimize the dangerous "charisma" of the high-cultural center, which has historically always been defined by its exclusion of those on the periphery?

I think there is a great deal of truth to this view of culture as a conflict between (dominating) center and (victimized) periphery.[22] But like all such institutional or sociological perspectives, it assumes a "macrosociological" or "anthropological" analysis of the origin of the center-periphery structure itself. In the third and final section of this chapter, I will provide such an analysis. And I will do so by beginning with a celebrated instance of the critic as charismatic personality.

III

Greenblatt begins his 1988 *Shakespearean Negotiations* with a portentous series of claims:

I began with the desire to speak with the dead.
This is a familiar, if unvoiced, motive in literary studies, a motive organized, professionalized, buried beneath thick

layers of bureaucratic decorum: literature professors are salaried, middle-class shamans. If I never believed that the dead could hear me, and if I knew that the dead could not speak, I was nonetheless certain that I could re-create a conversation with them.... It is paradoxical, of course, to seek the living will of the dead in fictions, in places where there was no live bodily being to begin with. But those who love literature tend to find more intensity in simulations—in the formal, self-conscious miming of life—than in any of the other textual traces left by the dead, for simulations are undertaken in full awareness of the absence of life they contrive to represent, and hence they may skillfully anticipate and compensate for the vanishing of the actual life that has empowered them. Conventional in my tastes, I found the most satisfying intensity of all in Shakespeare.[23]

In claiming that his project began with the desire to speak with the dead, Greenblatt invokes religion, the chief function of which is to attach the individual to a community that exists beyond the death of its individual members. In paying our respects to the dead and the unborn, we guarantee the continued existence of this community by simultaneously renewing our attachment to it. By presenting the literary text as the living voice of the dead, Greenblatt self-consciously reproduces the religious motive to sacralize the object as a deity ("Speak to me!"). Like Aladdin rubbing his lamp, Greenblatt's "touch of the real" magically produces presence where before there was absence.

But as Greenblatt himself implies ("it is paradoxical, of course, to seek the living will of the dead in fictions"), the world of the sacred is subject to the same representational paradoxes as the world of fiction. In presenting his private aesthetic experience of Shakespeare in the context of a desire for collective belonging, Greenblatt implicitly acknowledges that this sacred context has been lost forever, lost because it never existed apart from its representation. The sacred is constituted "performatively" by its representation. It is the historical function of ritual—but not literature—to attempt to reproduce the collective context of this originary experience, to re-create the experience of communal belonging that all cultural representation points to but only religion promises to deliver as a reality.

On first glance it may seem surprising that Greenblatt should choose to represent the sacred in these minimal, literary terms.[24] But this "minimization" of culture represents a renewed return of the aesthetic to its anthropological basis. The weak point of Greenblatt's criticism lies not in his anthropological intuitions, which are often profound, but quite simply in his lack of a more explicitly formulated anthropology, a lack that he perversely interprets as a virtue.[25] But without an anthropology to grant his literary intuitions broader critical purchase, Greenblatt is forced to conclude that his criticism begins and ends not in anthropology but in the figure of the artist, even if this artist has now been "deconstructed" into the fragments of the Renaissance period and its mysterious "Shakespearean negotiations."

Consider the problem for a moment from the hypothetical perspective of an originary anthropology. By interpreting the central object as the referent of the mimetic other's sign, I am participating in the collective act of signification. The latter imposes on the object a symbolic significance that exists over and above any previously given, nonsymbolic significance the object may have held for us (for instance, as an object of sexual or alimentary satisfaction). In the ritual context the central object is sacralized by us as something that deserves, not our destruction or appropriation, but our piety and respect. As René Girard and Eric Gans have powerfully shown in their respective analyses of the sacred, the object is too significant because it is too dangerous as an object of mimetic contagion to remain unguarded by prohibition and taboo.[26] By sacralizing the object, religion guarantees the object's cultural difference, securing it from the merely ephemeral needs of the body. The body's needs are of course real and must be taken care of if the body is to survive. But they do not determine what is sacred and what is profane. On the contrary, the distinction between profane and sacred is a consequence of the subordination of individual appetite in the face of the scene's potential for mimetic rivalry. In collectively designating the object as sacred, the conflict inherent to mimesis is momentarily deferred. The appetitive object now stands against us as a prohibition to unmediated appetite. Appropriation of it can now be pursued only within this context—that is, with the awareness that each individual's desire is in conflict with the desires of the others.

In the ritual context, the repelling force of the sacred appears to inhabit the central object, which is subsequently regarded as a god. But the perception of the object as a sacred figure or "totem" would not be possible without the prior mediation provided by the collectively produced sign. Thus, for example, in placing a taboo on the meat killed by the hunter, the community guarantees the subordination of the hunter's appetite to the needs of the group. These needs are not determined by the body (though they are necessarily constrained by it). They are determined by the desire for membership in the community itself, a membership that is secured only through constant and vigilant attention to the rituals of sacrifice through which this membership is both created and renewed. Ritual is thus itself a representation of originary deferral; it refers back to previous ritual events, which it meticulously attempts to both preserve and reproduce. As Gans puts it, what the theory proposes is that these commemorative reproductions must ultimately refer back to an originary event, "a hypothesis concerning the phenomenon of representation-in-general."[27] And the minimal structure of this hypothetical originary event must be symbolic deferral itself. In its most minimal anthropological sense, ritual interdiction is the reproduction of the originary deferral of desire before a central (appetitive) object.

Before returning to Greenblatt's purely aesthetic interpretation of the sacred, let us consider an actual historical example of ritual interdiction. In her fascinating discussion of the various types of prohibition among the Chewong tribe of the Malay Peninsula, Signe Howell refers to *punén*, a word used by the Chewong to acknowledge the potentially rivalrous desires of the tribe's members.[28] *Punén* is typically associated with the distribution of meat, the critical nature of which for the tribe needs no explanation. But it may also arise in the context of any desirable object that is not readily obtained by a tribe member:

> The Chewong take all possible precautions against provoking *punén*. All food caught in the forest is brought back and publicly revealed immediately…. As soon as a carcass is brought back, and before it has been divided up, someone of the hunter's family touches it with his finger and makes a round touching everyone present in the settlement, each time saying *"punén."*… This is another way of announcing to everyone present that the food will soon be theirs, and to refrain from desiring it yet awhile. (185)

What is interesting about the Chewong use of the word *punén* is that it refers neither to the object of desire nor indeed to desire, but to the danger of unfulfilled desire. The Chewong are extremely superstitious of desires that are provoked but remain unsatisfied. "Once a desire has been voiced," Howell writes, "the person who can satisfy it must immediately do so. If he refrains, the person refused will suffer the consequences of *punén*" (185). The slightest mishap that may subsequently befall the refused party will be unhesitatingly attributed to the fact that this individual's desire has remained unsatisfied and continues to fester malignantly, causing all kinds of misfortunes. The individual is, so to speak, haunted by *punén*, by the ill will or resentment that unfulfilled desire engenders.

The obligation to fulfill the other's desire is not, however, a recipe for multiplying desire. The latter is rather a feature of the modern "consumer" market, which operates by relentlessly promoting new products and therefore "new" desires among its participants. Among the Chewong, the reverse is true. Desire is a menace to be purged in collective ritual. The threat of *punén* keeps the individual from believing that she can indulge her desire outside the context of a strictly collective and hence rigidly egalitarian system of distribution. Howell observes that the Chewong "hardly ever make overt requests for anything, and the fear of *punén* may easily have prevented people from requesting gifts from me" (185). Only on one occasion was a gift explicitly requested of her. An old woman asked her for a whetstone. Howell gave her the object lest the woman were to come under the spell of *punén*, but the rest of the group "commented unfavorably" on this woman's evidently aberrant behavior (185).

Now reconsider Greenblatt's rather more elevated description of desire, the desire to speak with the dead. What differentiates his representation of desire from that of the Chewong? The most obvious difference is the latter's proximity to the general problem of economic distribution. The Chewong ceremoniously provoke desire when appetitive fulfillment is all but guaranteed. The *punén* ritual is a pretext to the actual eating of the object. Yet this apparent difference in functionality, though fundamental, is not metaphysical or ontological. For what structures desire in both cases is given not by the real physical object, but by the preceding cultural or ritual task of *representing the object as collectively significant*. The object must be *sacralized*. The difference is thus primarily a temporal one. Whereas the Chewong permit the collective representation of desire only within the context of imminent appetitive satisfaction, Greenblatt's desire to speak with the dead can never be satisfied. The focus on the subject's unfulfillable desire—a representation that would no doubt be considered scandalous or "blasphemous" by the rigidly egalitarian Chewong—distinguishes Greenblatt's "charismatic" representation of desire from the Chewong's prohibition against all such charismatic representations.

This is not to say that the Chewong know no such desire. On the contrary, all desires are publicly acknowledged but also publicly constrained; the utterance *punén* reminds the group that they must, in Howell's words, "refrain from desiring [the meat] yet awhile" (185). The word is a solemn reminder of the need to defer one's desire in the face of extreme provocation. The ceremony of touching each member of the tribe with the same finger that touched the meat heightens the ambivalence—the paradoxicality—of the desiring relation. On the one hand, it emphasizes the physical proximity between the individual and the desire object; on the other, it undermines this physical or *indexical* proximity by placing the meat under the symbolic or metaphoric taboo of *punén*. By touching first the meat and then each member of the tribe, the person whose task it is to distribute the meat indicates to each member that he will receive his just share but that he must also await this anticipated satisfaction. The word is a temporary substitute for the object, not simply in the linguistic or indexical sense that it indicates the presence of the object (as in the deictic "There!"), but more powerfully and more fundamentally in the ritual sense that it designates the object as bound by a taboo. To repeat, *punén* does not refer to the meat itself but to the misfortune visited upon those who fail to defer their desire for appetitive gratification.

The ritual invocation of *punén* is thus occasioned by critical moments in the collective life of the tribe, exemplified by the ethical problem of distributing scarce and therefore desirable resources such as meat. Deferral in this context is limited to the time that elapses between the ritual centralization of the meat and its eventual consumption. But the key performative or aesthetic moment in this process of economic distribution occurs when the word *punén* is substituted for the thing. Desire is first provoked, and then renounced. The carcass is publicly presented where all can see it, but only so that the onlookers can be reminded, one by one, of the association between the meat and its prohibition. The individual contemplates the entire portion of meat, but this subjective and therefore also germinally aesthetic moment of contemplation is permitted only within the collective context that is itself strongly reinforced by the repeated utterance of the word *punén* to each individual. The threat of *punén*, which is ultimately none other than the collective threat or "mimetic presence" of the other tribe members, hangs over the consciousness of each spectator contemplating the desire object.

It is this paradoxical experience of collective membership that Greenblatt seeks to re-create fictionally in his opening to *Shakespearean Negotiations*. By translating the critic's aesthetic experience into this ritual context ("literature professors are salaried, middle-class shamans"), Greenblatt authenticates his aesthetic experience of Shakespeare. The hope is that the latter will thereby become not merely a private but a publicly shared experience and thus an instance of sacred membership. In paying attention to Greenblatt's text, we are being invited to share in this more elevated high-cultural depiction of literary desire. Like the shaman who becomes momentarily possessed by the voice of the other, Greenblatt becomes a vessel through which we may peer briefly into immortality. Greenblatt deserves our attention because he has been touched by literature, and above all by Shakespeare.

As these remarks suggest, there is more than a hint of romanticism in this view of the sacred. Greenblatt may be influenced here by Geertz, whose theory of ritual shares much with the modern "post-romantic" idea of literature as an attempt to compensate for the loss of religion. Bereft of its practical economic function in rituals such as those of the Chewong, the representation of desire becomes instead an end in itself. But what this exclusive focus on the aesthetic tends to forget or repress is the anthropological origin of the aesthetic in the originary scene that includes not merely the aesthetic but the linguistic, sacred, and economic moments.

Despite its one-sided idealism, there is nonetheless a genuine anthropological truth to the romantic doctrine. The aesthetic moment of the originary scene occurs when the peripheral spectators contemplate the central object *before* it is divided up in the sacrificial feast. As Gans argues in his analysis of the aesthetic, what makes this contemplation specifically aesthetic is the "oscillation between imaginary possession and recognized inviolability."[29] On the one hand, the originary sign points us to the content we desire; on the other, it forbids us access to it. The generativity of this experience is a consequence of our recognition that we cannot violate the mediation provided by the sign without also violating the aesthetic experience.

We have already seen how this structure of imaginary possession and recognized inviolability informs the Chewong's use of the word *punén*. In placing an interdiction upon the meat, the desires of the tribe members are both recognized and deferred. The close proximity of the meat exacerbates desire, but the utterance of the word *punén* reminds the individual that the object is inviolable. The practical function of this paradoxical process of representing an object in order to forbid its appropriation is to defer or contain the conflict that is likely to break out when multiple desires are focused on a scarce object. The time purchased by representing the object as *punén* allows it to be more peaceably and equitably divided among the group. Desire is inseparable from this ethical economy of deferral.

Greenblatt implicitly accepts the priority of the aesthetic mediation of the sign. Indeed, he makes this priority the generative basis for his whole idea of a cultural poetics. But what Greenblatt ignores in his "poetics" of culture is the economic conclusion to the originary event. The aesthetic sign is thus divorced from its basis in a unified anthropology. But the consequence of this deanthropologization of the aesthetic is that literature is understood to be a unique product of Shakespeare, or as the new historicist is wont to put it, of the particular "cultural period" in which Shakespeare wrote his plays. But this is far too ambitious a hypothesis to serve as the basis of culture, for it thereby assumes, consciously or not, that culture is coterminous with "the age of Shakespeare." Despite its many protestations to the contrary, the new historicism is thus the mirror image of the unabashed romanticism of such "traditionalists" as Harold Bloom.

In his major theoretical essay on the sacred, "Religion as a Cultural System," Geertz argues, as Nietzsche did of Greek tragedy, that Balinese drama is "not merely a spectacle to be watched but a ritual to be enacted. There is," Geertz insists, "no aesthetic distance here separating actors from audience."[30] The outsider's detachment from the event he beholds creates a thrilling sense of alienation in the contemplating ethnographer, who feels excluded from the solidarity he senses among those he observes. "Where for 'visitors' religious performances can only be presentations of a particular religious perspective, and thus aesthetically appreciated or scientifically dissected, for participants they are in addition enactments, materializations, realizations of it—not only models of what they believe, but also models *for* the believing of it. In these plastic dramas," Geertz concludes, "men attain their faith as they portray it."[31] The sacred is wherever the modern observer is not. As in

Hamlet's first stage appearance, which finds the prince dressed in black and lurking resentfully on the periphery of his uncle's brilliant court scene, all the ethnographer can do is contemplate the scandal of his dispossession from the center.

But that is not all one can do, at least not from the "etic" perspective of a minimal anthropology rather than the "emic" perspective of the "culture of criticism." High secular culture, like religion before it, is a historical institution. It therefore can also be transcended historically. But this "end of culture" is also a return to its minimal beginning in the formulation of an anthropology. This is a more positive and constructive interpretation of the recently much-debated "end of theory." Contrary to Greenblatt's and Geertz's implied historical arguments, the aesthetic is not specific to any particular literary period, because it is not specific to literature at all. It is an originary category of language, which originates as a deferral of the indexical sign/object relationship in favor of the symbolic sign/sign relationship. Both religious and aesthetic uses of language depend upon this deferring function for their power. The difference is that religion defers the individual's relationship to the object by collectively sacralizing it, whereas literature exploits the sign's originary deferring function to designate the object *as a fiction*. In aesthetic contemplation, we return to the formally closed structure of the sign in our subjective experience of the object. It is on the model of the formal closure of the sign that we understand the object as a Gestalt—that is, as a coherent pattern or "imitation" of the formal sign. It is for this reason that literature, but not religion, is capable of reflecting hypothetically on its anthropological origin. Because the aesthetic insists on the necessity that the individual's subjective experience of the world is mediated by the collectively produced sign, it therefore also stands closer to the generative source of a theoretical anthropology, which begins not with the object but with the representation of the object. The best criticism implicitly understands the anthropological discovery power of literature. But it perversely refuses to grant this understanding anything other than a tentative basis in the institutional history of literature itself. It is therefore forced to interpret literary history not in terms of a history of increasingly more powerful reflections on the hypothetical event of anthropological origin, but as an ad hoc collection of aesthetic "periods" that may be studied synchronically, but from which all sense of a larger historical-anthropological narrative has been abortively, and I think quite illogically, removed.

Why then do we still need theory? We need theory because we need the humanities in which theory flourishes. In an era in which the biological sciences of the human, the protohuman, and the parahuman (for example, evolutionary and cognitive psychology, cognitive linguistics, biological anthropology, neuroscience, and primatology) are increasingly refining our sense of the continuity between human and animal life, we need the humanities because only the humanities are founded on the anthropological truth that the human is differentiated not ultimately by its biology but by its capacity to use and interpret symbolic signs. This does not mean we must go back to reading poetry as an abstract reflection of "the human condition." It means we must take seriously the postulate that the minimal basis for any theory of culture is hypothetical and anthropological. From this perspective, cultural criticism begins not with the maximal historical assumption that the aesthetic is an institution to be derived "empirically" from an ad hoc examination of various arbitrarily chosen cultural works or periods. Rather, it begins with a minimal hypothesis that seeks to explain the originary basis for those institutions deemed indispensable for cultural and aesthetic analysis (for example, language, art, ritual, and economic exchange). Without such a hypothesis we cannot expect criticism to last much beyond its own narrow self-justifications of institutional membership. In the final analysis, knowing how to enter into the "culture of criticism" means much more than knowing how to gain membership into an academic elite. It means recognizing membership in its most minimal sense, as members of the originary anthropological community, the only community we have ever known and are ever likely to know.

PART III

TWO ORIGINARY ANALYSES

Chapter 5

Shakespeare and the Idea of the Modern

In an essay of admirable historicizing rigor, Margreta de Grazia states that "no work in the English literary canon has been so closely identified with the beginnings of the modern age as *Hamlet*."[1] De Grazia cites Harold Bloom as the most recent example of this identification.[2] She could just as easily have cited William Kerrigan, who is no less convinced of the importance of *Hamlet*'s romantic origins. "Shakespeare's revenge tragedy," Kerrigan writes, "was present at the birth of Romantic individualism, at the early tests of the doctrine of organic unity, at the discovery of the oedipus complex, at the center of the mythy shenanigans in Joyce's *Ulysses*."[3]

Does this mean that the modern era begins in 1600 when Shakespeare wrote *Hamlet*? Yes and no. Yes, because that is indeed when *Hamlet* first made its way from Shakespeare's brain to the page and thence to the stage. No, because the play was much too ahead of its time to be appreciated as, well, modern. Instead it had to rely on all the standard gags of Elizabethan revenge tragedy: murder, madness, the obligatory ghost, and plenty of violence. No doubt there were many who resented the upstart playwright's popularity and therefore preferred to point to this rather "primitive" or "old-fashioned" element in his theater. It would take Shakespeare some time to shake this reputation for Saxon savagery.

Two hundred years, in fact. As both Kerrigan and de Grazia agree, before the romantics Shakespeare wasn't the child of modernity that he is today. But here their agreement ends. Whereas Kerrigan embraces Shakespeare's modernity, de Grazia resists it. More precisely, whereas Kerrigan's *Hamlet* begins positively and definitively with the romantics, de Grazia's begins well before that, indeed, before *Hamlet* was even written, in the "dark ages" of medieval ritual culture.

Since Kerrigan's idea of modernity has until relatively recently been the dominant one, I will discuss him first. De Grazia's new-historicist position in fact constitutes a direct critique of the tradition Kerrigan so passionately and, it must be admitted, convincingly defends. It is therefore best understood as a response to him. After summarizing their debate, I will go on to propose, in the second and much longer part of my argument, an anthropological solution to it.

Romantic Shakespeare

"It all begins with the Romantic Germans," Kerrigan starts his chapter "*Hamlet* in History" by saying, and then goes on to show how Johann Wolfgang von Goethe and, even more so, Friedrich and August Wilhelm von Schlegel, and G. W. F. Hegel provided us with the idea of *Hamlet* as the quintessential modern work. But what does Kerrigan mean by "modern"? Kerrigan's use of this term is not strictly speaking historical. The modern is not a datable empirical fact, or even a datable period with a well-defined beginning and end (compare "the Elizabethan period"). It is rather a literary-historical category: history *mediated* by literature. For Kerrigan, the site of the modern is thus the literary text itself. But since the text is nothing without interpretation, the modern must also be an interpretation. Modern interpretation begins when the romantics foregrounded the problem of Hamlet's delay, which had for so long remained in the background of previous criticism, including criticism before *Hamlet* was written (Aristotle's, for example). Only after Shakespeare wrote *Hamlet*, and only after the romantics interpreted it, could we talk of plot in the modern sense, that is, in a sense that updated Aristotle for modern times, for example, by codifying "the aesthetics of a drama based on pure individualism of character" (*HP* 8).

Kerrigan thus accepts as inaugural or originary the problem of Hamlet's delay. Its very originarity is also what makes it "modern," in that it constitutes a moment in history we are unable to transcend. "When Schlegel proposed that *Hamlet* was the first modern drama," Kerrigan enthusiastically writes, "he set a problem that no amount of historical scholarship can resolve" (*HP* 29). And it cannot resolve it because there is no historical solution to it, only better or worse *literary* interpretations.[4]

In implicit if not explicit debate with Kerrigan, de Grazia questions the significance of this literary origin. What about the "real" historical origin of *Hamlet* in 1600? And what about the period before the romantics, from 1600 to 1800, that Kerrigan silently passes over? De Grazia worries about this omission, and she takes her main critical task to be to return us to this neglected period. For as Kerrigan's account seems to exemplify with breathtaking vengeance, "these interstitial two centuries tend to be phased out by Hamlet's identification with the modern" in 1800 ("HBT" 356).

Let us attempt to put this debate in broader perspective. The scandal implied in pointing out the "barbaric" or premodern origins of so illustrious and thoroughly romanticized a work as *Hamlet* gives de Grazia's essay considerable polemical edge. Indeed, her argument recalls T. S. Eliot's snub of Coleridge, when Eliot argued, contra Coleridge, that *Hamlet*'s "intractability" stems not from anything to do with the psychology of the prince, but from the play's being "superposed upon much cruder material which persists even in the final form."[5] Though de Grazia does not mention Eliot in her survey of *Hamlet* criticism, her historicist debunking shares much in common with his 1919 essay. Having neatly lined her romantic ducks in a row, she, like Eliot, turns her back on them, announcing instead a new-historicist "turnabout," a theoretical shift from "the hero of modern consciousness to the ghost from a premodern system of belief" ("HBT" 374). In medieval religion de Grazia discovers what the romantics had either repressed or ignored, the haunting trace of the other.[6]

Kerrigan, on the other hand, seems to have no interest in being "new" in this historicist sense. Instead he pronounces himself, rather disingenuously, to be so unfashionably old-fashioned as to be idiosyncratic. He is thus new in his very unconcern with newness. While the avant-garde have been immersing themselves in postmodern theory, Kerrigan remains a stubborn "modern," which is to say, he still believes in the transformative power of what used to be called high culture. And therein lies the deeper target of de Grazia's historicism, namely, Kerrigan's unrepentant romantic belief in the aesthetic text as a vehicle of personal transformation or self-discovery.[7] Eschewing generative inwardness of any kind, de Grazia's aim is to historicize *Hamlet*, not to update the prince for the presentist needs of the modern consumer, whose relentless low-cultural appetite for new models of desire obscures from view the high-cultural recognition of the origin of desire in *Hamlet* itself. In obvious dissonance with Kerrigan's conviction that *Hamlet* will never cease to transcend the merely ephemeral products of marketplace or consumer culture, de Grazia regards the text with all the ironic disenchantment of the apostate, the one whose belief in the literary text's transcendence has been rudely and noisily shattered by the profane distractions of the modern world.

We should not be surprised by de Grazia's "apostasy." On the contrary, we should be more surprised by Kerrigan's refusal to follow suit. For it has been apparent for some time that the era of high Western culture is drawing to a close. There are still a few "last stands" being made by defenders of this tradition, of which Kerrigan's is undoubtedly one of the best and most interesting. But as even he seems to recognize, the days of the master literary critic are over.[8] The rise of "theory" in literature departments is a response to this decline.[9] But the literary object has not simply disappeared. It has been subsumed by a broader anthropological category. That category is culture. But culture is much older than literature. It is as old as the human itself. Literature has enjoyed enormous cultural centrality for the duration of the modern era (roughly, since Shakespeare's day). But this centrality is nothing when compared to the historical longevity of its cultural precursor, which is religion.[10]

Anthropological Aesthetics

In Eric Gans's "generative anthropology," the neoclassical aesthetic is the first modern aesthetic.[11] For Gans, the aesthetic manifests itself in a historical "sequence of hypotheses of [human] origin" that together map "the rise and fall of the esthetic as an anthropological discovery procedure" (*OT* 25). I have already alluded to the fall of the aesthetic, that is, to the demise of high literary culture, in my summary of the debate between Kerrigan and de Grazia. What Gans's aesthetic history allows us to grasp more clearly is that their debate on modernity is really an allegory for the rise and fall of the aesthetic as the West's principal source of anthropological discovery. Kerrigan sees the rise of the aesthetic, which establishes its ascendancy in the romantic and postromantic eras, whereas de Grazia sees only its fall, in the postmodern turn to theory and the subsequent new-historicist project of digging up historical exotica left in the margins of the old high culture. This is not to say that Kerrigan is totally unaware of this fall, only that he chooses to interpret it as premature, thus making a space for his continued discipleship of the romantics.[12] De Grazia, on the other hand, interprets her "modernity" in terms of her rejection of the romantic aesthetic defended by Kerrigan. But—and this is crucial—she offers no anthropology capable of replacing the aesthetic tradition she rejects.[13]

Romantic Anthropology

As Kerrigan convincingly shows, the romantic *Hamlet* assumes a generative distinction between ancient and modern. Anthropologically speaking, this difference was presented as a transition from an ethical system based in collective ritual to one based in the interiority of the modern subject.[14] Hegel's analysis of *Hamlet* is exemplary of the romantic critical enterprise as a whole. Whereas a classical hero like Oedipus is destined to suffer for crimes he is totally ignorant of, the romantic Hamlet suffers because he internalizes as a representation—for example, in the figure of the ghost, the player's speech, and the Mousetrap play—the crimes his uncle has committed. For the classical hero, torment comes from without; at the end of the play, Oedipus is ritually banished for transgressing taboos (parricide and incest) that preexist his capacity to understand or control them. For the modern hero, torment comes from within; haunted by the memory of his father's death, Hamlet invents fictional scenes by which he attempts to relieve himself of his ethical duty to revenge. For Hegel, as indeed for most moderns, this internalization of the classical scene of collective sacrifice is considered an ethical advance. Hamlet's celebrated delay is also a symptom of his exemplary modernity. By internalizing the scene of his uncle's crime rather than blindly reproducing its ethical structure in an act of revenge (like Laertes, like Fortinbras), Hamlet points the way toward a more open ethical system, one in which individual desire is liberated from the constraining forces of ritual interdiction and integrated into the productive forces of the modern exchange system.[15] Hence the currency of A. C. Bradley's remark in 1904 that "the tragedy of *Hamlet* with Hamlet left out has become the symbol of extreme absurdity."[16] For the romantics, what the play is above all about is the mind of its ambivalently "liberated" protagonist.

But if the romantics only invented the problem of Hamlet's delay, what enabled them to come up with the idea of delay in the first place? De Grazia's reply is that it was the plot of *Hamlet* that provided the ultimate source for the romantic infatuation with the procrastinating prince. By translating a dramatic narrative of suspended action (delayed revenge) into a narrative of psychological hesitation, the romantics reversed the historical priority of dramatic performance over internal reflection. In effect, they argued that the dramatic performance originated in the internal "psychological" scene of the prince's mind, whose capacious imagination they took as a model for their own.

Historically speaking, de Grazia is certainly right to say that the drama preexists the character. Without the collective context of the dramatic performance, there can be no individual view of this same scene. But it is precisely in this difference between the collective and individual "scenes of representation" that we can begin to discern the anthropology latent in the romantic interpretation of *Hamlet*.

Classical Anthropology

Drama assumes the difference between the individual spectator and the "scenes" performed on stage before the viewer. Like the frame of a painting, the limits of the stage represent the formal boundary between the fictional world of the play and the real world of the spectator. The question as to what scenes are appropriate to represent aesthetically was originally answered by the Greeks, who took their subject matter from the myths and legends that preceded them.

But the reception of myth differs from the reception of mythical *content*. The audience of the former is not so much a spectator as a participant. The point of myth is not to tell fictions that may be contemplated whenever it is convenient for the individual to do so, but far more urgently to "incorporate" the individual into the collective life of the community.[17] The power of myth is therefore never exclusively a product of the aesthetic effect it produces during the occasion of its particular performance. The boundary between myth and literature is a condition of the capacity of the text to survive by the power of its performance alone, independently of the historically specific beliefs that are necessary if a community's myths and rituals are to survive. It is for this reason that we are still able to appreciate Greek tragedy independently of its original ritual context, or why we read "Homer" as literature rather than as an authorless communal myth or folktale.

The Greeks were the first to institute an aesthetic distinct from the ritual scenes that historically preceded them and which still provided the festive occasion for their performance (as in the Dionysian festival in Athens). As Gans notes, the "classical esthetic is the first and simplest" because its sole claim to the significance of its (usually mythical) content is presence on stage (*OT* 132). Oedipus has no need to justify his appearance on stage; he is, as the priest says in his opening speech, "Greatest in all men's eyes," because his greatness has existed in the Greek imaginary since time immemorial.[18]

Neoclassical Anthropology

By Shakespeare's day, the classical aesthetic was firmly established as the historical source for all future aesthetics. To the question, "What should be represented on stage?" the neoclassicists replied by pointing to the Greeks. Hence the inevitable quarrel between ancient and modern.[19] The neoclassicists were the first historical anthropologists because they were the first to recognize, as a condition of their aesthetic project, their historical distance from their aesthetic precursors. As modernism's flirtation with the idea of the primitive suggests, the origin of anthropology lies ultimately in this "aesthetic" distinction between ancient and modern.[20] The contemporary idea of distinct aesthetic periods ("classical," "medieval," "Renaissance") is a continuation of a historical development begun by the Greeks, when they liberated the aesthetic from the "eternal present" of ritual. But these aesthetics are not, despite what the romantics and their modernist heirs believed, the instigators of actual historical change. The formulation of new aesthetics is possible only on the basis of new systems of social organization. Historically speaking, the difference between ancient and modern is less a formal-aesthetic than an ethical difference. What intervenes between the Greeks and Shakespeare is the ethical revolution that is Christianity. In this specifically anthropological sense, the intervening "Middle Ages" are just as "modern" as the Renaissance.[21]

According to Gans, the most obvious consequence of Christianity for the classical aesthetic is that the automatic privilege granted to the protagonist of Greek tragedy becomes suspect. "The unquestioned exemplarity that separates the classical protagonist from the world of the spectator," Gans writes, "is no longer sufficient. Significance is no longer self-evident; it must be explicitly derived from the locus of the scene" (*OT* 151). In the face of Christianity's moral doctrine of spiritual election, it becomes increasingly difficult to justify the ethical inequalities of the social order. The Shakespearean protagonist is a representative of this moral sentiment, not in the sense that he is a romantic revolutionary who fights for "liberty, fraternity, and equality," but in the more fundamental sense that he is a resenter of the social order. None of the kings of Shakespeare's history plays, despite their obvious centrality on stage and within the social order they represent, are free of resentment toward those around them, whom they imagine as rivals to the very centrality they have themselves usurped. From Richard III to Henry V,

Shakespeare's kings are obsessed with the idea of their status as usurpers because they participate in the same resentment that makes it impossible for them to accept their invulnerability at the center. Shakespeare's theme of usurpation is thus much more than a political category. It implies the awareness that the throne is in reality an "aesthetic scene" that preexists the individual's place on it. Centrality becomes a role to be played, defined by the protagonist's self-consciousness of his distance from it.[22]

Before Shakespeare's radical staging of the "scene" of resentful inwardness, this distance was most often reflected in the self-conscious belatedness of the neoclassical work, which is forced to borrow from its classical precursors. For example, Marlowe's *Dido, Queen of Carthage* focuses not on Virgil's hero, but on the death of his African queen. Dido "imitates" Aeneas's tragic account of the fall of Troy. At Dido's insistence, Aeneas describes, in a narrative of gratuitous pathos, his own near-sacrifice at the hands of Achilles' avenging son Pyrrhus and his bloody Myrmidons. But Aeneas miraculously escapes from this imagined tragedy when Venus shields him with a magic "invisibility" cloud. With the central sacrificial position left vacant, Dido wastes no time usurping it. Marlowe's tragedy concludes with Dido imagining herself the true victim of the classical scene:

> Now, Dido, with these relics burn thyself,
> And make Aeneas famous through the world
> For perjury and slaughter of a queen.[23]

In Marlowe, the self-consciousness of the imitation is in danger of destroying the desired tragic effect. When Dido's sister Anna and the queen's former suitor Iarbas both kill themselves in imitation of the queen, the tragedy risks turning into farce. To a certain extent this is a danger implicit in all imitation. There is, for example, already a sense of belatedness present in Virgil; the Roman poet's depiction of Dido's death competes with the Homeric account of Hector's death. But in neither the Roman nor the Greek case is this lateness a subject for reflection on the anthropology of the scene of representation itself.

In Shakespeare, this belatedness with respect to classical precursors becomes more than an exercise in self-conscious imitation. It provides the occasion for a sustained reflection on the openness of the center to all humanity. For the Shakespearean protagonist, the center is an object of both intense desire and intense envy. What drives the plot of Shakespeare's more mature work is the protagonist's awareness of the center's openness to the periphery. This is the neoclassical's anthropological modification of the Aristotelian assumption that plot preexists character. Put in René Girard's terms of the mimetic triangle, without the mediation of the center provided by the mimetic other, there would be no center for the subject to desire, and hence no plot to drive the narrative of usurpation.[24]

The royal protagonists of Shakespeare's histories are all too aware that they are performing roles on stage rather than reproducing mythical-historical scenes from the past. Shakespeare's kings know they cannot take history for granted. They can of course be assumed to possess a historical significance that precedes them; the enormous popularity of historical subject-matter in Shakespeare's day is at least partially explained by the preexisting ideological significance of Tudor history among the Elizabethans. But unlike the classical figure, the neoclassical hero is aware that his historical significance must be continually renewed by the aesthetic scene itself.[25]

Thus no sacred ancestry can serve to put an end to rival claims on the center. On the contrary, it becomes all the more imperative to cite these ancestries as further instances of narrative legitimation. Henry V's convoluted claim to the throne of France is not just a pretext for the young king's aggressive war-mongering. It is a symptom of his awareness of his displacement from the center. Nor are the more patriotic elements of the play free of resentment. Harry's great speech on the eve of the battle of Agincourt is usually understood as an example of rousing patriotism. When Harry declares, "For he today that sheds his blood with me / Shall be my brother," he is in the mode of the revolutionary (4.3.61–63).[26] By emphasizing his fundamental equality with the common soldier, Harry abandons the ritual hierarchy of sacred kingship and embraces the fraternity and equality of his "band of brothers" (4.3.60). But Harry's "happy few" (4.3.60) constitute a new center more exclusive than the old when his "band of brothers" is explicitly opposed to England itself, to those "one ten thousand … gentlemen in England now abed" (4.3.17, 64). Westmorland, who wishes those "one ten thousand" were present to assist in the fight, sees only the fact that they are vastly outnumbered by the French, and quite reasonably desires more favorable odds. Harry, the more advanced student of desire, responds not by attempting to assuage Westmorland's natural fear of violent death, but by showing him the aesthetic potential of the scene in which they are about to centralize their marginality. The real climax of the speech occurs some seven lines before the speech ends, in the haunting and intensely imagined line, "We few, we happy few, we band of brothers" (4.3.60). Harry's "patriotism" defines itself not with but against all Englishmen, whom he imagines as competitors to his desire for significance.

Shakespearean Anthropology

Let us listen to Henry V once more, this time to the lines directly preceding those already quoted:

> This day is called the feast of Crispian.
> He that outlives this day and comes safe home
> Will stand a-tiptoe when this day is named
> And rouse him at the name of Crispian.
> He that shall see this day and live old age
> Will yearly on the vigil feast his neighbours,
> And say "Tomorrow is Saint Crispian."
> Then will he strip his sleeve and show his scars,
> And say "These wounds I had on Crispin's day."
> Old men forget; yet all shall be forgot
> But he'll remember, with advantages,
> What feats he did that day. Then shall our names,
> Familiar in his mouth as household words,
> Harry the King, Bedford and Exeter,
> Warwick and Talbot, Salisbury and Gloucester,
> Be in their flowing cups freshly remembered.
> This story shall the good man teach his son,
> And Crispin Crispian shall ne'er go by
> From this day to the ending of the world
> But we in it shall be remembered,
> We few, we happy few, we band of brothers. (4.3.40–60)

In his discussion of the generative scene of collective memory, Anthony Dawson notes that the paradoxicality of Harry's speech, which embeds in the historical past the scene of its own future retelling, grants this past the status of an "originary event."[27] The scene points forward to its own future significance in the immortalization of Harry's band of brothers through the memories passed down from "the good man" to his son. But this future significance is also being enacted before the audience in the theater, who identify with Harry's onstage audience precisely because they already know the outcome of Harry's prediction. Dawson argues that these metatheatrical moments are more than simply an example of dramatic irony.[28] Shakespeare, he suggests, is here staging in explicitly theatrical form a kind of "social memory" that was formerly devoted to the purely ritual "stage" of sacred commemoration.[29]

Dawson is certainly not alone when he suggests that in the background to such "originary" scenes of remembrance in Shakespeare lies a long-term cultural process of deritualization, in which the old sacred guarantees become increasingly decentered and recycled by a commercial marketplace, including the marketplace of the theater.[30] This change in the balance between the centripetal forces of the sacred and the centrifugal forces of the market is the real crux for discussions of the modern. But what exactly is meant by deritualization in these accounts of Shakespeare's pivotal position between ritual and aesthetic culture, between the premodern and the modern?

To answer this question, we need to begin our history much earlier than the religious controversies immediately preceding Shakespeare's day. Deritualization implies a movement away from the sacred. But the sacred did not begin with the historical controversies of the Reformation. A historical analysis of these controversies can therefore never fully explain the emergence of aesthetic institutions such as the theater from the ritual context, whether these are located in Reformation England or, going back still further, in Periclean Athens.[31]

In Gans's originary hypothesis, the sacred is that which stands at the center, maximally opposed to the individual desires of the peripheral human community. In ritual sacrifice, only the central sacred figure is able to withstand the multiple, conflictive desires among the members of the human periphery. As Girard suggests, the god functions as an "external mediator," upon whom all desire is collectively projected and so purged.[32] The god is thus both a victim and a hero. In the first moment, he functions as the repository for frustrated desire (the scapegoat); in the second, he is deified as the restorer of order (the god).

In Girard's formulation of the founding murder, the central figure is not a god but a human who stands in the place of the god. For Girard, the god always was a human; the sacrifice upon which the god depends was originally and foundationally the murder of his human victim. As

Gans points out, implicit in Girard's originary scene of sacrifice is the fundamental difference between the peripheral human sign and its central sacred object. We know the victim only by designating it as sacred, which means minimally situating the victim/object at the center of the human scene of representation that we call symbolic culture.[33]

In Gans's revision of the Girardian mimetic crisis, what stands at the center in the originary scene is not another human but the *figure* of humanity as such, which is the god. The usurpation of the role of the central figure by the humans on the periphery is implied by the desiring structure of the scene. Like Hamlet on the margins of Claudius's court, the peripheral subject remains attracted to the scene because his attention is mediated by the attentions of the others on the periphery. The sacred is the originary historical site of all such figurations. Insofar as the theater is a form of dramatic figuration, it necessarily partakes of this same "symbolic" relationship to the sacred object.

But there is a difference. The aesthetic manifests itself historically as an *effect* rather than as the sacred reproduction of history. Ritual is historical only in the "unconscious" sense that it attempts to reproduce as faithfully as possible previous ritual, which is to say, historically significant or collectively memorable events. There is no self-conscious attempt to differentiate between past and present in the ritual act. On the contrary, such attempts are likely to be regarded as a theft of the sacred—a sacrilege—and the perpetrator of difference will, like the unfortunate Pentheus in Euripides' *Bacchae*, not go unpunished for his "modernist" act of desecration.

As these remarks suggest, the modern is less a formal or generic category of literature than a term we use to differentiate between different degrees of centralization in the general cultural business of linguistic, aesthetic, sacred, and economic exchange. The universally observed historical movement from compact ritual societies, in which economic exchange remains bound by a centralized ritual "superstructure," toward the modern exchange system, which eschews ritual centralization of any kind, leaves in its wake a vacuum. This vacuum is filled by what we call high culture. Literature is the culture of the market because the market is the locus of cultural desacralization.[34]

But desacralization does not happen overnight. Because the market is centerless, culture responds by recentralizing in imaginary or aesthetic form—that is, on the stage of the theater, or in the pages of the novel, or within the frame of the painting—the old figures of the ritual order.

Henry V's great speech on the eve of the battle of Agincourt is an example of this imaginary recentralization. Shakespeare looks back to the old institution of kingship in order to look forward to the new social order in which each individual soul is elected, like Harry himself, to the center of world history. This may not be the radical revolutionary historicism of the romantic, who rejects the existing social order wholesale, but it is a precursor of it.

Reconsider this difference between the romantic and neoclassical ideas of aesthetic centralization. In contrast to the romantic model of subjectivity, Henry V still understands himself as a *rival* for a significance that precedes his own being. Hence his reference to the Christian martyrs Crispin and Crispian. Harry understands his own significance on this Christian model of victimary self-centralization. Obviously this has nothing to do with military strategy. Like the victimized saints themselves, significance or sainthood is inversely proportional to military strength. By increasing the likelihood of their sacrifice at Agincourt, Harry also increases the chance for his "happy few" to achieve aesthetic immortality. By the end of his speech, Harry has successfully communicated the cultural productivity of resentment to the previously queasy Westmorland, who now wishes that "you and I alone ... could fight this royal battle!" (4.3.74–75). Westmorland finally catches on that significance is a role to be played on stage, rather than a real battle that acquires significance from the empiricism of actual history.

In the plays of his middle period, including *Henry V, Julius Caesar* and *Hamlet*, Shakespeare's protagonists become increasingly obsessed with the aesthetics of the scene in which they imagine their destruction. Brutus is a transitional figure between Henry V and Hamlet. Like Henry, he recognizes his own belatedness with respect to the scene of his immortalization. But unlike Henry, who can at least claim to be the legitimate heir of his father's throne, Brutus is forced to imagine Julius Caesar's centrality as a usurpation. With increasing sharpness, Shakespeare will trace the passage of desire from its "comic" fulfillment in the collective appropriation and distribution of the central object (*Henry V* ends with a marriage) to its "tragic" source in the imagination of the peripheral subject. This renewed focus on the periphery is reflected in the secondary or "marginal" status of Shakespeare's tragic heroes. Brutus is to Julius Caesar, as Hamlet is to Claudius. Both protagonists are driven by resentment of the more central other. Brutus at home dreaming of the scene of his own centralization anticipates Hamlet "hallucinating" characters (the ghost, Pyrrhus, Lucianus) who can "purge" his resentment of Claudius.

In the history plays, this more lucid depiction of the structure of resentment tends to be obscured by the fact that the action inevitably centers on the dominant figure of the social order, which is the king. Hence the "stagy" artifice of Harry's disguise as a common soldier when he delivers his memorable soliloquy on the hollowness of the king's "thrice-gorgeous ceremony" (*Henry V* 4.1.263), as though donning the cloak of a peripheral subject has demonstrated to the king the emptiness of the center he occupies. In Richard II, whom Walter Pater extolled as the most "exquisite poet" of Shakespeare's kings,[35] we find another example of this doubling of center and periphery within the protagonist. Richard is more interested in imagining, while he is still king, the scene of his own sacrifice than in actually defending himself against the upstart Bolingbroke. An early prototype of Hamlet, Richard is fascinated by the prospect of his own death, not so much because he suffers from melancholia, as because he resentfully identifies with the omnipotent power of death itself. After learning that he has been abandoned by his Welsh allies and that his court favorites have been executed by Bolingbroke, Richard's response is to "sit upon the ground / And tell sad stories of the death of kings."[36] The long speech that ensues appears to be triggered by deep sorrow for what has befallen his friends, but beneath the ostensibly mournful tone is a much darker identification with the destructive power of the resentful protagonist of Richard's sad story: "the antic" "Death" who, "scoffing" and "grinning" at the king's "state" and "pomp" allows him "a little scene" before he "Comes at the last and with a little pin / Bores through his castle wall, and farewell, king!" (3.2.162–70).

The scene of Richard's resentful identification with death as the ultimate leveler of social inequality strikes us as perverse, or at the very least extremely ill-advised, because it takes place while Richard is still king. What indeed has this man to envy? But the point of resentment is not that, as Nietzsche believed, it is exclusive to slaves rather than masters, but that it is a universal condition of human subjectivity. Henry V, in disguise as a common soldier bitterly soliloquizing on the "thrice gorgeous ceremony" (*Henry V* 4.1.263) of a king is as much a resenter of the social order as Richard II denouncing the "pomp" and "state" of the monarch's "little scene" (*Richard II* 3.2.163–64).

This resentment reaches its most lucid depiction in *Hamlet*. Even before Hamlet sees the ghost, he is presented as a menace to the court. Dressed in black and defiantly ignoring the king's admonishment that he "throw to earth / This unprevailing woe,"[37] Hamlet's hostility is motivated not by revenge, for which he has as yet no motive, but resentment. Indeed, the whole point of delaying Hamlet's interview with the ghost seems to be to show us that Hamlet's resentment is generative of the scene in which the ghost reveals the secret of Claudius's crime. Hence W. W. Greg's still pertinent remark that Hamlet can reasonably be said to have "hallucinated" the ghost.[38] Despite the torrent of criticism Greg's original argument inspired, the most belligerent of which was undoubtedly Dover Wilson's, I do not think that its kernel of truth has ever been adequately explored.[39] Most of the original commentators rely on the standard retort that the ghost can hardly be a figment of Hamlet's imagination because it has also been seen by Marcellus, Barnardo, and Horatio. But the question of Hamlet's motivation cannot be decided by giving a headcount of the other witnesses. The very fact that it appears only to a handful of minor characters before word of its appearance gets to Hamlet is itself extremely significant, because it suggests that only from a position sufficiently removed from the centralizing or homogenizing influence of Claudius's court can the "difference" of the ghost be noticed. This seems to be the point behind Shakespeare's insistence that Gertrude is incapable of seeing the ghost, even when Hamlet is there to point to its presence.

After the nighttime mystery of the opening ghost scene, the action switches to Claudius's brilliant court scene. If we omit the "mythical" content of the ghost for a moment, we arrive at the following official narrative efficiently delivered by Claudius: (1) there has been a recent change in the seat of power in Denmark, the old king having died and his younger brother having taken the queen's hand in marriage and thereby the throne; (2) Denmark is preparing to defend itself from an external threat that, pushed underground by the former king's reign, now reemerges to test the new king's leadership. The only figure to challenge this official interpretation is Hamlet, but he does so not by direct refutation but by his menacing stage presence. Dressed in black on an occasion intended to celebrate the new king's marriage and coronation, Hamlet's resentment of Claudius is more pregnantly communicated by his stage presence than any speech could hope to convey.

But the very fact that this first challenge remains unspoken only increases our desire for an explanation. Commentators, from Coleridge to A. C. Bradley and Freud, have hastened to defend Hamlet's opening resentful posture and the delay upon which it feeds. Coleridge interpreted the prince's delay as the product of his "vivid imagination," which sends him into "endless reasoning and hesitating."[40] Bradley, accepting the romantic position, suggested that this was the effect, not the cause, of the particular predicament in which Hamlet finds himself; the one-two punch of a father's death and a mother's overhasty remarriage triggers the condition of stultifying resentment and deep melancholy in which the audience first observes the prince.[41] Finally, Freud and Ernest Jones proposed that, far from being unusual, Hamlet's resentment was all too typical.[42] Hamlet resents Claudius because he sees in him the unfolding of his own "unconscious" desire to unseat his father and marry his mother.

Of the three interpretations only the Freudian one puts its finger on the key issue, which is that Hamlet uses Claudius as a proxy for indulging his interdicted desires. But contrary to the Freudian view, desire is not first experienced then repressed. The Freudian notion of the unconscious as a repository of forbidden Oedipal desires is rather the consequence of the mediated status of *all* desire. What prevents the fulfillment of desire is not the repressive law of the father, but the fact that in order to be desired the object must be situated at the center of the scene of representation, where possession is possible only within the fictive space of the individual imagination. This is the source of the romantic intuition that Hamlet is the ultimate poet-figure, a procrastinator who would rather delay his usurpation of the center because he understands that its aesthetic power depends upon this delay. But the flip-side to the delayed fulfillment of desire is the buildup of resentment within the prince's diseased imagination. It was Wilson Knight who first pointed to the significance of Hamlet's resentment as a structural feature of the play.[43] Calling Hamlet the "ambassador of death" (32), Knight noted the Danish prince's resentful dependency on the scene he affects to despise. This dependency is evident in Hamlet's first stage appearance. Surrounded by Gertrude, Polonius, Ophelia, Laertes, and his other courtiers, the king dominates the stage. But this centrality is menacingly undercut by the black-clad prince, whose pregnant silence and snarling asides make clear from the start that this center is under attack, not indeed from Fortinbras, but from within the very same scene occupied by Claudius. The exemplary modern, Hamlet criticizes the scene that provides him with his *raison d'être*. He expresses with unparalleled lucidity the awareness that the scene of representation preexists the individual's right to appear on it.

When Christianity opened the aesthetic scene to slaves as well as masters, appearance on it becomes problematic. The neoclassical solution is to represent not just the center, but the paradoxical relationship between center and periphery. The representation of this relationship reaches its fullest expression in *Hamlet*. The prince's ambivalent relationship to the scene usurped by his uncle reflects the paradoxical structure of the neoclassical aesthetic, which represents the center as a locus of usurpation from the periphery. In the play's violent and bloody conclusion, Hamlet becomes the unofficial "king" of Denmark for the briefest of moments. Between his murder of Claudius and his own (delayed) death by Laertes's poisoned sword, he momentarily occupies the paradoxical position of the kings of Shakespeare's history plays. Like them, he is both the subject and the object of resentment. Hamlet's single "command" during his brief occupation of the center is to persuade Horatio to remove himself, by putting aside the poisoned cup, from the mimetic center's contagious violence. This forward-thinking action by the dying prince/king has one purpose: so Horatio can "tell my story" (5.2.354).

Hamlet is thus a modern "before his time" in a sense similar to the happy few of Harry's speech at Agincourt. Aware that his election to the center of the spectator's desire depends upon Horatio's ability to tell his story, Hamlet usurps the center at exactly the point where his own life is about to end. No longer a resentful spectator of Claudius's centrality, he becomes himself an object of resentment: ours. With impeccable timing, Hamlet transforms himself from a resentful prince competing metatheatrically with the spectator's (delayed) desire for the sacrificial dénouement of traditional revenge tragedy into its glorious and bloody fulfillment. From our mimetic rival, Hamlet transforms himself into our mimetic victim, the object of a spectacle that fulfills our desire not for delay, but closure.

Chapter 6

A Race of Devils: *Frankenstein*, Romanticism, and the Tragedy of Human Origin

The spirit that I have seen
May be a devil ...
(Hamlet)

a race of devils would be propagated upon the earth ...
(Victor Frankenstein)

Almost two centuries after the nineteen-year-old Mary Shelley wrote *Frankenstein*, her monster is so firmly entrenched in the popular imagination that the novel's title is frequently mistaken for the name of the monster himself. The desire to associate the monster with a proper name is natural enough, for by naming him we implicitly accept him as our moral equal. But "our" moral reciprocity with the monster is undermined by the ethical reality depicted by the novel. No one else sees fit to name the monster. Is this why Shelley leaves her monster unnamed? Is his anonymity a condition of his subaltern status, the permanent victim or scapegoat of society?

In fact the novel's representation of scapegoating is more subtle than that. To be sure, the monster recalls his encounter with society in terms of a narrative of persecution. From his first contact with human society when he is expelled from the village "grievously bruised by stones and many other kinds of missile weapons,"[1] he consistently casts himself in the role of scapegoat or victim. But the fact that his account comes to us in heavily mediated form, that is, nested within the narratives of two previous speakers—speakers who "imitate" to varying degrees the monster's righteous sense of moral indignation—should warn us against reading his narrative with too much credulity. In what follows, I will not rehearse the usual claims for the monster's "otherness," his status as a victim of one or another political injustice or "ism" (racism, colonialism, imperialism, sexism, scientific rationalism, ethnocentrism, etc.). Rather, I will delve beneath the victimary reading to grasp its underlying anthropological source.[2]

As J. L. Austin recognized, naming works by a curious paradox. The individual is both singled out from the group ("*you* are the unique bearer of this name") but also incorporated into it ("*we* give this name to you"). But this paradox is that of the originary anthropological scene of representation, which defines its center only by excluding its periphery. According to Eric Gans, alienation from the center is the condition of human consciousness, insofar as the latter is defined as existing only within the context of that scene. *Frankenstein* is a prolonged meditation on the experience of resentful dispossession from the anthropological birthright of the originary scene. But since none of us is present at this scene, which is by definition available to us only as a representation (Derrida), we share the same belatedness or supplementarity as the solitary protagonists/narrators of *Frankenstein*. Paradoxically, the experience of dispossession, voiced and acted upon with increasing violence by first Walton, then Victor, and finally the monster himself, defines the condition of membership in the community one also accuses of rejection. What was formerly protected by the public scene of sacrificial ritual is now opened to appropriation by the resentful "secular" periphery.

The romantics interpreted this opening of the center to the peripheral self as an indication of the more fundamental role of the aesthetic in establishing the self's relationship to the social order. But the romantic faith in the aesthetic as the key to social organization turned out to be an illusion, a substitution of one (religious) asymmetry for another far more terrifying one. The attempt to make good on the harmony promised by the aesthetic imagination, to expel resentment once and for all in a centrally managed "final solution," failed, as all such projects must fail if humanity is to survive. This failure is anticipated by Shelley's novel, which describes both the failure of aesthetics to transcend politics and the reason for this failure in the persistence of the self's resentment toward the center. What the monster acquires in his aesthetic education is not the paradise of linguistic and moral reciprocity but a lesson in what Gans calls "victimary rhetoric."[3] He is the *reductio ad absurdum* of the technique whereby the romantic artist justifies his claim to our attention by announcing the scandal of his worldly anonymity.

Victimary Rhetoric

In Mary Shelley's day, the celebrated master of victimary rhetoric was Jean-Jacques Rousseau. *Frankenstein* was composed on the shores of

Lake Geneva where Rousseau was born. The scenes of Victor languishing in his sailboat come directly from Rousseau's *Reveries of the Solitary Walker*, which we know (from her journal) Mary Shelley read at the time.[4] Percy Shelley and Byron sailed the lake in imitation of Rousseau. Together with Mary, they read and discussed his work constantly. It is impossible to grasp the irony of *Frankenstein* without some sense of this context. Consider, for example, the opening lines of Rousseau's *Reveries*:

> So now I am alone in the world, with no brother, neighbour or friend, nor any company left me but my own. The most sociable and loving of men has with one accord been cast out by all the rest . . . . Could I, in my right mind, suppose that I, the very same man who I was then and am still today, would be taken beyond all doubt for a monster, a poisoner, an assassin, that I would become the horror of the human race, the laughing-stock of the rabble, that all the recognition I would receive from passers-by would be to be spat upon, and that an entire generation would of one accord take pleasure in burying me alive? (27–28)

In order to place *Frankenstein* in its specific intellectual and literary context, we need to grasp its relationship to Rousseau, particularly the Rousseau of the *Reveries*. But in order to grasp the anthropology implicit in *Frankenstein* and romanticism more generally, we also need to step back from this context to see why Rousseau's language of persecution is much more than just a literary strategy adopted and parodied by Mary Shelley. It implies a fundamental ethical paradigm shift, the long-term historical effects of which we are only just beginning to recognize.

In his discussion of the ethical significance of victimary thinking after World War II, Gans describes Rousseau as "the greatest contributor to the arsenal of modern victimary rhetoric."[5] As the label implies, victimary rhetoric is the language of the victim. The latter is defined by his or her marginality with respect to the social order. The initiation of individuals into this order is the traditional task of culture, which works by the "conservative" practice of extrapolating on the basis of previous tradition. Tradition thus serves as the "natural" or unquestioned model for present practice. This is the argument of Edmund Burke in his *Reflections on the Revolution in France*. But it is also the argument of the early anthropologists of traditional religious societies, such as those

documented by Arnold van Gennep in his *Rites of Passage* (first published in French in 1908).

Victimary rhetoric expresses the awareness that this conservative
practice benefits the establishment rather than the individual. But because the individual is defined only in relation to the establishment,
victims of this order must make their case on the basis of their relative
exclusion from it. In other words, victimary rhetoric is based on a dynamic or generative understanding of the individual's relationship to the
"closed" political and economic structures of ritual society.[6] Victimary
rhetoric is concerned not with sacred transcendence, but with historical
transcendence. It is the rhetoric of and for historical change.

But victimary rhetoric is based on a paradox. For how are we to use
the language of the victim without ourselves becoming victims? How
are we to flaunt the aesthetic of the peripheral sign without succumb-
ing to the tragedy of the center? Rousseau's answer to this paradox,
which Gans takes as prophetic of romanticism in general, was to deny
the validity of the center altogether. The peripheral individual becomes
a world unto himself, a new center who needs only to "write" himself
autobiographically into existence.

This is indeed the argument of the first paragraph of the *Reveries*.
After describing how he has been expelled from society by "one accord,"
Rousseau proceeds to deny the very existence of that society: "So now
they are strangers and foreigners to me; they no longer exist for me,
since such is their will" (27). Having turned his back on society, Rousseau is free to devote his attention to the chief object of his writing, himself: "But I, detached as I am from them and from the whole world, what
am I? This must now be the object of my inquiry" (27). Having removed
himself from the violence of the sacrificial center, Rousseau is free to
turn his attention to himself as an autobiographical subject, which is to
say, a textual subject who "names" himself into existence. It is this shift
from self-as-content to self-as-form that makes Rousseau the crucial
figure in the emergence of the romantic aesthetic. "The *Rêveries*," Gans
writes, "are the first work to exhibit a modern sense of textuality; the
praxis of textual production becomes not merely a recuperative but a
transcendental experience."[7]

Frankenstein exhibits a similar concern for the text as the locus of
personal transcendence. But Mary Shelley also departs from the naïve
victimary persona of Rousseau's *Reveries*. By multiplying the number
of her narrative personae, she returns the text to the collective (and

therefore more overtly agonistic) context of classical tragedy. But this agon, which in classical tragedy takes the "sacrificial" form of the designation of the scapegoat, is rerouted through Rousseau's personal aesthetic of the peripheral narrative subject. Consequently, there is no catharsis or purging of emotion in the expulsion of a victim. What takes place is rather a contest between successive narrators who compete for the attentions of the reader by designating their own victimhood. The unquestioned victor in this struggle is the monster, whose very anonymity suggests a literary textuality that encompasses the selves of the other two narrators, Walton and Victor. The fact that the monster has now become more or less synonymous in the popular imagination with the name "Frankenstein" demonstrates the greater centrality of his narrative in our imaginations than those of the other two "lesser" victims. Of the three narrators, Victor dies before the narrative ends and Walton is forced to turn back a defeated man left only with the letters to his sister, the text of *Frankenstein*. The monster's death is anticipated by the text but not represented. The last sentence of the novel describes him being "borne away by the waves and lost in darkness and distance" (198). The text pays its respects to the reader by pointing to but not representing the scene of the monster's death. This is as close as any textual subject can get to making himself the sacrificial subject of his own tragedy.

This paradox between the monster as both narrator and victim, or, in originary terms, between peripheral sign and sacred center, is everywhere apparent in Shelley's novel. It is most clearly illustrated by the question, Why is the monster so aesthetically repulsive? The obvious answer is to point out that in the novel monstrosity exists, quite literally, in the eye of the beholder. For despite the fact that those who see the monster are instantly repulsed by him (so much so that they automatically condemn him), it is also true that any sympathy he does manage to elicit is a consequence of his capacity for language. The latter response is self-evidently true of the novel's readers. Lacking a perceptual image of his hideousness, we have no difficulty identifying with what he says. What guarantees our attachment to this being is not the collective desire to identify a scapegoat, whose sacrifice explains and therefore purges the community of its collective misfortunes. It is far more ambivalently the aesthetic or literary desire to permit his sacrifice *within the formal limits of the text itself.* Our identification of the victim as a moral being is a consequence of this formal limitation. In the fictional world of the text, the scapegoat of sacrificial ritual is transformed into the protagonist of literary narrative. In thus delaying the passage from sign to object, from text to worldly sacrifice, we identify the object as another instance of the form of the sign. This is the source of our intuition of the literary, the notion that the work is a self-contained form expressing a unique "generative" content. Within the limits of this form and our identification with its content, the sacrificial victim is not merely someone to vilify. He becomes someone to imitate.

Literary identification with the victim is not original to Mary Shelley's novel. As I have suggested, Rousseau exploited it as a means to ensure his own literary immortality. Insofar as Shelley recognized and parodied this tactic, she understood both the originality and the naïveté of Rousseau's position. But not even Rousseau can be granted the privilege of having invented victimary identification. The latter is implicit in Greek tragedy. Indeed, it is the underlying assumption of all acts of aesthetic identification. In order to understand the originality of Mary Shelley's contribution to aesthetic history, we must therefore first make a brief detour through this history. This will require us to consider not only Greek tragedy, but its first radical revision in the "neoclassical" drama of the early modern period. Thence we will return to *Frankenstein*, as a specifically romantic incarnation of classical tragedy. The romantic text's greater self-awareness of its status as an anthropological discovery procedure also indicates its historical distance from the classical prototype. In the case of *Frankenstein*, this greater self-consciousness is suggested by the desiring relation existing between narrator and narratee, and ultimately between author and reader. Within the fictional world inhabited (temporarily) by the reader's imagination, the author functions as the transcendent or "external" mediator of the latter's "monstrous" desires.

Tragedy and the Culture of Resentment

The horrific nature of the monster's physical appearance is both a tribute to and a parody of classical tragedy. It points to the violence of the *sparagmos* suffered by those, like Oedipus, who attempt to usurp the central position toward which all human desire tends. As Gans notes in his discussion of the classical aesthetic, in Greek tragedy the central position is structurally given by the tragic protagonist. His presence on stage is sufficient guarantee of his centrality. The Greek amphitheater reflects the spatial or "scenic" structure of human desire. In observing the onstage actions of the protagonist, the spectators participate vicariously in his being. But in classical tragedy, the indulgence of the spectator's desire for central being is "purged" when, in a sudden reversal, which Aristotle took to be a condition of the well-constructed tragedy, the hero is revealed to be a monster, a criminal guilty of transgressing the social order's most sacred taboos. Greek tragedy is structured by (but without ever thematizing) the ambivalence of this relationship between central protagonist and desiring spectator. Oedipus begins his quest for the murderer of Laius as the most admired of men, but the play ends with the recognition that he is in fact the source of Thebes's pollution, the cause of the plague decimating the city.

Classical tragedy is a literary thematization of ritual sacrifice. It repays the literary desire to identify with the central victim with a narrative that ends in the horror that such a "monstrous" desire leads to. But classical tragedy does not thematize desire as "novelistic," which is to say, mediated by the scene of representation.[8] The latter is the explicitly Judeo-Christian contribution to Western culture. The radical iconoclasm of the Protestant Reformation that preceded the spectacular experiments of the Elizabethan and Jacobean stage is not an evacuation of the spectator's desire in the classical scene but a further opening to it. This opening in the aesthetic sphere corresponds to an opening in the economic sphere. The early modern period is the first historical period to possess a reasonably "free" market, that is, one not ritually constrained by an ontological hierarchy of the human, as was the case, for example, in the slave-driven economies of the Greek and Roman empires. But the rise of the market in the West is not, as some have rather optimistically understood it to be, the "end of history."[9] The free circulation of desire in the goods and services bought and sold in the marketplace leads to a concomitant rise in the overall level of resentment in those who feel unfairly marginalized by this system. But because in a genuinely free market this desire is also always changing, so is resentment. In an open economy, it therefore becomes increasingly difficult to mobilize resentment collectively in a "final [sacrificial] solution." Resentment is rather recuperated by the market itself, a phenomenon well known by those who nostalgically bemoan the "commercialization" of the once-radical counterculture of, for example, the 1960s. But as peripheral countercultures become homogenized by the dominant culture, new resentments emerge together with new countercultures which in turn become the object of a new recuperation. This dynamic situation contrasts with the social mechanisms governing Girard's analyses of so-called "sacrificial" cultures. As Girard shows in *Violence and the Sacred*, in the "closed" systems of ritual cultures, desire and resentment are periodically purged in sacrificial ritual. In the "open" societies of the modern market, on the other hand, desire and resentment are made a condition of the exchange system itself.

The systemic and dynamic nature of the "counterculture" of resentment is first portrayed on the stage of the Renaissance dramatists, the most celebrated example of which is *Hamlet*. Wilson Knight called Hamlet the "ambassador of death" because of the prince's obsession not just with death but with the failure of Claudius and his court to adopt the prince's resentful point of view.[10] Hamlet's resentment or "melancholy" is not merely a consequence of his father's unexpected death and his mother's overhasty remarriage. It is, as Knight suggested, a structural feature of the play. Thus, in what Gans calls "the most pregnant scene of modern tragedy" (*OT* 156), Hamlet first appears dressed in black, shocking us with his disdain for the king and his court. Silent for most of the scene, Hamlet is drawn only reluctantly into the dialogue of the central figures, and then not without his signature irony when he mocks the efforts of his king and queen to coax him into a better humor.

In his analysis of the "neoclassical aesthetic" represented by the drama of Marlowe, Shakespeare, and Racine, Gans argues that the classical scene of the Greeks, with its straightforward opposition between "high" center and "low" periphery, becomes problematic. The protagonist's centrality in Greek tragedy is unquestioned. Neither he nor the audience questions his right to be represented on stage. But in the neoclassical aesthetic, this "unquestioned exemplarity that separates the classical protagonist from the world of the spectator is no longer sufficient." Instead, "it must be derived from the locus of the scene" (*OT* 151).

Gans attributes this change in aesthetic structure to a change in ethical structure. The neoclassical aesthetic reflects the historical changes wrought by Christianity during the Middle Ages: "The so-called Middle Ages were the cocoon in which the modern bourgeoisie gradually came to maturity, to emerge in the early modern era as the bearer of a new social order" (*OT* 150). More precisely, by making "every human being an equal participant in the sacred," Christianity subverts the "worldly hierarchy" that is an ontological assumption of the Greek and Roman empires (*OT* 151). This "ontological hierarchy of the human" (*OT* 151) is an unexamined assumption of the classical aesthetic, which justifies its opposition between tragic protagonist and peripheral spectator by appropriating its central figures from the "preselected" religious categories of myth or historical legend. The problem confronting the humanist scholars of the Renaissance was how to reproduce the classical aesthetic in the context of this radical change in ethical structure. How were they to reconcile the moral message of Christianity's "equality of souls" with the worldly hierarchy implicit in the classical opposition between central protagonist and peripheral spectator?

The solution, Gans argues, was to put the classical scene, with its unproblematic opposition between center and periphery, on stage. The neoclassical protagonist attacks what he takes to be the source of the old classical opposition, the central figure of the scene of representation. Hamlet's resentful stance toward his uncle's court exemplifies this structure. In the prince's first stage appearance, we contemplate the brilliance of the public scene with Claudius at its center. Our response is in this sense similar to that of the audience of Greek tragedy. We immediately identify with the king, whose presumed centrality is given by the mythology of the "divine right" of kings. But then our attention is drawn away from Claudius and toward the prince, whose significance is not given but generated by his "supplementarity" with respect to the more central figure. This supplementarity is above all a "literary" or, as Girard would say, "novelistic" strategy of resentment. The prince undermines the court's unthinking imitation of the king's "festive" actions by his eccentric dress and sardonic asides. In this manner, Hamlet insidiously woos our attention away from the king and toward himself, to the point that by the end of the play he has successfully inverted the original hierarchy between center and periphery. The displaced prince is now at the center of our imagination, and Claudius is dispatched, like the "incestuous, murd'rous, damnèd" (*Hamlet* 5.2.326) villain he is, to the monstrous position of the originary scapegoat.

What is truly remarkable about this literary strategy, and what is all too easily forgotten in the heaps of criticism that continue to mythologize the Danish prince as the "real" persecuted victim of Claudius's villainy, is that this persecution is explicitly represented by Shakespeare as internal to Hamlet's resentful imagination. As W. W. Greg pointed out long ago, the actual evidence Hamlet uncovers against Claudius remains to the end subjective, which is to say, mediated by Hamlet's private imagination.[11] This is obvious enough in the case of the Mousetrap play, which Hamlet devises as a trap to catch the conscience of the king. But it is also evident in the sole witness to Claudius's crime—the ghost.

Critics indignant of the idea that Hamlet could also be the quintessential modern man of resentment like to point out that the ghost is objective (and by implication therefore also a credible witness), for it is seen by no less than four characters. But this proves nothing except that Hamlet is not alone in his resentment. More to the point, of these four characters only Hamlet is able to converse with the ghost, and then only privately, the implication being that only Hamlet is "poetic" enough to imagine within his private "literary" theater a concrete object of his resentment.

The first critics to discern the resentful structure of *Hamlet* were the romantics. Not coincidentally, they were also the first to understand Hamlet as a poet—the Hamlet of the soliloquies rather than the Hamlet who avenges his father. Hence Coleridge made Hamlet's delay the central problem of the tragedy. What is significant about Hamlet, Coleridge argued, is not that he kills, but that he talks an awful lot about killing. Hamlet is an eloquent poet, but a reluctant murderer. Indeed, he is a reluctant murderer precisely because he is such a good poet. As Coleridge put it, no doubt thinking as much of himself as the dark prince, he has that "aversion to action which prevails among such as have a world within themselves."[12]

It is easy to make fun of Coleridge's narcissism, as indeed it is to make fun of anyone who enjoys taking opium and reaching deep into his inner soul. But the intuition behind the romantic interpretation of *Hamlet* is basically sound. Deprived of what Friedrich Schiller called a "naïve" belief in the legitimacy of the traditional figures of authority (for example, in the patriarchal family, church, or state), the romantic looks inward for signs of his election to the center, for "that within which passes show" (*Hamlet* 1.2.85). But what he finds there is not an awareness of his own divinity, but a sense of his distance from past tradition. This is the source of the protagonist's resentment.

It is also the source of the historicity of modernity. *Frankenstein* is a variation on this peculiarly modern obsession with the resentful rejection of history, which is to say, the rejection of tradition. Shelley adopts the myth of the monster (the "ghost story" of folktale, referred to briefly in her preface to the 1831 edition) and attaches to it the sentimental category of the *Bildungsroman*. But by denying her monster entry into the human community, Shelley reverses the typical sentimental trajectory. The result is tragedy, but of a distinctly ironic and romantic type. *Frankenstein* is *Oedipus Tyrannus* without the tyranny.[13] At least Oedipus gets to rule Thebes for a few years (just long enough to marry his mother and raise a family). Shelley doesn't even grant her central protagonist the possibility of a minimal social integration within the nuclear family. The monster thus bears a closer resemblance to the infant Oedipus abandoned on Mount Cithaeron than to the adult male who marries a queen to become a king. The romantic infatuation with the child is the counterpart to the romantic denigration of tradition, which is inevitably a preoccupation of adults rather than children. The child's perceived innocence in the face of the harmful effects of the social order is also the basis of the psychoanalytic model of desire (though Freud himself suffered no illusions about the necessity of civilization). The child-monster of Shelley's youthful ghost story is the prototype of so many subsequent victims of the repressive social order, of which Marx's proletariat is only the most famous nineteenth-century example.

The Rhetoric of Monstrosity

Like the divine figures of countless myths and legends, Victor's monster is a projection of human desire. But where the myth sacralizes the object of desire as forbidden to human appropriation, literature encourages us to identify with the central figure as a fellow human being. The latter is thus not an equivalent of the divine figure of myth, whose original status as the scapegoat of the community has been forgotten or repressed. He is a wholly human protagonist, a being no different from the hearer or spectator who listens to his story. But it is precisely this lack of divine or sacred difference that makes our attention to his story a specifically "textual" problem, one to be resolved, as in Rousseau's *Reveries*, by the text itself rather than designated as external to it. Our devotion to the text is rewarded not by any material benefits (as in collective ritual, which typically ends with a communal feast). What we gain in attending to the text is instead a purely imaginary satisfaction, a literary catharsis in which our attention to this content is ultimately expelled when we reach a satisfactory sense of closure.

The simplest example of this literary catharsis is provided by the classical aesthetic. In attending to the desires of the tragic protagonist, we imagine ourselves in his place, the sole possessor of the forbidden center that in ritual and myth is always represented by a god. Our desire for centrality is first indulged in an imaginary self-centralization, but then expelled or purged in a catharsis when we learn that the tragic hero, with whom we have identified during the performance, is in fact guilty of a monstrous crime or sacrilege. The *locus classicus* is Oedipus, whose twin crimes of parricide and incest Sophocles makes dependent upon the narrative of Oedipus's own "hubristic" desire to save Thebes from the plague, to be, as the priest at the beginning of the play says, "Greatest in all men's eyes."[14] The specifically romantic contribution to the tragic aesthetic of the Greeks is to conceive of the sacrificial victim as no longer a negative model, the real-life imitation of which is considered a monstrosity to be avoided at all costs, but on the contrary as a model of desire in general. Romantic protagonists, unlike their classical counterparts, wear their monstrosity proudly on their sleeves. This is Rousseau's contribution to romanticism.

The romantic aesthetic is thus based on a constitutive paradox. The more marginal the protagonist, the greater his claim to centrality. But since centralization implies marginality, the romantic aesthetic operates by continually raising the stakes of the latter. *Frankenstein*'s nested series of narrators, as we move from Walton to Victor to the monster himself, illustrates this competitive agon for the center from the margins. Each narrator usurps the narrative of his precursor by upping the ante of the claim to victimhood. But the overall effect is to erase the distinctiveness of the individual voices. After listening to each character explain how he is more persecuted than the others, we get the impression that we are no longer listening to a series of distinct voices but to a blend of voices, all stridently proclaiming their ultimate victimary status. Everyone has the same tired story of persecution to tell. Walton is persecuted by his dead father who wouldn't allow him to go to sea. Victor is persecuted by an unsympathetic father who denigrates his youthful reading of the alchemists. At the university, after some initial modest success ("I made some discoveries in the improvement of some chemical instruments, which procured me great esteem and admiration at the university" [36]), he is ostracized because he turns his attention to the occult, which promises a transcendence unavailable to the mere technical researcher (whom Victor caricatures in his description of the modern man of science, Krempe). This preoccupation with the occult culminates in the construction of the monster, an event which signifies Victor's lasting attachment to the "novelistic" or "literary" scene of his own persecution. The monster and Victor are textbook examples of Girard's monstrous double. Each feels morally certain that he is the victim of the other's persecution. Even the characters within each narrator's story are emblematic of the narrative structure of resentment, beginning with the story of Beaufort victimized by his ill-luck in the marketplace and ending with the monster's account of the victimized De Lacey family. Monstrosity, Shelley suggests, is the natural endpoint of this mimetic rivalry. It is the inevitable outcome of Victor's obsessive desire for transcendence, which is to say, for the prestige and glory he associates with scientific discovery.

At the generative center of the novel lies the monster's aesthetic contemplation of the De Lacey home. It functions as the *mise-en-scène* of the literary trajectory of desire. The monster's desiring relation to the De Laceys mirrors the oscillation of the aesthetic sign in the originary scene. In the first moment of desire, we identify with the object pointed to by the sign. But this experience of identification is limited by the fact that it is, after all, only imaginary. The moment of aesthetic detachment gives way to an act of aggression toward an object that is no longer imaginary but real. In the originary scene, the buildup of resentment is unleashed in a collective act of mimetic aggression, when the participants converge violently on the central object that had once withheld itself from their appropriative gestures.

In the De Lacey episode, Shelley represents this oscillation between the individual's aesthetic identification with the object and its resentful destruction in the *sparagmos*. The narrative of the monster's acquisition of language takes place as a scene, in which the monster situates himself on the periphery of his protectors' home. From his outside position in the "hovel" or woodshed attached to the cottage, he can contemplate unobserved, by way of "a small and almost imperceptible chink through which the eye could just penetrate" (89), the actions of his family. It is his position on the periphery of the scene that enables him to construct this idealized image of the cottagers as his protectors and benefactors. That these peasants are described as a noble French family brought low by the misfortune of political circumstance does not undermine the sentimentality of the image. On the contrary, it dignifies the "low" subject matter with the romantic narrative of persecution. In the new romantic dispensation, beggars are the true victims of the social order. But, as Shelley shows, the dispensation is itself dependent on an aesthetic fiction. As long as the monster can refrain from introducing himself into the aesthetic scene before him, he is free to imagine himself a member of this intimate world of egalitarian domestic relations. The wall separating the monster from his "benefactors" represents the formal barrier separating the individual spectator from the aesthetic object, or, in other terms, the form of the artwork from its internal content. Once the monster crosses this threshold the image collapses, and he is left with nothing but a deserted cottage. In thus moving from the aesthetic ideal to its worldly counterpart, the subjective experience of the community as an aesthetic totality gives way to the objective experience of the individual's necessary peripherality. The monster discovers he is alone. It is the scandal of this discovery that triggers resentment. Mary Shelley insists both on the necessity of resentment and its deferral. On the brink of releasing his resentment in a violent act of physical destruction, the monster is reminded momentarily of his former attachment to the aesthetic whole:

For the first time the feelings of revenge and hatred filled my bosom, and I did not strive to control them, but allowing myself to be borne away by the stream, I bent my mind towards injury and death. *When I thought of my friends, of the mild voice of De Lacey, the gentle eyes of Agatha, and the exquisite beauty of the Arabian, these thoughts vanished and a gush of tears somewhat soothed me.* But again when I reflected that they had spurned and deserted me, anger returned, a rage of anger, and unable to injure anything human, I turned my fury towards inanimate objects. (118; emphasis added)

The passage reproduces the characteristic oscillation of aesthetic experience. The monster's desire to vent his rage in an act of destruction is deferred momentarily by the soothing images of his protectors. But in contemplating these images of the objects he loves, he is reminded of their absence in reality. In a fit of rage, he turns from the image back to reality.[15] After destroying "every vestige of cultivation in the garden," the monster lights a firebrand and dances "with fury around the devoted cottage" (118). His dance climaxes with the setting of the moon, at which point he lights the cottage and watches it burn with vengeful satisfaction. In his desire to satisfy his resentment, the monster pays scant empirical respect to the notion of economic scarcity. Instead, in an action that is more reminiscent of the "conspicuous consumption" of a potlatch, but notably without the collective ritual context, he destroys the garden he had once worked so lovingly, and burns the "devoted cottage" that was his shelter. Never again will he be associated with the economic necessities of food and shelter. Instead, he will become the monstrous embodiment of human desire and resentment.

Less a person than an idea, the monster represents the negative underside of the romantic view that the self is originary. Divorced of its attachment to the traditionally defined public center, the self is forced to reinvent itself as unique and self-originating. But then the self is confronted by a multiplicity of other selves who seek to affirm *their* originality. The belief in personal uniqueness thus risks being exposed as an illusion, a fantasy nurtured by the sheltered world of the child, but undermined by the reality of the marketplace. Upon entry into the adult world, which in the romantic era is increasingly synonymous with the competitive world of the bourgeoisie, the self finds it hard to sustain the original optimism of its childhood. The prospect of success or failure in the market is mirrored by the wild swings in mood of the romantic protagonist. Until his death, Victor oscillates between extreme optimism and extreme despair. Toward the end, he is sustained only by the prospect of final victory over his monstrous double. But the more he conceives this victory as an act of ultimate transcendence, the more hopeless and despairing his situation becomes. The north pole represents both the transcendence and the futility of this vision. On the one hand, it is a place of "eternal light," on the other, of "desolation and frost" (1).

The retreat of the romantic subject into the sublimity of nature, where he is supposedly free to commune in private with the world spirit, is in reality a retreat from the challenge of a world governed by nothing more stable than the centerless exchange system. For there is no ultimate (sacrificial) transcendence of desire. Despite Victor's repeated attempts to locate a personal scene wholly impervious to the fortunes of mimetic desire, each attempt fails. Nowhere is this more apparent than in the scene of his encounter with the monster on the ice field below Mont Blanc. Standing amidst the impressive majesty of this scene, Victor addresses the mountains as if they are gods: "Wandering spirits, if indeed ye wander, and do not rest in your narrow beds, allow me this faint happiness, or take me, as your companion, away from the joys of life" (80). Yet no sooner has he uttered this prayer for sanctuary from the rivalrous world of mediated desire, than the latter abruptly returns to haunt him. He sees the "figure of a man, at some distance, advancing towards me with superhuman speed" (80). Prayer leads not to the hoped-for transcendence of desire but to its worldly antithesis—the mimetic confrontation between two rivals who compete for the attentions of a third, the reader of the text. Religious transcendence is transformed into narrative desire, the literary culture of and for the marketplace.

The Literary Subject and the Marketplace

Walton's early letters chart the dynamics of literary desire as it oscillates between the optimism and despair experienced by the participant of
the modern exchange system. We know, for example, that this twenty-
eight-year-old has had a rather spotty career, replete with false starts and
hesitations. First he wanted to be a poet. "I imagined," Walton writes in
his first letter, "that I also might obtain a niche in the temple where the
names of Homer and Shakespeare are consecrated" (2). But his artistic
aspirations only lead to failure and disappointment. Then, with the help
of an unexpected inheritance from a cousin, he receives the financial resources to pursue an early childhood dream of becoming a great explorer
and seafarer. He had formerly been banned from this career by both his
father and his uncle. But with a fortune now at his disposal, Walton is
no longer dependent upon his family; he is free to indulge his childhood
desire, a desire that was first planted by his "passionately fond" reading
of the "history of all the voyages made for purposes of discovery" in his
uncle's library (2).

As in Victor's narrative, the objects of Walton's desiring imagination
are represented as transcendent or sacred with respect to those familiar
objects rendered profane by their everyday traffic in the world of vulgar
"bourgeois" market relations. Walton, like all the other young romantics
in this novel, defines himself by his disdain for the quotidian world of
the bourgeoisie. This disdain has an obvious Oedipal dimension and
is associated most often with the repressive regime of the father. Victor describes Henry Clerval's father as "a narrow-minded trader," who
sees nothing but "idleness and ruin" in his son's desire to pursue "a liberal education" (30). Victor also implies, rather ungratefully, that when
his father dismisses his romantic interest in the alchemy of Cornelius
Agrippa, the father is to blame for his son's misfortunes.[16] Even Walton
implies that his father is an obstacle to his desire because he has forbidden him from going to sea. But this interdiction is short-lived. After
acquiring independent wealth through an inheritance, Walton "buys"
himself passage on board various whaling ships. Here is Walton's account of his "qualifications" for his present expedition:

Six years have passed since I resolved on my present undertak-
ing. I can, even now, remember the hour from which I dedicated myself to this great enterprise. I commenced by inuring

my body to hardship. I accompanied the whale-fishers on several expeditions to the North Sea; I voluntarily endured cold,
famine, thirst, and want of sleep; I often worked harder than
the common sailors during the day and devoted my nights to
the study of mathematics, the theory of medicine, and those
branches of physical science from which a naval adventurer
might derive the greatest practical advantage. Twice I actually
hired myself as an under-mate in a Greenland whaler, and ac-
quitted myself to admiration. I must own I felt a little proud
when my captain offered me the second dignity in the vessel
and entreated me to remain with the greatest earnestness, so
valuable did he consider my services. (2–3)

What is most remarkable about this passage is its deadpan sincerity.
Walton lacks any sense of irony concerning his authenticity. Like a Hol-
lywood celebrity, he simply accepts the status bestowed on him by his
adoring audience (his sister). But as today's celebrities well know, or are
quickly forced to discover, public admiration can easily turn to public
vilification. Walton is no exception to this rule. Let us therefore read
his text with a little dose of irony, which is to say, literary *ressentiment*.
  What motivates Walton's seafaring adventures is not economic necessity, which is presumably the motivation of the "common sailors,"
with whom he is so keen to rub shoulders. It is, rather, the desire for an
intangible—one is tempted to say, sacred—experience. But the irony
is that this intangible experience is itself represented as a commodity.
Walton *buys* his passage on board these whaling ships. (How else are we
to explain the fact that he is only able to go to sea once he has acquired
his cousin's fortune?) One need not even deny Walton the satisfaction
of believing he "works" harder than the regular sailors, nor assume that
he must be lying when he claims that twice he "actually hired" himself
as an "under-mate" and was rewarded with a job offer of "second dignity" by the captain. For "work" here implies not the material labor upon
which the economic viability of the whaler is based, but the altogether
less easily measurable economy of Walton's desire for a singular transcendent experience. Walton's desire to experience the life of a whaler
marks the beginning of a new economy of desire, the fledgling consumer economy. Walton is a precursor of the modern eco-tourist. Whaler
by day, scientist by night, he works "harder" than anyone else, because
he alone understands that the end of these "careers" is self-fulfillment

rather than the dross of economic production. Walton is a prototype of the modern consumer.

This is why Walton cannot seriously accept an offer to remain permanently as "the second dignity" on board a Greenland whaler. As he exhausts each new experience, his desire moves on to pursue a different one. This is the real motivation of his trip to the north pole. The latter is attractive because it remains untainted by human presence. Like the "undiscovered solitudes" of the "heavenly bodies," it remains "a land never before imprinted by the foot of man" (1–2). The openness of the terrain is a metaphor of Walton's infinite desire. The latter suffices to guarantee the romantic subject's quest for centrality. Feeling the north wind blow on his face, Walton's "daydreams become more fervent and vivid" as he tries "in vain to be persuaded that the pole is the seat of frost and desolation" (1). Walton genuinely believes he deserves "to accomplish some great purpose" (3), not because he is the best sailor and navigator in England, but simply because his imagination is more vivid than anyone else's, or at least so he believes. What ultimately qualifies Walton to become an intrepid explorer is not the six years he claims to have spent hardening himself to a sailor's way of life, but his one-year apprenticeship as a disciple of the poets in his uncle's library.

But all this changes when he meets Victor. Walton's boyhood dreams of becoming a great protagonist, to be universally admired and sympathized with, are effortlessly trumped by the more experienced "poet." Shelley transfers our desire from the solitary and friendless Walton to the yet-more-solitary and yet-more-friendless Victor. As Victor's relationship to Walton demonstrates, the poet works by mediating the desires of his readers. The trick is not to point directly to the object, but to narrate the story of the object's (permanent) absence. Victor leads Walton through a suspenseful story that makes Walton's letters to his sister seem like the amateurish and desultory creations they are. Victor's more powerful eloquence overwhelms the "illiterate" (5) would-be poet Walton. The latter immediately grasps he is in the presence of a master storyteller and becomes Victor's disciple, carefully recording the words of the great poet. Victor, of course, realizes this too, and he pauses dramatically to comment on the reaction of his disciple at precisely the moment when he seems to be on the point of revealing his great "secret":

I see by your eagerness and the wonder and hope which your eyes express, my friend, that you expect to be informed of the

secret with which I am acquainted; that cannot be; listen pa-
tiently until the end of my story, and you will easily perceive
why I am reserved upon that subject. I will not lead you on,
unguarded and ardent as I then was, to your destruction and
infallible misery. Learn from me, if not by my precepts, at least
by my example. (37–38)

Learn *by my example*, not by my precepts. That is, learn by imitating my
actions, not by interpreting my words. The instruction is paradoxical
because in order to grasp the precept to imitate the model's actions, one
must interpret the model's actions as a precept, which is to say, as words.
But this is already to remove oneself from the aura of direct imitation,
the originary model of which is the aborted gesture of mimetic appropriation. By treating the other as a subject of language, one removes
oneself from the crisis of unmediated mimetic relations.

Victor understands all too well that his narrative power over Walton
is secured by his ability to continue to mediate Walton's desire. Indeed,
Victor must consider himself extremely fortunate to have come across
such a willing literary disciple. (Compare, for example, the reaction of
the magistrate, who dismisses Victor's story with cynical professional
condescension.) This asymmetrical relationship between narrator and
listener, model and disciple, is sealed in the moment when Victor, near
death and stranded on an iceberg, refuses to accept Walton as his res-
cuer. Instead, he politely inquires whither Walton is bound, consenting
to come on board only when he learns he will be joining a "voyage of
discovery towards the northern pole" (10). Victor recognizes in Walton
a fellow romantic, a reader ripe for the mediation of desire by the literary
subject. The "secret" that Victor demonstrates in his story is the necessary presence of the mimetic other for the story to continue. Without
a reader to (as Walton puts it) "participate my joy" (4), there can be no
periphery to define the center. And without a periphery, there can be no
narrative of desire for the center.

Frankenstein unfolds as a movement from periphery to center, as
the reader's desire passes through progressively more violent narratives
of persecution. The endpoint of this desire is the "monstrosity" of the
sparagmos, the convergence of the periphery on the central victim. Both
Victor and the monster justify their hold on the reader's imagination in
terms of this victimization. Thus the story of their victimization lasts
only as long as the reader is willing to participate in, or identify with,

their persecution. On his deathbed Victor expresses a hope that Walton may continue the persecution of the monster. But this is too much to ask of the reader, who after some two hundred pages of relentless victimary rhetoric, is only too happy to see the protagonist and his monster die. Their claim on our imagination has long outstayed its welcome. In the final pages of the novel, we are quickly returned from center to periphery, from the "tragic" deaths of Victor and the monster, who predicts his own magnificent "funeral pile" where he can "exult in the agony of the torturing flames" (198), to the altogether more "bourgeois" image of Walton returning home to his sister, tail between his legs.

When Walton, confronted by his mutinous crew, agrees to turn his boat around rather than pursue individual glory, he removes himself from the tragic trajectory of Victor's narrative. This reversal is also that of the reader, whose desire has been fulfilled (at last!) in the sacrifice of the protagonist, Victor. But Victor's death is hardly a tragedy in the traditional sense; we are neither horrified nor cathartically purged by it, for his death has been predicted from the beginning by the text itself, when his feeble and exhausted body is pulled from the ice by Walton's crew. We are more likely frustrated by Victor's massive ego. Not even death seems to bring humility to this egocentric character.

This failure of the desiring imagination to respect reality is imitated by his truest disciple, the monster. In a veritable parody of his master's victimary discourse, the monster addresses the dead body of Victor in order to assert his superiority over his victim: "Blasted as thou wert, my agony was still superior to thine, for the bitter sting of remorse will not cease to rankle in my wounds until death shall close them forever" (198). The reaction seems tasteless and crass, until we realize that it is merely a duplication of Victor's reaction to the characters he "kills" in his story. On the eve of Justine's execution, Victor can only imagine the superiority of his suffering: "Despair! Who dared talk of that? That poor victim, who on the morrow was to pass the awful boundary between life and death, felt not, as I did, such deep and bitter agony. I gnashed my teeth and ground them together, uttered a groan that came from my inmost soul" (70).

Victor's "literary" suffering in imitation of Justine's is a prelude to further attempts by the narrator to imitate victimhood. Justine's death is but the second in a series of horrible murders that Victor promises to recount to his infatuated listener. In a perverse elegy to his remaining characters, who exist fictionally on a sort of literary death row, Victor addresses them with the paradoxical pleasure of an aesthetic spectator: "Ye weep, unhappy ones, but these are not your last tears! Again shall you raise the funeral wail, and the sound of your lamentations shall again and again be heard! . . . Thus spoke my prophetic soul, as, torn by remorse, horror, and despair, I beheld those I loved spend vain sorrow upon the graves of William and Justine, the first hapless victims to my unhallowed arts" (71).

Like the monster's observation of his beloved cottagers, this is tragic metafiction. And like Hamlet's prophecy of his uncle's villainy ("O my prophetic soul!" [1.5.40]), which Shelley explicitly alludes to in this passage, Victor's metafiction demonstrates the reader's complicity in the act of sacrifice. In these moments of metafiction, Hamlet, Victor, and the monster stand outside the world of their victims and comment on their tragic fates. The commentary reproduces the formal opposition, derived from classical tragedy, between central victim and desiring spectator. But unlike classical tragedy, this opposition is thematized in the work itself. *Frankenstein*, with its concentric arrangement of multiple narrators, represents the narrative relationship between text and reader as a desire on the part of the reader for the sacrifice of the work's protagonist. Hence the increasing monstrosity of the narrators, as we move from Walton, who is a rather timid and childish "bad boy," to Victor, who is a self-confessed "monster," to the monster himself, who is Victor's mimetic double, the natural endpoint of the reader's insatiable desire for victims. Walton's decision to abort his voyage of discovery is by contrast, as Victor himself suggests, a recipe for mediocrity. No one wants to hear the story of a loser.

But the loser of this story is also the ultimate winner. Of the three narrators, only Walton survives to tell his tale. He is also the only character who appears to grasp the hypocrisy of the victimary rhetoric that pervades the speech of the other two narrators. After the monster makes a great show of mourning over his dead master's body, Walton points to the creature's hypocrisy, which is also Victor's: "It is well that you come here to whine over the desolation that you have made. You throw a torch into a pile of buildings, and when they are consumed, you sit among the ruins and lament the fall. Hypocritical fiend!" (196).

As a "mere" peripheral consumer of desire, Walton stands outside the tragic cycle of desire figured by Victor and his monstrous appropriation of the sacrificial center. But Walton's peripheral relationship to Victor and his monster is a reflection of the centerless world of the market.

The latter operates not by channeling resentment into a monolithic public center, where it is periodically purged in ritual sacrifice, but by distributing resentment throughout the centerless periphery of the exchange system itself. But the recuperation of resentment by the market also leads to the radical proliferation of the victimary rhetorics of those who feel unfairly excluded by this system. Rousseau is the exemplary model of the romantic exile-cum-celebrity. He turned Hamlet's purely literary strategy of resentment toward the center into a worldly practice, the success of which is measured concretely in terms of the "brand-name" status of the literary persona. Rousseau was the first theoretician of the social order to transform resentment into a marketable product. *Frankenstein* is both an adoption of and an ironic commentary on this strategy. The monster figures the reader's complicity in worldly resentment. But this resentment is "contained" by the text when Walton, out of respect for his crew, abandons his intended expedition to the north pole, thereby also implicitly rejecting Victor's dying wish that he pursue the monster to the ends of the earth. Walton thus refuses to adopt the victimary position modeled for us by Victor and the monster. Instead, he offers us *Frankenstein*. Walton's desire for transcendence is transformed into a few hours of literary satisfaction. He returns us to the place where he began: in his uncle's library reading of great voyages of discovery.

Notes

Notes to Introduction

1. The American sociologist Randall Collins has recently reinterpreted Weber's historical thesis concerning the demise of the patrimonial household and the rise of the modern state as an opening for aesthetic interaction. Formerly the aesthetic was controlled by the ritual center. Artists were servants of this center, in the sense that they depended upon the patronage system of the patrimonial household. But once the ritual center was dissolved in the early modern era, the aesthetic was released from its subservience and permitted to flourish on the periphery, as an instrument of the bourgeois marketplace: "The realm of consumption is now separated from the places where production takes place and where politically and economically based power relations are enacted. Consumption now takes place in private, or at least outside of situations where it is marked by socially visible rank. The center of gravity of daily life switches to the realm of consumption. This is reinforced by the growth of consumer industries, including entertainment and the hardware that delivers it, into the largest and most visible part of the economy. A side-result has been to increase the salaries as well as the pervasiveness of entertainment stars; by contrast, in a patrimonial society, entertainers were merely servants, dependent upon patronage of the big households. Entertainment stars are the contemporary sacred objects, because they are the only widely visible points of attention in this private sphere, where relationships are casual (which is to say, deritualized) and free of work and power relations." *Interaction Ritual Chains* (Princeton, NJ: Princeton University Press, 2004), 290–91.

2. This is explicit in Derrida, but it is apparent in the work of many other critics. For example, in analyzing Shakespeare's scenes of cultural memory, Anthony Dawson, in "The Arithmetic of Memory: Shakespeare's Theatre and the National Past," *Shakespeare Survey* 52 (1999): 54–67, proposes that Shakespeare's theater is an attempt to represent "an originary event, one that is strangely both present and absent" (54–55). For my analysis of Shakespeare's originary scenes, see chapter 5. The preeminent anthropological theorist of the originary is not Derrida, however, but Eric Gans. See, for example, Eric Gans, *Originary Thinking: Elements of Generative Anthropology* (Stanford, CA: Stanford University Press, 1993).

3. Derrida's deep sympathy for postromantic and modernist authors, from Baudelaire and Kafka, to Beckett and Joyce, reflects the lineage of deconstruction in the postromantic aesthetic tradition.

4. For a recent welcome addition to the handful of scholarship devoted to discussing Gans's work, see Adam Katz, ed., *The Originary Hypothesis: A Minimal Proposal for Humanistic Inquiry* (Aurora, CO: The Davies Group Publishers, 2007).

Notes to Chapter 1. Cognitive Science and the Problem of Representation

1. Monika Fludernik, Donald Freeman, and Margaret H. Freeman, in "Metaphor and Beyond: An Introduction," *Poetics Today* 20 (1999): 383–396, predict that the "poetics … for the new millennium" will be a cognitive poetics (395). Alan Richardson, in "Cognitive Science and the Future of Literary Studies," *Philosophy and Literature* 23 (1999): 157–173, and Mary Thomas Crane and Alan Richardson, in "Literary Studies and Cognitive Science: Toward a New Interdisciplinarity" *Mosaic* 32.2 (1999): 123–40, review the situation and conclude that literary studies is lagging behind in its attention to the "cognitive revolution." But undoubtedly the most outspoken commentator is Mark Turner in *Reading Minds: The Study of English in the Age of Cognitive Science* (Princeton, NJ: Princeton University Press, 1991). In his polemical introduction, "Professing English in the Age of Cognitive Science," he claims that "contemporary critical theory … is ungrounded and fragmented" and derides it as a "self-sustaining" and "self-feeding" "mandarin activity," "unrestrained by laws of entropy" (3). The point of this polemic seems entirely political, aimed at those discontented with "theory" in the humanities. This is unfortunate because it gives the impression that cognitive science is not likewise heavily theoretical. Turner paints a rather misleading picture in which the fresh, childlike wonder of cognitive science can reclaim the lost innocence of literary studies by removing it from the grip of a cynical and increasingly senile "critical theory" and returning it to the simpler, happier days of object perception and object manipulation.
2. This is the substance of the criticism of Michael Fischer, in "Literary Change and Cognitive Science" (Review of Spolsky, *Gaps in Nature: Literary Interpretation and the Modular Mind*), *Poetics Today* 17 (1996): 362–65, Sabine Gross, in "Cognitive Readings: or, the Disappearance of Literature in the Mind," *Poetics Today* 18 (1997): 271–297, and Tony Jackson, in "Questioning Interdisciplinarity: Cognitive Science, Evolutionary Psychology, and Literary Criticism," *Poetics Today* 21 (2000): 319–347.
3. In this respect, Gross 1997 is exemplary. Her criticism of Turner is motivated by the assumption that literature is somehow more powerful than cognitive science when it comes to explaining the human condition. But the real debate is not over whose interpretive strategy should be privileged in

the exercise of interpreting literary texts, but what enables us to engage in this exercise in the first place. On this score, Turner at least has a hypothesis, whatever one may think of its scientific pretensions.

4. Paul Miers, in "The Other Side of Representation: Critical Theory and the New Cognitivism," *Modern Language Notes* 107 (1992): 950–975, is one of the few commentators to recognize that the major difficulty for what he calls the "new cognitivism" is its theory of representation. Jackson remarks in his healthily skeptical review of cognitive approaches to literature that the dispute between poststructuralism and cognitive science properly begins with a theory of representation; however, he does not develop this notion.

5. See Richard Dawkins, *The Selfish Gene*, 2nd ed. (Oxford: Oxford University Press, 1989); and Daniel C. Dennett, *Darwin's Dangerous Idea: Evolution and the Meanings of Life* (New York: Simon & Schuster, 1995).

6. For applications of these four perspectives to language, see Robin Dunbar, "Theory of Mind and the Evolution of Language," in *Approaches to the Evolution of Languages: Social and Cognitive Bases*, ed. James Hurford et al. (Cambridge: Cambridge University Press, 1998), 92–110, esp. 92–93; and Matt D. Hauser, *The Evolution of Communication* (Cambridge, MA: Massachusetts Institute of Technology Press, 1996), 2. See also Thomas Sebeok, *Signs: An Introduction to Semiotics* (Toronto: University of Toronto Press, 1994), 39.

7. See Robin Dunbar, "Mimesis and the Executive Suite: Missing Links in the Origin of Language," in *Approaches to the Evolution of Language: Social and Cognitive Bases*, ed. James Hurford, Michael Studdert-Kennedy, and Chris Knight (Cambridge: Cambridge University Press, 1998), 92–110.

8. See, for example, Merlin Donald, *Origins of the Modern Mind: Three Stages in the Evolution of Culture and Cognition* (Cambridge, MA: Harvard University Press, 1991), and Steven Pinker, *The Language Instinct* (New York: HarperCollins, 1994).

9. See, for example, F. R. H. Englefield, *Language: Its Origin and its Relation to Thought*, ed. G. A. Wells and D. R. Oppenheimer (London: Pemberton, 1977).

10. See Robert M. Seyfarth, Dorothy Cheney, and Peter Marler, "Monkey Responses to Three Different Alarm Calls: Evidence of Predator Classification and Semantic Communication" *Science* 210 (1980): 801–803.

11. See Terrence Deacon, *The Symbolic Species: The Co-Evolution of Language and the Brain* (New York: Norton, 1997), esp. 330–31.

12. See, for example, Derek Bickerton, *Language and Species* (Chicago: University of Chicago Press, 1990), and *Language and Human Behavior* (Seattle: University of Washington Press, 1995), esp. 28–29. See also William

Calvin and Derek Bickerton, *Lingua Ex Machina: Reconciling Darwin and Chomsky with the Human Brain* (Cambridge, MA: Massachusetts Institute of Technology Press, 2000).

13. For the original research involving vervet monkey alarm calls, see Seyfarth et al. "Monkey Responses to Three Different Alarm Calls." For a synthetic review of the literature on animal communication, see Hauser, *The Evolution of Communication*. For a critical assessment of the relation between vervet monkey calls and human language, see Robbins Burling, "Primate Calls, Human Language, and Nonverbal Communication" *Current Anthropology* 34.1 (1993): 25–53, and Terrence Deacon, *The Symbolic Species.*

14. In his *Introduction to the Science of Religion* (London: Longmans, 1873), Max Müller suggested that "One of the earliest objects that would strike and stir the mind of man and for which a sign or a name would soon be wanted is surely the sun.... Think of man at the very dawn of time.... Think of the Sun awakening the eyes of man from sleep, and his mind from slumber! Was not the Sunrise to him the first wonder, the first beginning of all reflection, all thought, all philosophy!" (366–68).

15. Geoffrey F. Miller, "Sexual Selection for Cultural Displays," in *The Evolution of Culture: An Interdisciplinary View* eds. Robin Dunbar et al. (New Brunswick, NJ: Rutgers University Press, 1999), 72.

16. As Durkheim shows, in *The Elementary Forms of the Religious Life* (New York: The Free Press, 1965), the "momentary impressions" (103) that characterize perceptual experience "could not serve as a basis for these stable and permanent systems of ideas and practices which constitute religions" (103). Rather, "religion responds to quite another need than that of adapting ourselves to sensible objects" (102). The origin of religion therefore cannot be discovered in the "intrinsic properties" of objects (261): "The world of religious things is not one particular aspect of empirical nature; *it is superimposed upon it* [Durkheim's emphasis]" (261).

17. George Lakoff and Mark Johnson, *Metaphors We Live By* (Chicago: University of Chicago Press, 1980); and Mark Turner, *The Literary Mind* (New York: Oxford University Press 1996).

18. Lakoff and Johnson, *Metaphors We Live By*, 58.

19. Turner, *The Literary Mind*, 17.

20. For the idea of displacement, see Charles F. Hockett and Robert Ascher, "The Human Revolution" *Current Anthropology* 5 (1964): 135–68; and Robbins Burling "Primate Calls, Human Language, and Nonverbal Communication," *Current Anthropology* 34 (1993): 25–53. For decoupling, see John Tooby and Leda Cosmides, "Does Beauty Build Adapted Minds? Towards an Evolutionary Theory of Aesthetics, Fiction and the Arts,"

SubStance 94/95: (2001): 6–27; and Paul Hernadi, "Literature and Evolution," *SubStance* 94/95 (2001): 55–71.

21. I take this example from an early work by Lakoff and Johnson, but the same problem recurs in, for example, Lakoff and Turner, *More than Cool Reason: A Field Guide to Poetic Metaphor* (Chicago: Chicago University Press, 1989), esp. 113; and Lakoff and Johnson, *Philosophy in the Flesh: The Embodied Mind and Its Challenge to Western Thought* (New York: Basic Books, 1999), esp. 45–59.

22. Lakoff and Johnson, *Metaphors We Live By*, 59; hereafter cited in text as *MWL*.

23. Turner, *The Literary Mind*, 4–5; hereafter cited in text as *LM*.

24. The term is actually due to Mark Johnson, in *The Body in the Mind: The Bodily Basis of Meaning, Imagination, and Reason* (Chicago: University of Chicago Press, 1987). See Turner (*LM* 22–25) for a brief account of the main research.

25. In general, Deacon's book has been very well received by the scientific community. See, for example, William Calvin, "Talking Heads," review of Terrence Deacon, *New York Times on the Web*, August 10, 1997, http://www.nytimes.com/books/97/08/10/reviews/970810.10calvint.html (accessed October 17, 2000); Ralph Holloway, "Language's Source: A Particularly Human Confluence of Hard Wiring and Soft," review of Terrence Deacon, *American Scientist* 86 (1998): 184–86; James Hurford, Review of Terrence Deacon, *Times Literary Supplement*, October 23, 1998, 32; Richard Hudson, Review of Terrence Deacon, *Journal of Pragmatics* 33 (1998): 129–35; Michael Ruse, "The Evolution of Symbols," review of Terrence Deacon, *The Semiotic Review of Books* 9.3 (1998), http://www.chass.utoronto.ca/epc/srb/srb/evolution.html (accessed February 19, 2001); Mark Turner, "Poetry for the Newborn Brain," review of Terrence Deacon, *Bostonia* 1 (1998): 72–73. From the humanities, on the other hand, there has been little interest in Deacon thus far; for a notable exception, see Eric Gans, "The Little Bang: The Early Origin of Language," *Anthropoetics* 5 no. 1 (1999), http://www.anthropoetics.ucla.edu/ap0501/gans.htm (accessed April 15, 2002). Given my criticism of Turner's *The Literary Mind*, the reader may be surprised to see his name in the above list. But Turner's brief review, though very favorable, seems not to notice the radicality of Deacon's argument that human neurobiology has been shaped by something as abstract as a word.

26. See Deacon, *The Symbolic Species*, 34.

27. Deacon is certainly not the first to put the problem in this way, but I think his account represents the best recent synthesis of evolutionary neuroscience and semiotic theory. Similar arguments for the anthropological specificity of the difference between the sign-as-index and the sign-as-symbol, can be

found in Ernst Cassirer, *An Essay on Man: An Introduction to a Philosophy of Human Culture* (New Haven, CT: Yale University Press, 1944), 24–25, and in Derek Bickerton's already cited work (e.g., *Language and Human Behavior*, 1995). See also the work of anthropologist Leslie White, in particular, *The Science of Culture* (New York: Farrar, Straus and Cudahy, 1949), esp. 22–39, and *Ethnological Essays*, ed. Beth Dillingham and Robert L. Carneiro (Albuquerque: University of New Mexico Press, 1987), esp. 259–72. Also noteworthy is Ralph Holloway's insightful analysis of hominid tool-making in "Culture: A Human Domain," *Current Anthropology* 10.4 (1969): 395–412. Holloway finds evidence for the origin of the specific difference of human cognition in tool-making, in that it requires the symbolic process of the "imposition of arbitrary form on the environment" (395). See also Burling, "Primate Calls, Human Language, and Nonverbal Communication," for an excellent discussion of the difference between the "digital" linguistic system and the "analogue" primate-call system. For the contrary argument that no essential difference between human language and animal communication exists, see Englefield, *Language: Its Origin and Its Relation to Thought*.

28. See Charles Saunders Peirce, "Logic as Semiotic: The Theory of Signs," in *The Philosophical Writings of Peirce*, ed. J. Buchler, 98–119 (New York: Dover Books, 1956). See also Sebeok, *Signs*, 68.

29. For examples of the confusion that Deacon's evolutionary application of Peirce's semiotic categories has caused among linguists, see the reviews by Hurford and Hudson. I think the confusion points to a genuine difference between a metaphysics that takes symbolic reference for granted, as linguistics in general does, and an evolutionary perspective that attempts to ground symbolic reference in more basic referential processes. For example, what Deacon calls "iconic reference" may seem unrecognizable to followers of Peirce, because he grounds this referential process in basic categorization. The beauty of Deacon's solution is that it puts the evolutionary problem of human origin in terms of a semiotic processing problem.

30. *The Symbolic Species*, 78.

31. Deacon notes that the tendency to interpret animal communication systems as simply less advanced forms of language, though superficially plausible, is actually perverse in the extreme because it implicitly treats all forms of communication as exceptions to what is in fact itself an exception, namely, language. Researchers who are eager to see in monkey alarm calls the rudimentary nouns and phrases of full-blown language, should take note of what Deacon says on this score: "One reason we have such a difficulty [i.e., in distinguishing between signals learned by rote and true symbolic understanding] is that we don't know how to talk about communication apart

from language. We look for the analogues of words and phrases in animal calls, we inquire about whether gestures have meanings, we consider the presence of combination and sequencing of calls and gestures as indicating primitive syntax. On the surface this might seem to be just an extension of the comparative method: looking for the evolutionary antecedents of these language features. But there is a serious problem with using language as the model for analyzing other species' communication in hindsight. It leads us to treat every other form of communication as exceptions to a rule based on the one most exceptional and divergent case. No analytic method could be more perverse" (52).

32. According to my calculations there are only 36 possible ordered pairs. But Deacon's point still stands.

33. See Sue Savage-Rumbaugh, *Ape Language: From Conditioned Response to Symbol* (New York: Columbia University Press, 1986), 93–94.

34. See John Searle, *The Construction of Social Reality* (New York: The Free Press, 1995). I agree with Searle's basic point that social institutions require a symbolizing function (i.e., language) because, in order to represent duties, rights and obligations, we have to go beyond the straightforward perception of objects. I think, however, that he underestimates the difficulty of explaining this shift from perception to symbolic representation. His formula "X counts as Y in context C" (55) is very far from being an anthropological hypothesis for the origin of representation precisely because it downplays the "evolutionary anomaly" of language. Why should such a symbolizing function be selected for in the first place?

35. This opposition between top-down symbolic functions and bottom-up indexical functions is the equivalent of the old philosophical dichotomy between nature and culture. The latter is really a debate about the origin of meaning or, in evolutionary terms, the origin of intentional design or artifice in nature. Deacon emphasizes the design-oriented or teleological structure of the symbolic system: "the shift from associative predictions to symbolic predictions is initially a change in mnemonic strategy, a recoding. It is a way of offloading redundant details from working memory, by recognizing higher-order regularity in the mess of associations, a trick that can accomplish the same task without having to hold all the details in mind. Unfortunately, nature seldom offers such nice neat logical systems that can help organize our associations. *There are not many chances to use such strategies, so not much selection for this sort of process. We are forced to create artificial systems that have the appropriate properties*" (89; emphasis added). Another way of putting Deacon's point is to say that symbols depend upon intentionality, which is evident in the artificiality of the symbolic reference system. Or in evolutionary terms: with the advent of the symbolic reference

system, we get for the first time in evolutionary history the reality of intentional design. For example, archeologists who believe they have discovered physical evidence for symbolic abilities in early humans—e.g., highly regulated patterns or marks on fossilized bone—are responding positively (i.e., symbolically) to the following question: Were the marks produced by natural processes (e.g., by the claws and teeth of animal scavengers), or are they the result of intentional design, which is to say, of meaning? Note that this question is not even debated when the evidence in question is, for example, the sixteen-thousand-year-old cave paintings in Lascaux, because we assume that our own (symbolic) experience of the art is shared by that of the original artists: we have no difficulty in attributing intentional (aesthetic or ritual) design to the representation. The same interpretation applies, though admittedly less starkly, to the Oldowan stone choppers and flakes (about 1.9 millions years old), which were presumably used for butchering meat by early hominids. The reason the distinction is less clear in the case of Paleolithic tools is because the function of the tool can be predicted on the basis of the physical shape of the stone itself. But one cannot predict the function of the paintings from the physics and chemistry of the paint.

36. In suggesting that specifically anthropological categories are so constituted, I do not mean to imply that *all* ontological categories are symbolic. The failure to distinguish between specifically anthropological categories and more universal biological, chemical, and physical categories is a feature of cultural idealism. Cultural idealists hold that, because even scientific models of the world depend upon symbolic representation, we cannot assume a distinction between categories that preexist such representation and categories that are (in some sense) constituted by it. It would follow that science is every bit as constructive of the facts as religion or myth. For example, Stanley Fish, in *Is There a Text in this Class?* (Cambridge, MA: Harvard University Press, 1980), believes that there is no way to distinguish between "institutional facts" (e.g., the fact that certain bits of paper issued by the Federal Reserve count as money) and "brute facts" (e.g., the fact that those same bits of paper are cellulose fibers) (240). The chemistry of paper is just another "set of discourse agreements ... as to what can be stipulated as a fact" (242). Of course, in a trivial sense, Fish is right. Without symbolic representation, there could be no scientific explanation of the chemical structure of the world and no common meaning for words. But chemistry and literary criticism still differ in the level of reality (subatomic, atomic, molecular, cellular, psychological, social, cultural, etc.) each discipline aims to interpret. It is not trivial to say that literature aims to constitute a community of readers by deferring reference to a nonsymbolic reality. But to apply the same func-

tional explanation to chemistry is to impose on the ontological categories of atomic and molecular structure the causal model of anthropological explanation. As always, cultural idealism is typified by an excessive optimism concerning the constitutive power of language, an optimism shared by the cosmologies of mythical explanation. But to understand myth as a primitive form of natural science is simply a category error. What mythical explanation is ultimately concerned with is not the natural world "in itself," but the natural world as distilled through the lens of the always unstable ethical—i.e., inter-human—relationship. To the mythical mind, when disasters like earthquake and famine strike, it is never due to natural causes. It is rather the intentional design of some vengeful (divine or human) agent.

37. As Gérard Genette, in *Narrative Discourse: An Essay in Method*, trans. Jane E. Lewin (Ithaca, NY: Cornell University Press, 1980), 26–27, has shown, the analysis of narrative assumes a symbolic relationship between signs and events. But beyond assuming the formal necessity of this relationship, narratology has given little attention to what motivates it. My assumption is that the significance of this relationship is most fruitfully understood by way of a hypothesis of their coeval origin.

38. In terms of genetic assimilation or Baldwinian evolution, for example, a behavioral pattern of recurring migration to cooler climates can select for individuals with warmer coats should the cooler region become increasingly important for survival; or, more dramatically, invariant features among sign, neural processing, and environment can lead to the hardwiring of vervet monkey alarm calls. Applied to the issue of language origin, this would mean that the universal features of language postulated by cognitive scientists like Pinker as candidates for adaptive success must be susceptible to Baldwinian evolution. But Deacon shows that there is in fact no correlation between the deep grammatical structure of language and the structure of neural processing and concludes that the genetic assimilation of grammar by Baldwinian evolution is biologically implausible. John Searle, in *The Rediscovery of Mind* (Cambridge, MA: Massachusetts Institute of Technology Press, 1992), reaches a similar conclusion when he argues that the postulation of deep unconscious rules to explain language acquisition confuses the distinction between causal and functional explanation. In seeking a causal explanation, there is no reason why we should assume that the underlying unconscious neural mechanisms should mirror the grammatical patterns of language. What Searle objects to is the move from a functional explanation, based on observable grammatical patterns, to a causal explanation that must reproduce those patterns at some *deep unconscious* level. But postulating deep unconscious rules of universal grammar

adds no "further predictive or explanatory power" and so the explanation is not in fact "causally efficacious" (244).

39. Turner, *The Literary Mind*, 7.

40. Merlin Donald, "Mimesis and the Executive Suite: Missing Links in the Origin of Language," in *Approaches to the Evolution of Languages: Social and Cognitive Bases*, ed. James Hurford, Michael Studdert-Kennedy, and Chris Knight (Cambridge: Cambridge University Press, 1998), 50.

41. This is particularly evident in *Reading Minds*, where Turner claims that certain patterns in the brain are "inherently meaningful" (46). But this is not to speak of "human meaning" at all.

42. Cf.: "A concept does not have hard edges. If we think of a concept as an activated set of links in a pattern, then different links in the pattern will have different degrees of strength, and there will be no clear boundary to how strong any link must be to qualify as belonging to the pattern. Concepts fade out at their boundaries, as opposed to stopping abruptly" (Turner, *Reading Minds*, 45).

43. Cf. esp. Deacon: "Once we abandon the idealization that language is plugged into the brain in modules, and recognize it as merely a new use of existing structures, there is no reason to expect that language functions should map in any direct way onto the structural-functional divisions of cortex. It is far more reasonable to expect language processes to be broken up into subfunctions that have more to do with neural logic than with linguistic logic" (288).

44. See Lakoff and Johnson, *Metaphors We Live By*, 59; Turner, *The Literary Mind*, 18.

45. Turner, *The Literary Mind*, 7, 17.

46. Consider, for example, Robin Fox, in *Kinship and Marriage: An Anthropological Perspective* (Cambridge: Cambridge University Press, 1983): "A consanguine is someone who is defined *by the society* as a consanguine, and 'blood' relationship in a genetic sense has not necessarily anything to do with it, although on the whole these tend to coincide in most societies in the world" (34).

47. See, for example, Leslie White, *The Evolution of Culture: The Development of Civilization to the Fall of Rome* (New York: McGraw-Hill, 1959); Robin Fox, *The Red Lamp of Incest* (London: Hutchinson, 1980); and Chris Knight, *Blood Relations: Menstruation and the Origins of Culture* (New Haven, CT: Yale University Press, 1991).

48. White, in *The Evolution of Culture*, 82–83, recognizes the inseparability between the origin of language and the origin of kinship systems, but tends to regard the former as a wholly unproblematic evolutionary occurrence.

49. At this point, it may be objected that I am simply misreading the cognitivist project, which aims to attack classical metaphysics and its rigid

adherence to mind/body dualism. How can I deny that symbolic thought must make use of more biologically primitive cognitive functions? In developing a theory of representation, surely we must first study how categories are formed at this basic cognitive level? For example, on the basis of Eleanor Rosch's work, Lakoff argues, in *Women, Fire, and Dangerous Things: What Categories Reveal about the Mind* (Chicago: University of Chicago Press, 1987), that our concepts exhibit "prototype" effects. Thus we tend to think of sparrows as more representative or more prototypical of the category *bird* than penguins, which suggests that "prototypes act as *cognitive reference points*" from which inferences can be drawn (45). However, my point is not to deny that we make use of prototypes in drawing inferences, but that we cannot take such inferential processes as a sufficient explanation of symbolic reference.

50. See John Searle, *The Rediscovery of Mind*, 36.

51. I don't wish to imply that cognitivists simply ignore cultural influences on the individual. On the contrary, they frequently acknowledge that all kinds of external pressures, from material bodily needs to sociocultural conventions, shape cognition. But never is there any reflection on the ontological difference between perceptual and cultural representations. Instead of being explained, this difference is assumed, for example, in Lakoff and Johnson's distinction between direct experience and indirect experience (*Metaphors We Live By* 178) or Turner's distinction between story and parable (*The Literary Mind* 4–5). I think the reason for this omission is obvious: cognitivists interpret the emergence of culture as a gradual outgrowth from more basic sensorimotor functions. For them, ultimately, culture must be reducible to an ontology of the brain, the only other alternative being a return to old-fashioned mind/body dualism.

52. For example, in *The Literary Mind*, Turner, after asserting that "story, projection, and parable ... are the root of human thought" (12), gives this definition of story: "The basic stories we know best are small stories of events in space: The wind blows a cloud through the sky, a child throws a rock, a mother pours milk into a glass, a whale swims through the water" (13). To the objection that these are not stories at all but simply evidence of basic sensorimotor abilities, Turner responds that, given the fact that "five billion different human beings all recognize and execute" these "small spatial stories," "we have a hard time imagining that the capacity can be interesting" (13). But, Turner continues, we should not be misled by appearances, because this is in fact "the chief puzzle of cognitive science" (13) and "if you do not have this capacity [i.e., for producing small spatial stories], you do not have a human mind" (13). But one cannot dismiss the distinction between the commonsense and the "scientific" notion of

story simply by stating that science inquires into "boring" (13), unnotice-able things (like perception) rather than the exciting things (like Achilles' wrath or Goldilocks' encounter with three bears). In grounding the pri-macy of his cognitivist notion of "story" in its anthropological universal-ity, Turner fails to realize that his idea of story is biologically universal as well. The ability to remember sequences of perceivable events, like clouds blowing through the sky or milk pouring into a glass, is hardly unique to human beings, and it is certainly very far from our normal understanding of what a story is. His claim that such capacities are indispensable for having a human mind, therefore, seems overstated at best, and simply mistaken at worst, since these are the conditions for having any conscious mind at all, whether human or animal!

53. The term "hopeful monster" is due to Richard Goldschmidt (see Dan-iel Dennett, *Darwin's Dangerous Idea*, 288). The idea is that evolution can throw up dramatic macromutations leading to radically new forms and lines of descent for micromutation to work on. For a review, see Richard Goldschmidt, "Evolution, as Viewed by One Geneticist," *American Scientist* 40 (1952): 84–135. The most famous "hopeful monster" theory of human language is Noam Chomsky's idea of an innate universal grammar. For a critique of Chomsky, see Deacon, *The Symbolic Species*, 35.

54. See, for example, Noam Chomsky, *Language and Mind* (New York: Harcourt Brace Jovanovich, 1972), Steven Pinker, *The Language Instinct*, and Derek Bickerton, *Language and Human Behavior*. For the counter-argument to the innateness hypothesis, as well as for a useful review of the main issues, see Geoffrey Sampson, *Educating Eve: The "Language Instinct" Debate* (London: Cassell, 1997).

55. David Lodge, *The Modes of Modern Writing: Metaphor, Metonymy, and the Typology of Modern Literature* (London: University of Chicago Press, 1977), 75.

56. As Miers notes in his 1992 critique of the "new cognitivism," Turner cannot appeal to the sheer weight of his empirical data because his interpre-tation of this data already implies a theory of representation—in Turner's case, a theory of meaning grounded in a "natural link between language and the body" (967). Miers's main point is that the "cognitivism" espoused by the likes of Turner and Lakoff mistakenly interprets "the presentation of embodiment as if it were not already a re-presentation" (967). I agree with this criticism, but I think that Miers too ultimately underestimates the anthropological nature of the problem of representation. He suggests that the discovery of its "neural recipe," as highly distributed processes in the brain, ends the "dialectic adventure" begun by Hegel and continued by Derrida, and launches a new theory of representation grounded in a

genuine cognitive science, which Miers is always anxious to distinguish from its "reactionary" use by Lakoff and Turner (954). To say the least, I am skeptical of the possibility that cognitive science, whether reactionary or revolutionary, can provide us with an understanding of representation superior to that of either the dialectic or the analytic tradition without at once also taking into consideration the *specifically anthropological context of this problem.*

57. Perceptive readers will note that I have omitted an intermediary step, in which Lakoff and Johnson first separate linguistic metaphor from conceptual metaphor. Conceptual metaphor is then grounded in nonmetaphoric concepts which, the authors claim, emerge from "direct physical experience" (*MWL* 57, 58). Thus, Lakoff and Johnson's schema goes as follows: direct experience → emergent concept → conceptual metaphor → language. It is revealing, however, that when the authors refer to direct physical experience, they do so only to embed the function of metaphor *within the very idea of experience.* Thus they speak of experience as generating "emergent concepts" and "emergent metaphors" (*MWL* 56, 58), as if language could be expected to emerge miraculously from basic sensory and motor functions. This is an instance of rhetoric reproducing the paradox of the origin, which no doubt a Derridean reading of Lakoff and Johnson would be quick to point out. The deconstructionists have a point, but I am far more optimistic than they about the possibility of a constructive solution to the paradox of symbolic reference.

58. See *The Literary Mind*, 5, 14–17.

59. David Herman, in "Parables of Narrative Imagining," *Diacritics* 29 (1999): 20–36, also remarks on Turner's careless definition of narrative when he notes that narrative always involves "the remarkable and the tellable" and not "the stereotypical and expected" (26). Herman, however, does not elaborate on why symbolic reference always involves "the remarkable" instead of the predictable.

60. See also Mark Turner and Gilles Fauconnier, "A Mechanism of Creativity," *Poetics Today* 20 (1999): 397–418.

61. See Deacon, *The Symbolic Species*, 393–401.

62. See Thomas Hobbes, *Leviathan*, ed. Kenneth Minogue (London: J. M. Dent, 1994).

63. See Jean-Jacques Rousseau, *Discourse on the Origin of Inequality*, trans. Franklin Philip and ed. Patrick Coleman (Oxford: Oxford University Press, 1994).

64. See, for example, Michael Ruse, "The Evolution of Symbols."

65. As in, for example, Jacques Derrida, *Of Grammatology*, trans. Gayatri Spivak (Baltimore: Johns Hopkins University Press, 1974).

66. In his masterly study *The Rise of Anthropological Theory: A History of Theories of Culture*, updated ed. (Walnut Creek, CA: Altamira, 2001), Harris points his finger at Franz Boas, whose "historical particularism" was "inductive to the point of self-destruction" (286). Boas, Harris argues, was reacting to the evolutionism bequeathed to anthropology by the great nineteenth-century anthropologists: Herbert Spencer, Edward Tyler, and Lewis Henry Morgan. Leslie White, in *The Evolution of Culture* (New York: McGraw-Hill, 1959), similarly notes that "the schools of Boas, Radcliffe-Brown, and Malinowski" have all rejected the problem of the origin of culture and deride evolutionary theories of culture as "conjecture," "unverifiable," or "sheer speculation," but they fail to recognize that all scientific hypotheses are "speculative" in the sense that they are "built up with inferences" (70–72). In anthropology, the polemic between evolutionism and historical particularism continues to this day. To scholars in the humanities, this polemic may seem somewhat passé. Are we not all historical particularists in the Boasian sense? The very notion of literature departments divided along lines of national cultures implies the historical specificity—rather than the anthropological universality—of cultural explanation. Some rearguard actions continue to be fought in the name of liberal humanism: see, for example, Graham Good's critique of the rise of "Theory" in literature departments in *Humanism Betrayed: Theory, Ideology, and Culture in the Contemporary University* (Montreal & Kingston: McGill-Queen's University Press, 2001). But despite Good's misgivings, the message underlying his analysis is clear: historical particularism has won the day.

67. The difference goes to the heart of the language-instinct debate. Is language innate or is it something we learn? There is no question that *ontogenetically speaking* we are innately predisposed to acquire language. But the difficulty of an evolutionary answer to the question of the origin of language is precisely that the genetic predisposition of modern Homo sapiens is itself a consequence of adaptation *to* symbolic reference (e.g., if modern Homo sapiens is innately predisposed to acquire language, the same cannot be said of hominid ancestors like *Homo erectus* and, a fortiori, *Australopithecus*). It follows that we cannot simply appeal to genetic factors in explaining the phylogenetic origin of an institution like language. The whole point of Deacon's coevolutionary argument is that the origin of symbolic reference can only be explained as a response to socioecological pressures—which I think are also specifically anthropological pressures—and, furthermore, that these are ultimately only accessible in the form of a *deductive hypothesis* based on observations of both historical and contemporary human society. As Deacon puts it: "I believe symbolic reference itself is the only

conceivable selection pressure for such an extensive and otherwise counter-productive shift in learning emphasis [i.e., from index to symbol]. Symbol use itself must have been the prime mover for the prefrontalization of the brain in hominid evolution. Language has given rise to a brain which is strongly biased to employ the one mode of associative learning that is most critical to it" (336).

68. In *Expression and Meaning: Studies in the Theory of Speech Acts* (Cambridge: Cambridge University Press, 1979), 58, Searle poses the problem of fiction as a paradox between sense and reference: How is it that fictional sentences can mean without referring? For a critique of Searle's logical model of fiction, see my "Three Models of Fiction: The Logical, the Phenomenological, and the Anthropological (Searle, Ingarden, Gans)" *New Literary History* 29 (1998): 439–465.

69. See *The Elementary Forms of the Religious Life*, esp. 225–45, 255–62.

70. See *The Symbolic Species*, 261.

71. See Eric Gans, *Signs of Paradox: Irony, Resentment, and Other Mimetic Structures* (Stanford, CA: Stanford University Press, 1997), 13–36; hereafter cited in text as *SP*. For an introduction to Gans's idea of generative anthropology, see the *Anthropoetics* website, http:www.anthropoetics.ucla.edu. See also Wolfgang Iser, "What is Literary Anthropology? The Difference Between Explanatory and Exploratory Fictions," in *Revenge of the Aesthetic: The Place of Literature in Theory Today*, ed. Michael Clark, (Berkeley, CA: University of California Press, 2000), 157–79. The conversation between Iser and Gans is continued in my interview with Iser, "The Use of Fiction in Literary and Generative Anthropology: An Interview With Wolfgang Iser," *Anthropoetics* 3 no. 2 (1998), http://www.anthropoetics.ucla.edu/ ap0302/Iser_int.htm, and in Eric Gans, "Staging as an Anthropological Category," *New Literary History* 31 (2000): 45–56. See also Iser's brief account of generative anthropology in *How to Do Theory* (Oxford: Blackwell, 2006), 131–43. For more literary applications of Gans's work, see Matthew Schneider, "Problematic Differences: Conflictive Mimesis in Lessing's *Laokoon*," *Poetics Today* 20 (1999): 273–289, and Kevin Kohan, "James and the Originary Scene," *The Henry James Review* 22 (2001): 229–238.

72. Paul Watzlawick, Janet Helmick Beavin, and Don D. Jackson, *Pragmatics of Human Communication: A Study of Interactional Patterns, Pathologies, and Paradoxes* (New York: Norton, 1967), esp. 194–95.

73. Gregory Bateson, *Steps to an Ecology of Mind* (San Francisco: Chandler Publishing Company, 1972), esp. 201–27, 271–78.

74. See *Pragmatics of Human Communication*, 199–200.

75. For René Girard's mimetic theory, see *Deceit, Desire, and the Novel*, trans. by Yvonne Freccero (Baltimore: Johns Hopkins University Press,

1965); *Violence and the Sacred*, trans. (Baltimore: Johns Hopkins University Press, 1977); and *Things Hidden Since the Foundation of the World*, trans. Stephen Bann and Michael Metteer (Stanford, CA: Stanford University Press, 1987). For a different (but nonetheless highly provocative) approach to the origin of language, see Merlin Donald's *The Origins of the Modern Mind*; and his "Preconditions for the Evolution of Protolanguages," in *The Descent of the Mind: Psychological Perspectives on Hominid Evolution*, ed. Michael C. Corballis and Stephen E.G. Lea, (Oxford: Oxford University Press, 1999), 138–54. Donald is more concerned with the cognitive basis of presymbolic mimesis than with its conflictive social consequences, but he does note that, as an evolutionary strategy, the emergence of mimesis "might also have introduced some destabilizing elements, especially by amplifying both the opportunities for competition, and the potential social rewards of competitive success" ("Preconditions" 148).

76. Jane Goodall's *In the Shadow of Man* (Boston: Houghten Mifflin, 1971) is the classic ethological study of wild chimpanzees, but see also Franz de Waal, *Chimpanzee Politics: Power and Sex Among Apes* (New York: Harper & Row, 1982). Both accounts are vivid and highly engrossing depictions of chimpanzee social life.

77. See Bateson, *Steps to an Ecology of Mind*, 177–93.

78. My analysis is indebted to Gans's illuminating discussion of irony in *Signs of Paradox* , 64–74.

79. The relationship between imitation and language acquisition is discussed in more detail in chapter 2.

80. See Deacon, *The Symbolic Species*, 36.

81. For a painstaking philosophical discussion of the dualism implied by the distinction between natural and conventional meaning, see Bernard E. Rollin, *Natural and Conventional Meaning: An Examination of the Distinction* (The Hague: Mouton, 1976). I share Rollin's desire to reduce this (metaphysical) dualism to a (pragmatic) distinction, but I am skeptical of his appeal to psychology as an adequate answer to the origin of the distinction. In particular, I do not share Rollin's rather uncritical acceptance of "the principle that ontogeny recapitulates phylogeny" (97) for precisely the same reasons that I do not accept Lakoff and Johnson's reduction of meaning to perceptual association.

82. This analysis suggests a solution to the logical paradoxes generated by metaphysical discussions of ostension or pointing, which seek to reduce the latter to either an exclusively natural or conventional phenomenon (see Rollin, *Natural and Conventional Meaning*, 99–100). Meir Sternberg, in "The *Laokoon* Today: Interart Relations, Modern Projects and Projections," *Poetics Today* 20 (1999): 291–379, esp. 372ff., points out that the traditional

metaphysical dichotomy between arbitrary and natural signs can be more usefully understood in terms of the Peircean trichotomy of icon, index and symbol, with the index reconceived. Sternberg's point, I take it, is rather similar to Deacon's. Indexical reference provides the crucial missing link in rethinking the traditional dualisms between arbitrary and natural signification systems.

83. Irony is also the source of many a joke, including the following one that highlights the difference between indexical and symbolic thought in a way that nicely complements Boysen's candy experiment with chimpanzees. Two children, Dominic and Kate, are offered two slices of cake. One piece, however, is significantly larger than the other. "You choose!" says Kate, knowing that by committing Dominic to the first choice, she has also committed him to taking the smaller piece as politeness demands. To her dismay, Dominic instead helps himself to the larger piece. Indignant, Kate attempts to draw his attention to the infraction:

Kate: "Why did you take the larger piece?"
Dominic: "Which piece would you have taken?"
Kate: "Why, the smaller of course."
Dominic: "But that is what you have! Why are you now upset?"

The joke plays on the irony of substituting signs for things. Both Kate and Dominic are of course primarily concerned with getting the biggest piece of cake. But since both are also competent language users, each knows that the other's appetite is mediated by symbolic rules that dictate how desirable objects (like cake) should be appropriated. In this case, politeness requires that the smaller piece be taken when offered the choice. Knowing this, Kate offers the choice to Dominic. But Dominic surprises her, and us, by exploiting the irony latent in all such rules. If Kate really meant what she said, she should be content with the smaller piece. The joke plays on the fact that it is not sincerity that is important but merely civility. Sincerity, as the joke demonstrates, is the alibi used by the romantic who refuses to play by the rules of normative ethical conduct. (My thanks to Marina Ludwigs for bringing my attention to this joke, whose original version can be found in Astrid Lindgren's *Karlsson on the Roof*.)

84. Implied in this hierarchical shift from indexical reference by sequential association to true narrative representation is the presence of what psychologists call "theory of mind" (see Dunbar, "Theory of Mind and the Evolution of Language," 102). By this label, psychologists mean not a philosophy of mind, but simply the ability to judge other people's mental states, to distinguish between one's own beliefs and those of others. Intentionality or "theory of mind" may be multiplied to quite high levels, e.g., I believe that X believes that Y believes that X is sleeping with Y's

partner. In the case of fictional narratives, this layering is further complicated by the fact that all the intentional relationships between characters are subordinated to our sense of an overarching authorial presence, a sort of meta-intentionality that is not simply identical with the intentionality of the real author.

85. John Locke, *An Essay Concerning Human Understanding*, ed. Peter H. Nidditch (Oxford: Oxford University Press, 1975), 104.

Notes to Chapter 2. Imitation and Human Ontogeny

1. I'm afraid I don't have a specific reference for this criticism of Girard. Nor do I know if Girard himself has made any reference to imitation in human ontogeny. Nonetheless, in casual conversation I have repeatedly heard the claim that children demonstrate Girard's theory rather well. Recently, Matthew Taylor raised the issue on GABlog (July 24, 2006), http://dev. cdh.ucla.edu/GABlog/2006/07/toys-toddlers-and-taboos/. He pointed out that at least one social scientist has disputed the Girardian claim about mimetic rivalry among children. I would like to thank Matt for raising the question. I hope this article goes some way to providing an answer.

2. See, for example, Eric Gans, *Originary Thinking: Elements of Generative Anthropology* (Stanford, CA: Stanford University Press, 1993), especially chapter 4.

3. This seems to be the source of Derek Bickerton's objection that Tomasello's theory would be better served by postulating that language rather than intentionality were the originary basis of human culture. I tend to agree with Bickerton that Tomasello risks reifying the notion of intentionality, which he seems to regard as a purely biological phenomenon. It is more minimal to assume that once the joint attentional scene has emerged—protolanguage, in Bickerton's sense—then we can assume that specifically human forms of symbolic intentionality emerge with it. I think, however, that Tomasello's idea of the joint attentional scene already implies that human intentionality is a scenic phenomenon. I therefore will not dwell on his less parsimonious claim for the causative role of biological intentionality. For Bickerton's objection, see his response to the article by Michael Tomasello et al., "Understanding and Sharing Intentions: The Origins of Cultural Cognition," *Behavioral and Brain Sciences* 28 (2005): 675–735.

4. See Terrence Deacon, *The Symbolic Species: The Co-Evolution of Language and the Brain* (New York: Norton, 1997).

5. Eric Gans, "The Little Bang: The Early Origin of Language," *Anthropoetics* 5 no. 1 (1999), http://www.humnet.ucla.edu/humnet/anthropoetics/ ap0501/gans.htm (accessed May 27, 2008).

6. Eric Gans, *Signs of Paradox: Irony, Resentment, and Other Mimetic Structures* (Stanford, CA: Stanford University Press, 1997), 23.

Notes to Chapter 3. The Critic as Ethnographer

1. For the original research on vervet monkey alarm calls, see Robert M. Seyfarth, Dorothy Cheney, and Peter Marler, "Monkey Responses to Three Different Alarm Calls: Evidence of Predator Classification and Semantic Communication," *Science* 210 (1980): 801–3. For a discussion of the fundamental difference between language and nonhuman primate call systems, see Robbins Burling, "Primate Calls, Human Language, and Nonverbal Communication," *Current Anthropology* 34 (1993): 25–53.
2. For the evolutionary significance of the difference between index and symbol, see Terrence Deacon, *The Symbolic Species: The Co-Evolution of Language and the Brain* (New York: W. W. Norton, 1997). I discuss Deacon's work in chapter 1.
3. Stephen Greenblatt, "The Touch of the Real," *Representations* 59 (1997): 14.
4. See, for example, Greenblatt's work in *Renaissance Self-Fashioning: From More to Shakespeare* (Chicago: University of Chicago Press, 1980), 1–9; *Shakespearean Negotiations: The Circulation of Social Energy in Renaissance England* (Berkeley and Los Angeles: University of California Press, 1988), 1–20; and "Towards a Poetics of Culture," in *The New Historicism*, ed. H. Aram Veeser (New York: Routledge, 1989), 1–14. Similarly hesitant theoretical gestures can be found in the introductory chapter to his recent new historicist "manifesto" (coauthored with Catherine Gallagher), *Practicing New Historicism* (Chicago: University of Chicago Press, 2000), 1–19. In all of the above, Greenblatt resists the notion that one can define, in abstract theoretical terms, the business of cultural interpretation. Hence his insistence that cultural poetics (or "new historicism," as it is usually called) is a practice rather than a theory—which is to say, valued as the *expression* of a singular aesthetic experience rather than as a *representation* of an objectively established set of theoretical categories. That may in fact be true of the new historicism and other critical modes as they are currently conceived and practiced by their individual exponents. At least one agreeable consequence of the claim that one's practice is "untheorizable" is that it gives carte blanche to the critic, who may consequently continue to pursue his research without the impediment of having to justify it in terms of openly debatable theoretical premises, it being the mark of such premises that they also expose one's research to refutation, for example, on empirical or logical grounds.

5. Nowhere is this more apparent than in Shakespeare studies, where the desire to demonstrate the historical and ethnographic otherness of the text is felt to be all the more urgent given the monolithic "presentism" inherent in popular culture's recycling of the Bard for mass audiences. (Witness the steady stream of commercial movies based on the plays, which, as with most other products of contemporary popular culture, academic critics love to hate.) Add to this the assumption that Shakespeare wrote exclusively for the playhouse rather than the bookseller (but see Lukas Erne, *Shakespeare as Literary Dramatist* [Cambridge: Cambridge University Press, 2003], for a compelling counterargument to this assumption), and the critic is now able to argue for the unique performativity not just of the plays themselves, but of the different source texts that were previously held to be merely contingent versions of a single "authorial" play. On the principle that more is always better, we now have, for example, not one (judiciously conflated) text of *Hamlet*, but multiple texts of *Hamlet*. But what this insistence on the empirical "historicity" of the play-text tends to forget is that the material contingency of textual production (as the text makes its way from the playwright's pen to the actors, to the stage, to the audience, to the printing house, to the compositors, and so on) is not the origin of the general category of "text," but indeed its end. The precondition of the singular performance, whether on the stage or the page, is the historicity implicit in the category of textuality itself, which is to say, in the origin of representation. It is in this "originary" sense that we should understand the current interest in the "historicity of the text." Otherwise such interest risks becoming a crude fetishization of history: the equivalent in literary studies of ethnography's romanticization of the non-Western other. As its filiation with romanticism suggests, new historicism is always in danger of reducing its interest in "the historical" to a fetishization of the cultural differences of a particular aesthetic period.

6. For a detailed study of the romantic origins of speech-act theory, see Angela Esterhammer, *The Romantic Performative: Language and Action in British and German Romanticism* (Stanford, CA: Stanford University Press, 2000).

7. This is the more serious point behind Greenblatt's habit of beginning (or ending) his works of criticism with an extended personal anecdote. The tactic is ostensibly designed to differentiate the author from the pack, but, of course, now everybody is doing it, and the confessional mode, rather than being a revelation of the personal, instead tends to come off as affected and pretentious. For example, *Shakespearean Negotiations* begins with the statement: "I began with the desire to speak with the dead," after which we are told that literature professors are "middle-class shamans" who seek to

resurrect the voice of the dead through the self-conscious "textual traces" of fiction. But what this inward focus on the desiring self as a universal model of the literary (academic) reader obscures is the collective and mimetic context of desire. By paying our respects to the dead and the unborn in the *ritual* (not literary!) context, we reaffirm our desire for significance in the next world, thereby reminding ourselves of the ultimate insignificance of our less transcendent, more worldly (mimetic) desires. In an interesting (and inevitably slightly gossipy) take on the worldly mimetic context of Greenblatt's Hegelian desire for recognition or "authenticity of identity," Paul Stevens, in "Pretending to Be Real: Stephen Greenblatt and the Legacy of Popular Existentialism," *New Literary History* 33 (2002): 491–519, argues that Greenblatt's penchant for personal anecdote and name-dropping constitutes an attempt by the author to create an authentic identity for himself. The paradox for Stevens is that this runs counter to the high-theory idea that the self is decentered. Far from being postmodern, it turns out that Greenblatt is just another modern. I agree with this conclusion, but the basic analysis applies to many others besides Greenblatt. "Postmodern" academic criticism is characterized by this paradox between the glib deconstruction of the subject, on the one hand, and earnest professional cultivation of it, on the other. For pertinent analysis, see Mark Bauerlein, *Literary Criticism: An Autopsy* (Philadelphia: University of Pennsylvania Press, 1997); and "Political Dreams, Economic Woes, and Inquiry in the Humanities," *boundary 2* 27, no. 1 (2000): 197–216.

8. Attempts by primatologists to bring chimpanzees under the rubric of the other make the mistake of assuming that this category can be expanded beyond the bounds of anthropology. See, for example, Jane Goodall and Dale Peterson, *Visions of Caliban: On Chimpanzees and People* (Boston: Houghton Mifflin, 1993). But, unlike the subaltern other, who like Caliban is perfectly capable of dialogue, the chimpanzee (with the marginal exception of famous laboratory chimps like Kanzi) must indeed be "spoken for," as the essays by Goodall and Peterson so movingly demonstrate.

9. Already in *Renaissance Self-Fashioning*, Greenblatt invokes Geertz's "control mechanism" metaphor of culture as a parallel of his own metaphor of "self-fashioning," which he suggests is quite peculiar to the Renaissance: "Self-fashioning is in effect the Renaissance version of [Geertz's notion of] control mechanisms" (3). But what exactly is the point of borrowing from Geertz in this context? For in what sense is the "Renaissance version" of the control mechanism different from its "anthropological" prototype in Geertz? And if it is not different, why not? But Greenblatt prefers to ignore these questions concerning the relationship between anthropological explanation and literary history. Instead, as is customary in the literary

analysis of history, he treats the Renaissance as a discrete historical entity that can be conveniently interpreted on the model of the self-contained literary work: one pursues the relationships and contradictions within the boundaries of the given aesthetic period, without any consideration of the broader pattern of historical change that would connect it to other periods and ultimately to an anthropological theory.

10. For a characteristically sharp diagnosis of this problem, see Bauerlein's analysis of how critics use the terms "cultural poetics" and "cultural studies," in his *Literary Criticism*, 23–35.

11. See, in particular, Eric Gans, *The End of Culture: Toward a Generative Anthropology* (Berkeley and Los Angeles: University of California Press, 1985); and "The End of Culture," in *Signs of Paradox: Irony, Resentment, and Other Mimetic Structures* (Stanford, CA: Stanford University Press, 1997).

12. For a notable exception, however, see Wolfgang Iser's essay "What is Literary Anthropology? The Difference Between Explanatory and Exploratory Fictions," in *Revenge of the Aesthetic: The Place of Literature in Theory Today*, ed. Michael Clark (Berkeley and Los Angeles: University of California Press, 2000), 157–79, which compares Iser's "exploratory" model of literary anthropology to the "explanatory" model employed by Gans. The discussion is continued in Eric Gans, "Staging as an Anthropological Category," *New Literary History* 31 (2000): 45–56.

13. Why isn't Greenblatt theoretical? By the end of this chapter, I hope the reason will be obvious. At this point, suffice it to say that Greenblatt's insistence that new historicism is a "practice" rather than a "theory" is based on the profoundly antitheoretical (and deeply romantic) assumption that abstract generalization is inherently a betrayal of the truth. In privileging individual expression over theoretical representation, new historicism demonstrates its affinities with the romantic thinker's general distrust of the universalizing and static anthropologies of the Enlightenment. Yet, at the same time, we must be careful not to confuse the irreducibly subjective character of aesthetic experience with the possibility of theoretical dialogue on that experience. It is of course true that my experience of an artwork is not the same as yours, but it does not follow that, because of the necessarily subjective character of aesthetic experience, we therefore cannot attempt to formulate an aesthetic theory—a minimal literary anthropology—that attempts to explain the basis of that experience in objectively acceptable theoretical terms. That is indeed the point of aesthetic criticism, which remains dissatisfied with the mere subjective experience of art, but also seeks to confirm that experience by referring to other interpretations by other interpreters. In their idolization of the aesthetic, the new historicists (along with their various poetically minded precursors and progeny) betray their

romantic origins. But from the point of view of a minimal anthropology, it is inadequate to assume that the most profound thoughts, including those of the critic, are accessible only via aesthetic means. In seeking to emulate the aesthetic practice whereby the romantic artist taps into the life-spirit of the community, criticism forfeits its claim to be engaged in theory. Of course, the new historicism appears quite happy to accept this verdict. But that does not mean we have to too. On the contrary, an aesthetic criticism fully conscious of its own historicity is an invitation to a form of thinking that is resolutely anthropological in its theoretical presuppositions.

14. See, for example, Marvin Harris, "Anthropology and Postmodernism," in *Science, Materialism, and the Study of Culture*, ed. Martin F. Murphy and Maxine L. Margolis (Gainesville: University of Florida Press, 1995), 62–77; and James Lett, *Science, Reason, and Anthropology: The Principles of Rational Inquiry* (New York: Rowman and Littlefield, 1997), 105–6.

15. Clifford Geertz, *The Interpretation of Cultures* (New York: Basic Books, 1973), 44; hereafter cited in text.

16. Richard Dawkins, *The Selfish Gene*, 2nd ed. (Oxford: Oxford University Press, 1989), 254.

17. Geertz's favorite image of humanity without culture is the monster (see, for example, 49, 68, 99). One notes a curious parallel between Geertz's vision of the origin of culture and the monstrous titans of Greek mythology, whose champion stole fire from Zeus in order to give humanity culture. Geertz's monster appears to fulfill the same mediating function between heaven and earth, culture and nature, as these more obviously mythical figures.

18. For his idea of "protoculture," see Geertz, *Interpretation of Cultures*, 47. For a more recent example of the currently flourishing area of evolutionary approaches to culture, see the essays collected in *The Evolution of Culture: An Interdisciplinary View*, ed. Robin Dunbar, Chris Knight, and Camilla Power (New Brunswick, NJ: Rutgers University Press, 1999).

19. John Searle makes a similar point when he discusses the importance of language for the origin of "institutional facts." See *The Construction of Social Reality* (New York: Free Press, 1995), 66.

20. The classic analysis of the "rites of passage" is Arnold van Gennep's *The Rites of Passage*, trans. Monika B. Vizedom and Gabrielle L. Caffee (London: Routledge, 1960); first published in French as *Les rites de passage* in 1908.

21. I am adopting and modifying John Searle's notion of "direction of fit," which he uses in the more limited context of a discussion of types of speech acts. See "A Taxonomy of Illocutionary Acts," in his *Expression and Meaning: Studies in the Theory of Speech Acts* (Cambridge: Cambridge University

Press, 1979), 1–29. Searle eventually takes up some of the epistemological and anthropological issues implied by the word/object distinction in *The Construction of Social Reality*.

22. For the "evolutionary anomaly" of language, see Deacon, *The Symbolic Species*, 34.

23. The classic study of wild chimpanzees is Jane Goodall's *In the Shadow of Man* (Boston: Houghton Mifflin, 1971). For chimpanzee hunting and lethal intergroup raiding parties, see Richard Wrangham and Dale Peterson, *Demonic Males: Apes and the Origins of Human Violence* (Boston: Houghton Mifflin, 1996). I note in passing that both these studies emphasize the continuity between human and chimpanzee "culture," the scientific approach being essentially a project in reducing anthropological categories to imagined presymbolic biological precursors in other animals.

24. For a provocative analysis of how "scientific" accounts of human origin are far more mythically inspired than most scientists would like to believe, see Wiktor Stoczkowski, *Explaining Human Origins: Myth, Imagination and Conjecture*, trans. Mary Turton (Cambridge: Cambridge University Press, 2002).

25. J. L. Austin, *How to Do Things with Words* 2nd ed., ed. J. O. Urmson and Marina Sbisà (Cambridge, MA: Harvard University Press, 1962).

26. In speaking here of the "ostensive," I have in mind not Bertrand Russell's (deanthropologized) analytic notion of a "referring expression," but Eric Gans's suggestion that the ostensive is the minimal *linguistic* form of an originary, collectively constituted "scene" of representation. See Gans, "A Generative Taxonomy of Speech-Acts," in his *Originary Thinking: Elements of Generative Anthropology* (Stanford, CA: Stanford University Press, 1993), 62–85. This discussion of the anthropological context of the elementary forms of language is surely the most brilliant analysis of speech acts since Austin's original formulation of speech-act theory.

27. See the discussion of joint attention in chapter 2.

28. For a general account of "genetic assimilation," as well as the impossibility of genetically assimilating the symbolic function, see Deacon, *The Symbolic Species*, esp. 331–32.

29. See, in particular, René Girard, *Deceit, Desire, and the Novel: Self and Other in Literary Structure*, trans. Yvonne Freccero (Baltimore: Johns Hopkins University Press, 1965); *Violence and the Sacred*, trans. Patrick Gregory (Baltimore: Johns Hopkins University Press, 1977); and *Things Hidden Since the Foundation of the World*, trans. Stephen Bann and Michael Metteer (Stanford, CA: Stanford University Press, 1987).

30. A good example of this is the response from the specialists to Girard's major work on Shakespeare, *A Theater of Envy* (Oxford: Oxford University

Press, 1991). The specialists are of course never going to be very happy with a book whose central thesis tends to undermine their own assumption that Shakespeare must be understood "historically," which is to say, as a product of *his* time (the counterargument that this "historicism" is always ultimately *our* view of his time is labeled, derogatorily, as "ahistorical" or "presentist"). This deeply ingrained suspicion of a "master" theorist's intrusion into the specialist's historical domain explains the pattern to be observed among the various responses, which range from ambivalent admiration, on the one hand, to utter incomprehension, on the other. In the former, the admiration is "ambivalent" because, despite the obvious originality and power of Girard's readings of the plays, it is felt that these readings must inevitably be flawed *because they depend upon an explicitly formulated anthropology.* Girard is thus rejected not for his reading of Shakespeare (the brilliance of which is frequently, if also rather reluctantly, conceded), but for being *too transparent* about the theoretical assumptions that generate that reading. (Note the irony of a historical specialist rejecting Girard on the grounds of the latter's anthropology—without, of course, deeming it necessary to replace his anthropology with a better one.) At the other end of the spectrum of responses, one finds utter incomprehension, which is a more transparent defense of the status quo. Refusing to judge Girard on his own terms, this response resorts to the non sequitur that Girard fails to cite any recent Shakespeare scholarship (as though the mark of excellence in the world of ideas is the number of citations one includes of one's immediate peer group). In the end, however, what is striking is less what has been said by the specialists than the controversy Girard's book has inspired among them. At least most are agreed that it is too important to ignore, even if the advice they offer is to ignore it!

31. The recent discovery in monkeys of so-called "mirror neurons" (neurons that are activated irrespective of whether the test monkey is grasping an object or observing another individual performing the same gesture) provides interesting empirical evidence for the evolutionary importance of imitative behaviors among primates. See Maxim I. Stamenov and Vittorio Gallese, eds., *Mirror Neurons and the Evolution of Brain and Language* (Amsterdam: John Benjamins, 2002).

32. See, for example, Goodall's already-cited classic study, *In the Shadow of Man*, as well as the account by Frans B. M. de Waal in *Chimpanzee Politics: Power and Sex Among Apes* (New York: Harper & Row, 1982).

33. The provenance of the term "pragmatic paradox" ultimately derives from the psychological theory of Gregory Bateson by way of Paul Watzlawick. See Bateson, *Steps to an Ecology of Mind* (San Francisco: Chandler Publishing Company, 1972); and Paul Watzlawick, Janet Helmick Beavin,

and Don D. Jackson, *Pragmatics of Human Communication: A Study of Interactional Patterns, Pathologies, and Paradoxes* (New York: W. W. Norton, 1967). My reference to the term here, however, owes more to Eric Gans, who adopts Bateson's and Watzlawick's psychology of the "double bind" to describe the originary mimetic context of the symbolic sign. In a subtle but far-reaching modification of Girard's originary hypothesis, Gans suggests that the origin of culture is not to be located in a foundational act of protosacrificial murder, but in "an aborted gesture of appropriation" that defers mimetic conflict by representing, rather than appropriating, the central object. In Gans's formulation, no empirical claim is required as to the specific nature of the contested object. It is therefore ultimately unnecessary to decide whether the central object is another human (as Girard insists) or, as seems more likely, a hunted game animal. What is crucial is that the *sparagmos*, or rending of the object, be preceded by the moment of its (peaceful) representation. See Gans, *Signs of Paradox*, chap. 2.

34. See Gans, *Signs of Paradox*, 20, 38–39.

35. This may be taken to be the anthropological modification of the familiar Hegelian dialectic between master and slave. The question Hegel avoids asking is how the concept of freedom can emerge from the purely naturalistic state of the struggle for survival between master and slave. Despite Hegel's reference to slave-holding societies such as the ancient Greeks, the master-slave struggle is more appropriately applied to the non-symbolically instituted pecking orders observed by primatologists in chimpanzee societies.

36. The real origin for the new historicist denial of anthropology, however, is not Greenblatt, but Foucault. See Michel Foucault, *The Order of Things: An Archeology of the Human Sciences* (New York: Vintage, 1994); first published in French as *Les mots et les choses* in 1966.

Notes to Chapter 4. The Culture of Criticism

1. Clifford Geertz, *The Interpretation of Cultures* (New York: Basic Books, 1973), 47.

2. Jane Goodall, *In the Shadow of Man* (Boston: Houghton Mifflin, 1971), 37.

3. Ibid., 228.

4. Frans B. M. de Waal, "Cultural Primatology Comes of Age," *Nature* 399 (1999), 636.

5. "We" in the humanities, that is. For scientists, culture—far from being an insoluble epistemological paradox between knowing and doing, description and performance—is simply a matter of definition. If you define culture as the "non-genetic transmission of habits," as the primatologist

Frans de Waal does, then clearly there are many other social animals—in particular, chimpanzees—that have "culture." As always, the project of science has no time for the paradoxes of human self-understanding, so dear to those in the humanities.

6. The debate among scientists over the anthropological specificity of language is far from settled. For obvious reasons, primatologists prefer to downplay the difference between language and nonsymbolic forms of communication. However, for the view of a biological anthropologist, who accepts the "evolutionary anomaly" of language, see Terrence Deacon, *The Symbolic Species: The Co-Evolution of Language and the Brain* (New York: Norton, 1997). See also Michael Tomasello, *The Cultural Origins of Human Cognition* (Cambridge, MA: Harvard University Press, 1999). Tomasello suggests that so-called cultural traditions among different populations of chimpanzees are most plausibly explained not as genuine social or imitative learning but as "environmental shaping" (29). In a series of ingenious experiments with two-year-old children and chimpanzees, Tomasello notes that whereas children focus almost exclusively on imitating the experimenter's behavior, however "arbitrary" or bizarre it may appear (for example, using your head to flip on a light switch), among chimpanzees the focus is not on the experimenter's behavior but on the object or objects involved in the overall action. Tomasello suggests that the latter type of behavior is *emulative* rather than properly *imitative*, because the object is not the imitation of a model, but simply the achievement of a goal. For example, the chimpanzee may learn that the switch operates the light, but it will not also associate a particular type of behavior or gesture with the switch. Children perceive the switch from the start as mediated by the experimenter's gesture. In contrast, the chimps see the light switch as just a light switch, and the object receives no further symbolic or collective significance from the fact that it has been previously designated by the experimenter. Obviously, the ability to interpret a gesture as a symbolic sign requires a separation between mimetic gesture and object that is already latent within the attentional focus of the children but not the chimps. I have not come across any other scientific work that so clearly demonstrates the "scenic" origin of linguistic attention. It is a short step from Tomasello's theory of joint attention to René Girard's theory of mimetic desire and Eric Gans's theory of the ostensive sign. See René Girard, *Deceit, Desire, and the Novel*, trans. Yvonne Freccero (Baltimore: Johns Hopkins University Press, 1965); and Eric Gans, *Signs of Paradox: Irony, Resentment, and Other Mimetic Structures* (Stanford, CA: Stanford University Press, 1997).

7. Note that this analysis does not deny the cultural significance of the preexisting symbolic paradigms that enable the construction and testing of

particular empirical hypotheses. It is for this reason that Thomas Kuhn's notion of "paradigm shift" is useful for philosophers and historians who wish to understand the history of science. Whether it is useful for the scientists themselves seems doubtful. On the contrary, "normal" science advances only by assuming the transparency of the paradigm within which it operates. See Thomas Kuhn, *The Structure of Scientific Revolutions*, 2nd ed. (Chicago: University of Chicago Press, 1970).

8. Harold Bloom, *The Anxiety of Influence: A Theory of Poetry* (Oxford: Oxford University Press, 1973), 99, 107.

9. Terry Eagleton, *Literary Theory: An Introduction* (Minneapolis: University of Minnesota Press, 1983), viii, 185.

10. Stephen Greenblatt, "The Touch of the Real," *Representations* 59 (1997): 14.

11. Eagleton, *Literary Theory*, 209.

12. See, for example, John Guillory's Bourdieusian analysis of "cultural capital" in *Cultural Capital: The Problem of Literary Canon Formation* (Chicago: University of Chicago Press, 1993), or James J. Sosnoski, *Token Professionals and Master Critics: A Critique of Orthodoxy in Literary Studies* (Albany: SUNY Press, 1994).

13. Mark Bauerlein, *Literary Criticism: An Autopsy* (Philadelphia: University of Pennsylvania Press, 1997), 148.

14. Though the terms are Bauerlein's, my analysis of "belonging" owes more to Emile Durkheim, Arnold van Gennep, René Girard, Eric Gans, and Randall Collins. See Emile Durkheim, *The Elementary Forms of Religious Life*, trans. Karen E. Fields (New York: Free Press, 1995); and Arnold van Gennep, *The Rites of Passage*, trans. Monika B. Vizedom and Gabrielle L. Caffee (London: Routledge & Kegan Paul, 1960). For Girard's analysis of mimetic desire, see *Deceit, Desire, and the Novel*. His later works, *Violence and the Sacred*, trans. Patrick Gregory (Baltimore: Johns Hopkins University Press, 1977) and *Things Hidden Since the Foundation of the World*, trans. Stephen Bann and Michael Metteer (Stanford: Stanford University Press, 1987), develop the analysis in an explicitly anthropological direction. For Eric Gans's important modification of Girard's theory, see *The End of Culture: Toward a Generative Anthropology* (Berkeley: University of California Press, 1985). For Randall Collins's theory of "interaction ritual," see *Interaction Ritual Chains* (Princeton, NJ: Princeton University Press, 2004). The reader may be surprised not to see Michel Foucault in this list, but Foucault deanthropologizes Durkheim's analysis of the sacred. Compare, for example, this remark from "What Is an Author?": "In our culture … discourse was not originally a product, a thing, a kind of goods; it was essentially an act—an act placed in the bipolar field of sacred and the profane, the licit and the illicit, the religious and the blasphemous." *The Foucault Reader*, ed. Paul

Rabinow (New York: Pantheon Books, 1984), 108. For Foucault, all cultural differences can ultimately be traced back to differences of power. But what explains the concept of power? Is it anthropological, biological, or purely metaphysical? On this score, Foucault's theory represents a step backward from Durkheim.

15. "The equivocations of representational [i.e., political] criticism," Bauer-leins writes, "are subtle and complex, and unless one diagnoses its usages as the outcome of a pragmatic-representational opposition, much contemporary criticism will strike readers as confused, incoherent, or nonsensical. The following mini-essays on critical terms are designed to lift that incomprehension, to rationalize the confusions as natural consequences of criticism's anti-method proceedings. The intent is clarification. If the result should be a critique, I leave its consequences for my readers to draw." *Literary Criticism*, 15.

16. See Karl Popper, *Conjectures and Refutations: The Growth of Scientific Knowledge* (New York: Harper, 1963), esp. 35–39.

17. Of course, science too is an anthropological endeavor and therefore subject to the same desires and conflicts as the rest of humanity. In this sense, Kuhn's notion of "paradigm shift" explains far better than Popper's idealized notion of "falsifiability" the anthropology without which science could not exist. But precisely for that reason Kuhn's history of science is really a version of anthropology. There are, for example, no indications that Kuhn's idea of "paradigm shift" is changing the way scientist's formulate and test their hypotheses. And this is ultimately because these tests are, in the final analysis, always empirical tests. For a useful comparison of Popper and Kuhn, see Marvin Harris, *Cultural Materialism: The Struggle for a Science of Culture* (New York: Random House, 1979), 15–28.

18. Douglas Bruster, in *Shakespeare and the Question of Culture: Early Modern Literature and the Cultural Turn* (New York: Palgrave, 2003), has recently suggested that the new historicism is primarily "indebted to Geertz for the *style* of the thickly descriptive essay," a style that "entrances its reader with the accounts of things and events alternately wonderful, strange, violent, and odd" (36).

19. In *Cultural Capital* John Guillory states that the "perceived devaluation of the humanities curriculum is in reality a decline in its *market* value" (46). In an earlier and shorter version of the argument in "Canon," in *Critical Terms for Literary Study*, ed. Frank Lentricchia and Thomas McLaughlin (Chicago: University of Chicago Press, 1990), Guillory argues that modernism and difficult poets like John Donne were only allowed into the academic curriculum after the universities could offload the teaching of Standard English to the lower levels of education. Literature was now used

to do "something more"—namely, to defamiliarize students of precisely the "standard" reading practices they were required to learn at the primary levels ("Canon" 246). Academic literary study in the postwar period evolves, rather like the old modernism itself, as an attempt to scandalize the bourgeois subject produced by the liberal-democratic marketplace. In other words, it is by definition always marginal.

20. Richard Halpern, in *Shakespeare among the Moderns* (Ithaca, NY: Cornell University Press, 1997), has traced an interesting genealogy of modernism from T.S. Eliot through Northrop Frye to Stephen Greenblatt. "High modernism," Halpern writes, "not only dominated the cultural and critical reception of Shakespeare during the first half of our century, but continues to exert a powerful influence that is often unacknowledged or disavowed" (2).

21. Greenblatt, "Touch of the Real," 19; hereafter cited in text.

22. For a powerful analysis of Weber's concept of charisma in terms of the center-periphery structure of human societies, see Edward Shils, *Center and Periphery: Essays in Macrosociology* (Chicago: University of Chicago Press, 1975).

23. Stephen Greenblatt, *Shakespearean Negotiations: The Circulation of Social Energy in Renaissance England* (Berkeley: University of California Press, 1988), 1.

24. The representation is "literary" because Greenblatt isn't really a shaman conducting a ritual but a literature professor "pretending" to be a shaman. Less obviously, the representation is "minimal" because you don't have to believe in ghosts to get Greenblatt's point; all you need is a little imagination, like the actor who pretends he is Hamlet seeing a real ghost.

25. In *Practicing New Historicism* (Chicago: University of Chicago Press, 2000), Greenblatt and Catherine Gallagher cite Johann Gottfried von Herder as their forerunner, because Herder understood that anthropology depends on "an encounter with the singular, the specific, and the individual" (6). Yes, but the new historicist's encounter with the singular does not obviate a consideration of what makes this singularity relevant to *us*. Without an anthropology to justify the latter "etic" context, new historicism's emphasis on singularity is merely self-serving, because it implies that only the new historicist has privileged access to cultural "otherness." Mark Bauerlein observes that new historicism's "methodological frailty" is too often ignored because it otherwise seems to offer an "antidote to cultural imperialism." *Literary Criticism*, 29. Are we beginning to see the end of this political strategy of romantic victimary self-centralization in the humanities? No doubt it is too early to tell, but the recent publication by Columbia University Press of a 725-page anthology of essays that are

highly critical of criticism's strategy of victimary self-centralization suggests that the tide may be turning. See Daphne Patai and Will H. Corral, eds., *Theory's Empire: An Anthology of Dissent* (New York: Columbia University Press, 2005).

26. In *Violence and the Sacred* Girard views modernity as ambivalently poised between, on the one hand, primitive sacrifice, with its potentially endless cycle of violent retribution, and, on the other, its Weberian "rationalization" by the modern state. The latter is granted a monopoly on "good" or "sacred" violence: "In the final analysis, then, the judicial system and the institution of sacrifice share the same function, but the judicial system is infinitely more effective. However, it can only exist in conjunction with a firmly established political power. And like all modern technological advances, it is a two-edged sword, which can be used to oppress as well as to liberate" (23). Gans, more secular than Girard, suggests that the modern "exchange system has become at least conceivably capable of taking over the function, formerly carried out by religious institutions, of protecting the social order against the dangers of desire."*End of Culture*, 43.

27. Gans, *End of Culture*, 17.

28. Signe Howell, *Society and Cosmos: Chewong of Peninsular Malaysia* (Singapore: Oxford University Press, 1984), esp. 183–91; hereafter cited in text.

29. Eric Gans, *Originary Thinking: Elements of Generative Anthropology* (Stanford, CA: Stanford University Press, 1993), 118.

30. Geertz, *Interpretation of Cultures*, 116.

31. Ibid., 113–14.

Notes to Chapter 5. Shakespeare and the Idea of the Modern

1. Margreta de Grazia, "*Hamlet* before Its Time," *Modern Language Quarterly* 62 (2001), 355; hereafter cited in text as "HBT."

2. According to Harold Bloom, Hamlet is "the Western hero of consciousness," quoted in de Grazia, 355.

3. William Kerrigan, *Hamlet's Perfection* (Baltimore: Johns Hopkins University Press, 1994), xi–xii; hereafter cited in the text as *HP*.

4. "For finally," Kerrigan continues, "it is a literary call. It hardly matters that much of Renaissance dramatic theory was still wedded to Aristotle: Shakespeare might have been an original" (*HP* 29). Kerrigan's wager is, of course, that Shakespeare was "an original."

5. T. S. Eliot, "Hamlet and his Problems," *Selected Essays* (New York: Harcourt, 1950), 122. Like de Grazia's "new" historicism, Eliot's "old"

historicism is intended as a corrective to the excesses of the romantic critic. Eliot has no patience for the latter, whom he describes as "the critic
with a mind which is naturally of the creative order, but which through
some weakness in creative power exercises itself in criticism instead. These
minds [Eliot continues] often find in Hamlet a vicarious existence for
their own artistic realization. Such a mind had Goethe, who made Hamlet a Werther; and such had Coleridge, who made Hamlet a Coleridge....
We should be thankful Walter Pater did not fix his attention on this play"
(121). One notes the irony of a poet criticizing other poets for their insuf-
ficiently "objective" criticism. Eliot writes at the dawn of literature as a
"scientific" discipline. So, naturally, he is inclined to differentiate himself
from his precursors by invoking his alliance with this newly emerging
historical "science of literature."

6. "Can it be," de Grazia asks at the end of her essay, "that criticism, after
two centuries of pitching Hamlet toward the future, is turning its back
on the modern present?" De Grazia's wager is, of course, that it is. For
de Grazia, the ghost functions as a figure for a host of premodern religious issues, including "purgatory, patrilineality, real presence, embodied
memory, the justice of exact retribution, and the affinity between man
and earth (human and humus)" ("*Hamlet* before Its Time," 374–75). De
Grazia is thus not unlike Hamlet himself, who in his effort to become the
first successful interpreter of the ghost, to make it speak and thus to suc-
ceed where Barnardo, Marcellus, and Horatio have failed, must separate
himself, rather violently, from his fellow interpreters ("I'll make a ghost
of him that lets me").

7. "As I turned from the history of criticism to the play itself," Kerrigan
confides in his preface, "my work quickly lost its initial polemical edge.
Born of a sorrow that my generation of scholar-critics might have embar-
rassingly little to contribute to the understanding of Shakespeare's major
work, the book rapidly became a love affair with *Hamlet*" (*HP* xi). It is
hard to imagine a new historicist writing this way. Compare, for example,
Stephen Greenblatt in *Shakespearean Negotiations: The Circulation of Social
Energy in Renaissance England* (Berkeley and Los Angeles: University of
California Press, 1988): "If one longs, as I do, to reconstruct these negotiations, one dreams of finding an originary moment, a moment in which
the master hand shapes the concentrated social energy into the sublime
aesthetic object. But the quest is fruitless, for there is no originary moment, no pure act of untrammeled creation. In place of blazing genesis,
one begins to glimpse something that seems at first far less spectacular:
a subtle, elusive set of exchanges, a network of trades and trade-offs, a
jostling of competing representations, a negotiation between joint-stock

companies" (7). In Greenblatt, as in all new historicism, the romantic love affair with the aesthetic text is subconsciously diluted and flattened, via the deconstructionist notion of "textuality," to embrace not just literature but all history. There is a real anthropological point to this "flattening" of literature into history (Derrida would call it a "dissemination" or "supplementation" or, most originarily, a "*différance*"), but it tends to remain obscured by exaggerated polemics with mythical targets like the new criticism. New historicism's Oedipal relationship to the latter suggests that this polemic is really just an ironic form of literary piety. Hence the ease with which a "traditionalist" like Kerrigan can dismiss "theory" as so much petty rivalry among the brothers who have killed their father. But the solution to the "presentist" rivalries of theory is not to resurrect the dead father, as Hamlet seeks to do, but to minimize from within this mythical-literary scene the fundamental anthropological elements of rivalry itself.

8. Kerrigan's self-consciousness of his own marginalization comes across when he says "my book might be considered the minority report of a minority ambition" (*HP* xi). But his tendency is to explain this marginality in terms of his relationship to the contemporary critical vanguard ("theory") rather than in broader historical terms, which is the route I shall pursue here.

9. On this point, see Wolfgang Iser, "Changing Functions of Literature," in *Prospecting: From Reader Response to Literary Anthropology* (Baltimore: Johns Hopkins University Press, 1989), 197–214; Galin Tihanov, "Why Did Modern Literary Theory Originate in Central and Eastern Europe? (And Why Is It Now Dead?)," *Common Knowledge* 10 (2004): 61–81; and Stein Haugom Olsen, "Progress in Literary Studies," *New Literary History* 36 (2005): 341–358.

10. The classic discussion of the sacred remains Emile Durkheim's *The Elementary Forms of the Religious Life*, trans. Joseph Ward Swain (New York: Free Press, 1965); first published in French as *Les formes élémentaires de la vie religieuse* in 1912. For an intelligent and uncluttered summary of Durkheim's basic ideas, as well as for a lively analysis that attempts to show their continued relevance for the theory of culture today, see Roger Scruton, *An Intelligent Person's Guide to Modern Culture* (South Bend, IN: St. Augustine's Press, 2000). I admire the lucidity with which Scruton understands the fundamental anthropological problem of modern culture, but it seems to me that his solution is ultimately only a more rigorous defense of high culture than is available in, for example, Kerrigan. Having said that, Scruton still remains one of the few people to have grasped the magnitude of the problem. He is at his anthropological best when he

understands that the strongest defense of culture is not ultimately aesthetic but *religious*, which is very nearly to say, anthropological.

11. See Gans's account of aesthetic history in part two of *Originary Thinking: Elements of Generative Anthropology* (Stanford: Stanford University Press, 1993); hereafter cited in text as *OT*.

12. "Why," Kerrigan asks, "has my generation of literary intellectuals contributed so little to the elucidation of *Hamlet*?" He offers two explanations. Either we are fed up with the romantics whose "individualism ... promoted this play to its lofty status in world literature," or we are fed up with literature itself, there being "not much fresh and original to be said about *Hamlet*" or indeed any other great work (*HP* xi). Kerrigan of course rejects both answers. "Compared to *Oedipus Rex*," he writes, "*Hamlet* is still in its infancy. Its tradition is young and open, rich in questions, teeming with opportunity" (*HP* xi).

13. This point becomes most clear when one observes that the entire argument of "*Hamlet* before Its Time" is essentially an exercise in debunking exponents of the romantic aesthetic, from Coleridge to Derrida. To the question, "If what you say is true, what follows?" de Grazia ultimately has no answer. Instead, her final paragraph alludes very tentatively (via a footnote) to a list of names of possible critical reformers, including Anthony Low, Ann Rosalind Jones, Peter Stallybrass, and Stephen Greenblatt. But because this list is not backed up with a discussion of the fundamental ideas of any of these individuals, the gesture is in fact empty. The effect is, paradoxically enough, not unlike one of Derrida's own texts, a point de Grazia appears to acknowledge obliquely when she refers in the final paragraph to Derrida's remarks on the paradoxical figure of the ghost. Like Derrida's reading of metaphysics, de Grazia's argument is concerned with "deconstructing" the *Hamlet* of the romantics, not with advancing a new *Hamlet*, which is to say, a "new literary history."

14. This transition is also the subject of Katherine Maus's closely argued study, *Inwardness and Theater in the Renaissance* (Chicago: University of Chicago Press, 1995). Maus explains Hamlet's inwardness as a consequence of widespread ethical changes in the culture, including notably the religious changes produced by the Reformation.

15. Compare William Kerrigan and Gordon Braden in *The Idea of the Renaissance* (Baltimore: Johns Hopkins University Press, 1989): "The year after the peace of Westphalia, in an act of far-reaching symbolic import, England beheads its sovereign. If we posit that step as the symbolic climax to a general European Renaissance, it constitutes, despite its violence, a denial of Burckhardt's ultimately tragic scenario for the period, since it affirms a serious faith in the social potential of an individualistic

ethos.... The period at its end retrieves the seemingly failed enterprise of the Italian communes: the management of personal ambition as a civic resource" (40).

16. A. C. Bradley, *Shakespearean Tragedy: Lectures on Hamlet, Othello, King Lear, Macbeth*, 2nd ed. (London: Macmillan, 1905), 90.

17. For an analysis of the importance of the "rites of passage" in traditional religious societies, see Arnold van Gennep, *The Rites of Passage*, trans. Monika B. Vizedom and Gabrielle L. Caffee (London: Routledge, 1960); first published in French as *Les rites de passage* in 1908.

18. David Green, ed. *Sophocles I: Oedipus the King, Oedipus at Colonus, Antigone*, 2nd ed. (Chicago: Chicago University Press, 1991), 12.

19. Exactly how modern was Shakespeare in 1600? Did, for example, his small Latin and less Greek make him less modern than, say, Jonson? But the debate about Shakespeare's modernity does not hinge on his familiarity with classical texts, but on his sense of himself as a "literary" author competing for an audience (a market) that was also fast becoming a readership. On this last point, see Lukas Erne, *Shakespeare as Literary Dramatist* (Cambridge: Cambridge University Press, 2003). On the importance of Shakespeare's rivalry with Ben Jonson and of the "war of the theaters" as constitutive of literary authorship in general, see James P. Bednarz, *Shakespeare and the Poets' War* (New York: Columbia University Press, 2001).

20. It is for this reason that I find Richard Halpern's provocative argument in *Shakespeare among the Moderns* (Ithaca, NY: Cornell University Press, 1997) only partially convincing. Halpern's thesis is that modernism's fascination for the primitive, notably, in Sir James George Frazer and the Cambridge ritualists, was taken up by literary critics, first by arch-modernists like Wyndham Lewis and T. S. Eliot, but also by later academic critics like Northrop Frye and Stephen Greenblatt. For these critics Shakespeare represented the transition from primitive to modern. Halpern cites Eliot's notion of the "dissociation of sensibility" as a symptom of the modernist idealization of the primitive over the "fragmentation" of experience that is the lot of the modernist. But Halpern's thesis assumes that modern historical self-consciousness only begins with modernism's contact with the primitive other, a figure whose radical alterity forced the West to reconsider its own past as a source of difference rather than identity. But this is to ignore the historical self-consciousness inherent to the category of the aesthetic itself. The very idea of a "Renaissance" in which the art-forms of a previous era are revived and imitated is an illustration of the historicity of the aesthetic. No doubt this historical self-consciousness was more apparent to the successors of the Renaissance

than to its original practitioners, but the very notion that the classical art-forms could themselves be "revived" demonstrates a minimal awareness of the historical difference between ancient and modern.

21. This suggests an alternative interpretation of the "interstitial" period of the "Middle Ages" alluded to by de Grazia as another example of historical forgetting similar to the lost period of *Hamlet* criticism between 1600 and 1800 (*"Hamlet* before Its Time," 356). Insofar as the Middle Ages provided a new ethical context for the revitalization of the classical aesthetic, it is indeed erroneous to bracket the entire period as in some vague and undefined sense "premodern." The crucial factor is the integration of the aesthetic scene inaugurated by the Greeks into the ethical context of Christianity. As Gans suggests, in these terms the "medieval period already illustrates the same postclassical problematic as that of the Renaissance" (*Originary Thinking*, 150).

22. Kerrigan and Braden point to Richard, Duke of Gloucester as the first truly Shakespearean character, and offer this brilliant comment on his gleefully malicious opening soliloquy in *Richard III*: "the bitterness is itself something of an act. It is being cultivated as a resource. Richard's divorce from love is the detachment of Renaissance individualism, aware of its unlikeness to others as it sizes them up with exploitative intent. Machiavellian role-playing is the relevant art of such a medium; Richard is simply backing off to give it room to work." *The Idea of the Renaissance*, 65. Richard "backing off" to give himself room to work anticipates Hamlet delaying as he "backs off" from Claudius to put on plays.

23. Christopher Marlowe, *Dido Queen of Carthage and the Massacre at Paris*, ed. H. J. Oliver, The Revels Plays (Cambridge: Harvard University Press, 1968), 5.1.292–94.

24. See René Girard, *Deceit, Desire, and the Novel: Self and Other in Literary Structure*, trans. Yvonne Freccero (Baltimore: Johns Hopkins, 1965).

25. For a sensitive reading of how Shakespeare self-consciously reproduces the past in some of the tragedies, see Howard Felperin, *Shakespearean Representation: Mimesis and Modernity in Elizabethan Tragedy* (Princeton: Princeton University Press, 1977).

26. William Shakespeare, *King Henry V*, ed. T. W. Craik, The Arden Shakespeare (London: Thomson, 1995), 4.3.61–62. All quotations of *Henry V* are from this edition.

27. Anthony B. Dawson, "The Arithmetic of Memory: Shakespeare's Theatre and the National Past," *Shakespeare Survey* 52 (1999): 54.

28. For the analysis of the *hysteron proteron* effect as a purely dramatic or literary form of irony, see Marjorie Garber, "'What's Past Is Prologue': Temporality and Prophecy in Shakespeare's History Plays," in *Renaissance*

Genres: Essays on Theory, History, and Interpretation, ed. Barbara Kiefer Lewalski (Cambridge: Harvard University Press, 1986), 301–331.

29. For the idea of "social memory," see, in particular, James Fentress and Chris Wickham, *Social Memory* (Oxford: Blackwell, 1992).

30. See, for example, Lars Engle, *Shakespearean Pragmatism: Market of His Time* (Chicago: University of Chicago Press, 1993); and the debate between Anthony Dawson and Paul Yachnin in their co-authored, *The Culture of Playgoing in Shakespeare's England: A Collaborative Debate* (Cambridge: Cambridge University Press, 2001).

31. On this point I am in complete agreement with Eli Rozik, who in a recent reassessment, *The Roots of Theatre: Rethinking Ritual and other Theories of Origin* (Iowa City: University of Iowa Press, 2002), criticizes the commonplace view that the theater originates historically in ritual. Rozik argues instead that theater is "sui generis" and that any attempt to trace its origin "historically" to earlier ritual forms is therefore a category error. Rozik's own solution is to see the roots of theater in "the psychological constitution of human beings and sociocultural structures of human societies" (xiv). My view is that the "sui generis" character of institutions like ritual and theater must be addressed "minimally" in terms of an originary hypothesis.

32. See René Girard, *Violence and the Sacred*, trans. Patrick Gregory (Baltimore: Johns Hopkins University Press, 1977); and *Things Hidden Since the Foundation of the World*, trans. Stephen Bann and Michael Metteer (Stanford: Stanford University Press, 1987).

33. Gans's criticism of Girard's originary scene is original and far-reaching. The fundamental point Gans raises is that Girard's notion of an originary scene of victimage implies a theory of symbolic representation. By emphasizing the necessarily mediated status of the central object/victim of the originary scene, Gans removes from the original Girardian scenario the "naturalism" implied by Girard's assertion that it is the empirical presence of the victim as such that motivates the first moment of cultural "non-instinctual attention" (see Girard, *Things Hidden Since the Foundation of the World*, 99). To this assertion Gans responds by saying that the victim can only be a victim in this "non-instinctual," "cultural-symbolic" sense if it is assumed that the violent *sparagmos* of the "mimetic crisis" is preceded by an awareness that the focus of communal aggression—Girard's founding victim—is *already* a manifestation of the sacred, which is to say, this moment of non-instinctual attention must in fact take place before, rather than after, the first victim is dispatched. This is the basis for Gans's assertion that the *sparagmos* is preceded by the "aborted gesture of appropriation" (*Signs of Paradox*, 16), a moment in which the central object is designated

or represented to the mimetic other. Only this prior "symbolic" awareness can explain the difference of "mimetic" violence among humans from the sort of mimetic violence documented in many other social animals. For instance, chimpanzees appear to engage in group "murders" of conspecifics. But this does not mean that chimpanzees therefore have an understanding of the category of the sacred. The killing of a conspecific—or indeed of any living species, whether plant or animal—does not "naturally" evolve into an act of sacralization. The act of sacrifice is in the first place a *symbolic* act. The difference between humans and all other animals is to be found here. This is the originary ground of all anthropology, including the "cultural" anthropology of anthropology departments and the "literary" anthropology of literature departments. For a clear statement of the central issues, see Gans, "Differences," *Modern Language Notes* 96 (1981): 792–808; and especially *Signs of Paradox*, chap. 2.

34. For a fascinating sociological study of this tension between periphery and center in human societies, see Edward Shils, *Center and Periphery: Essays in Macrosociology* (Chicago and London: University of Chicago Press, 1975).

35. Walter Pater, "Shakespeare's English Kings," in *Richard II*, ed. Kenneth Muir, Signet Shakespeare, 2nd revised ed. (New York: Penguin, 1999), 151. No doubt this text is what T. S. Eliot had in mind when he expressed his relief that Walter Pater had not turned his attention to Hamlet. See note 5 above.

36. William Shakespeare, *King Richard II*, ed. Charles R. Forker, The Arden Shakespeare (London: Thompson, 2002), 3.2.155–56 (text references are to act, scene, and line of this edition).

37. William Shakespeare, *Hamlet*, ed. Harold Jenkins, The Arden Shakespeare (London and New York: Methuen, 1982), 1.2.106–7 (text references are to act, scene, and line of this edition).

38. See W. W. Greg, "Hamlet's Hallucination," *Modern Language Review* 12 (1917): 393–421.

39. See J. Dover Wilson, *What Happens in "Hamlet"*, 3rd ed. (Cambridge: Cambridge University Press, 1951), 138–97, esp. 159–60. For a review of the controversy, see Harold Jenkins's long note in his edition of *Hamlet*, 501–505. Jenkins himself sides with the traditional reading, and remains impatient with what he regards as the sheer "pointlessness" (503) of Greg's original argument. Jenkins's dismissal notwithstanding, Greg's "controversy" has experienced something of a minor revival among theorists who have been quick to point out the deconstructive, psychoanalytic, and occasionally even Marxian implications of Greg's analysis. For the Marxian reading, see Terrence Hawkes's entertaining, but ultimately misdi-

rected "Telmah," in *Shakespeare and the Question of Theory*, eds. Patricia Parker and Geoffrey Hartman (New York: Methuen, 1985), 310–32. For the deconstructive and psychoanalytic readings, see Ned Luckacher, *Primal Scenes: Literature, Philosophy, Psychoanalysis* (Ithaca: Cornell University Press, 1986), 178–235; Stanley Cavell, *Disowning Knowledge: In Six Plays of Shakespeare* (Cambridge: Cambridge University Press, 1987), 179–91; and Christopher Pye, *The Vanishing: Shakespeare, the Subject, and Early Modern Culture* (Durham: Duke University Press, 2000), 105–29.
40. Coleridge, *Lectures on Shakespeare and Milton*, quoted in *Critical Responses to "Hamlet," 1790–1838*, ed. David Farley-Hills, vol. 2 (New York: AMS Press, 1996), 54.
41. See Bradley, *Shakespearean Tragedy*, 118–19.
42. See Ernest Jones, *Hamlet and Oedipus* (New York: Norton, 1949).
43. See G. Wilson Knight, *The Wheel of Fire: Interpretations of Shakespearian Tragedy with Three New Essays*, 4th ed. (London: Methuen, 1949).

Notes to Chapter 6. A Race of Devils

1. Mary Shelley, *Frankenstein, Or, The Modern Prometheus* (New York: Signet, 2000), 87; hereafter cited in text. This edition is based on Mary Shelley's revised 1831 edition. The first edition was published in 1818, two years after it was begun.
2. Lawrence Lipking, in "*Frankenstein*, the True Story; or, Rousseau Judges Jean-Jacques," notes that "late-twentieth-century critics, when they look at Frankenstein's creation, no longer see a Monster, as earlier generations did; they now see a Creature." *Frankenstein*, ed. J. Paul Hunter (New York: Norton Critical Edition, 1996), 317. Lipking himself follows this "late-twentieth-century" preference for calling Shelley's protagonist a "creature" rather than a "monster." My own preference is for the older terminology because it is less fastidious about admitting the "monstrosity" of the protagonist's desire ("monster," from the Latin *monere*, "to warn," not, as some mistakenly believe, from *monstrare*, "to show"). Monstrosity is linked to the paradoxical experience of the sacred, which both attracts and repels.
3. Eric Gans, *Signs of Paradox: Irony, Resentment, and Other Mimetic Structures* (Stanford, CA: Stanford University Press, 1997), 176.
4. I am relying on David Marshall's excellent account of Mary Shelley's use of Rousseau, in *The Surprising Effects of Sympathy: Marivaux, Diderot, Rousseau, and Mary Shelley* (Chicago: University of Chicago Press, 1988).
5. *Signs of Paradox*, 180.
6. The centrality of sacred exchange in the "closed" economies of archaic societies is the premise of Mauss's celebrated analysis of the gift. See his *The*

Gift: The Form and Reason for Exchange in Archaic Societies, first published in French as *Essai sur le don* in 1923-24.

7. Eric Gans, *Originary Thinking: Elements of Generative Anthropology* (Stanford, CA: Stanford University Press, 1993), 162; hereafter cited in text as *OT.*

8. In *Deceit, Desire, and the Novel*, Girard reserves the term "novelistic" desire for those novelists who understand the mediated structure of desire— "*vérité romanesque*" rather than "*mensonge romantique*."

9. The most eloquent contemporary spokesperson of this view is Francis Fukuyama. See his *The End of History and the Last Man* (New York: Free Press, 1992).

10. Knight, *The Wheel of Fire: Interpretations of Shakespearian Tragedy with Three New Essays*, 4th ed. (London: Methuen, 1949), 32.

11. Greg, "Hamlet's Hallucination," *Modern Language Review* 12 (1917): 393–421.

12. Samuel Taylor Coleridge, *Coleridge's Criticism of Shakespeare*, ed. R. A. Foakes (Detroit: Wayne State University Press, 1989), 68.

13. On the importance of the Greek distinction between *tyrannos* (ruler by successful coup) and *basileus* (hereditary king), see Maurice Pope, "Addressing Oedipus," *Greece & Rome* 38 (1991): 156–170. It is no coincidence, Pope argues, that Sophocles almost always refers to Oedipus as *tyrannos* rather than *basileus*. The irony of the play is that Oedipus's discovery of his real or inherited kingship is what leads to his downfall. Oedipus's kingship is revealed to be inseparable from the tragedy of mimetic desire.

14. David Green, ed. *Sophocles I: Oedipus the King, Oedipus at Colonus, Antigone*, 2nd ed. (Chicago: Chicago University Press, 1991), 12.

15. The same oscillation characterizes the monster's contemplation of the miniature of Caroline Beaufort, which hangs from the neck of his first victim, William: "In spite of my malignity, it softened and attracted me. For a few moments I gazed with delight on her dark eyes, fringed by deep lashes, and her lovely lips; but presently my rage returned; I remembered that I was forever deprived of the delights that such beautiful creatures could bestow" (122).

16. More precisely, Victor's accusation is that his father didn't bother to explain why Agrippa is outdated. Victor claims that if he "had taken the pains to explain to me that the principles of Agrippa had been entirely exploded … I should certainly have thrown Agrippa aside" (24). But Victor is merely deluding himself here. Later, when Krempe "explodes" the scientific status of alchemy, Victor defiantly chooses to ignore him despite, or more likely because of, this "bourgeois" dismissal of the supernatural.

Bibliography

Austin, J. L. *How to Do Things with Words.* 2nd ed. Edited by J. O. Urmson and Marina Sbisà. Cambridge, MA: Harvard University Press, 1962.

Bateson, Gregory. *Steps to an Ecology of Mind.* San Francisco: Chandler Publishing Company, 1972.

Bauerlein, Mark. *Literary Criticism: An Autopsy.* Philadelphia: University of Pennsylvania Press, 1997.

———. "Political Dreams, Economic Woes, and Inquiry in the Humanities." *boundary 2* 27, no. 1 (2000): 197–216.

Bednarz, James P. *Shakespeare and the Poets' War.* New York: Columbia University Press, 2001.

Bickerton, Derek. *Language and Human Behavior.* Seattle: University of Washington Press, 1995.

———. *Language and Species.* Chicago: University of Chicago Press, 1990.

Bloom, Harold. *The Anxiety of Influence: A Theory of Poetry.* Oxford: Oxford University Press, 1973.

Bradley, A. C. *Shakespearean Tragedy: Lectures on Hamlet, Othello, King Lear, Macbeth.* 2nd ed. London: Macmillan, 1905.

Bruster, Douglas. *Shakespeare and the Question of Culture: Early Modern Literature and the Cultural Turn.* New York: Palgrave, 2003.

Burling, Robbins. "Primate Calls, Human Language, and Nonverbal Communication." *Current Anthropology* 34 (1993): 25–53.

Calvin, William. "Talking Heads" Review of Terrence Deacon, *New York Times on the Web.* August 10, 1997, http://www.nytimes.com/books/97/08/10/reviews/970810.10calvint.html (accessed October 17, 2000).

Calvin, William, and Derek Bickerton. *Lingua Ex Machina: Reconciling Darwin and Chomsky with the Human Brain.* Cambridge, MA: Massachusetts Institute of Technology Press, 2000.

Cassirer, Ernst. *An Essay on Man: An Introduction to a Philosophy of Human Culture.* New Haven, CT: Yale University Press, 1944.

Cavell, Stanley. *Disowning Knowledge: In Six Plays of Shakespeare.* Cambridge: Cambridge University Press, 1987.

Chomsky, Noam. *Language and Mind.* New York: Harcourt Brace Jovanovich, 1972.

Coleridge, Samuel Taylor. *Coleridge's Criticism of Shakespeare.* Edited by R. A. Foakes. Detroit: Wayne State University Press, 1989.

Collins, Randall. *Interaction Ritual Chains.* Princeton, NJ: Princeton University Press, 2004.

Crane, Mary Thomas, and Alan Richardson. "Literary Studies and Cognitive Science: Toward a New Interdisciplinarity." *Mosaic* 32, no. 2 (1999): 123–40.

Dawkins, Richard. *The Selfish Gene.* 2nd Ed. Oxford: Oxford University Press, 1989.

Dawson, Anthony B. "The Arithmetic of Memory: Shakespeare's Theatre and the National Past." *Shakespeare Survey* 52 (1999): 54–67.

Dawson, Anthony B., and Paul Yachnin. *The Culture of Playgoing in Shakespeare's England: A Collaborative Debate.* Cambridge: Cambridge University Press, 2001.

Deacon, Terrence. *The Symbolic Species: The Co-Evolution of Language and the Brain.* New York: Norton, 1997.

Dennett, Daniel C. *Darwin's Dangerous Idea: Evolution and the Meanings of Life.* New York: Simon & Schuster, 1995.

Derrida, Jacques. *Margins of Philosophy.* Translated by Alan Bass. Chicago: University of Chicago Press, 1982.

———. *Of Grammatology.* Translated by Gayatri Spivak. Baltimore: Johns Hopkins University Press, 1974.

Donald, Merlin. "Mimesis and the Executive Suite: Missing Links in the Origin of Language." In Hurford et al., 44–67.

———. *Origins of the Modern Mind: Three Stages in the Evolution of Culture and Cognition*. Cambridge, MA: Harvard University Press, 1991.

———. "Preconditions for the Evolution of Protolanguages." In *The Descent of the Mind: Psychological Perspectives on Hominid Evolution*, edited by Michael C. Corballis and Stephen E.G. Lea., 138–54. Oxford: Oxford University Press, 1999.

Dunbar, Robin. "Theory of Mind and the Evolution of Language." In Hurford et al. 92–110.

Dunbar, Robin, Chris Knight, and Camilla Power, eds. *The Evolution of Culture: An Interdisciplinary View*. New Brunswick, NJ: Rutgers University Press, 1999.

Durkheim, Emile. *The Elementary Forms of the Religious Life*. Translated by Joseph Ward Swain 1915. Reprint, New York: The Free Press, 1965.

Eagleton, Terry. *Literary Theory: An Introduction*. Minneapolis: University of Minnesota Press, 1983.

Eliot, T. S. *Selected Essays*. New York: Harcourt, 1950.

Engle, Lars. *Shakespearean Pragmatism: Market of His Time*. Chicago: University of Chicago Press, 1993.

Englefield, F. R. H. *Language: Its Origin and its Relation to Thought*. Edited by G. A. Wells and D. R. Oppenheimer. London: Pemberton, 1977.

Erne, Lukas. *Shakespeare as Literary Dramatist*. Cambridge: Cambridge University Press, 2003.

Esterhammer, Angela. *The Romantic Performative: Language and Action in British and German Romanticism*. Stanford, CA: Stanford University Press, 2000.

David Farley-Hills, ed. *Critical Responses to "Hamlet," 1790–1838*. Vol. 2. New York: AMS Press, 1996.

Felperin, Howard. *Shakespearean Representation: Mimesis and Modernity in Elizabethan Tragedy*. Princeton: Princeton University Press, 1977.

Fentress, James, and Chris Wickham. *Social Memory*. Oxford: Blackwell, 1992.

Fischer, Michael. "Literary Change and Cognitive Science" (Review of Spolsky, *Gaps in Nature: Literary Interpretation and the Modular Mind*). *Poetics Today* 17 (1996): 362–65.

Fish, Stanley. *Is There a Text in this Class?* Cambridge, MA: Harvard University Press, 1980.

Fludernik, Monika, Donald Freeman, and Margaret H. Freeman. "Metaphor and Beyond: An Introduction." *Poetics Today* 20 (1999): 383–396.

Foucault, Michel. *The Foucault Reader*, edited by Paul Rabinow. New York: Pantheon Books, 1984.

———. *The Order of Things: An Archeology of the Human Sciences*. New York: Vintage, 1994.

Fox, Robin. *Kinship and Marriage: An Anthropological Perspective*. Cambridge: Cambridge University Press, 1983.

———. *The Red Lamp of Incest*. London: Hutchinson, 1980.

Fukuyama, Francis. *The End of History and the Last Man*. New York: Free Press, 1992.

Gans, Eric. "Differences." *Modern Language Notes* 96 (1981): 792–808.

———. *The End of Culture: Toward a Generative Anthropology*. Berkeley and Los Angeles: University of California Press, 1985.

———. "The Little Bang: The Early Origin of Language." *Anthropoetics* 5 no. 1 (1999), http://www.anthropoetics.ucla.edu/ap0501/gans.htm (accessed April 15, 2002).

———. *Originary Thinking: Elements of Generative Anthropology*. Stanford, CA: Stanford University Press, 1993.

———. *Signs of Paradox: Irony, Resentment, and Other Mimetic Structures*. Stanford, CA: Stanford University Press, 1997.

———. "Staging as an Anthropological Category." *New Literary History* 31 (2000): 45–56.

Garber, Marjorie. "'What's Past Is Prologue': Temporality and Prophecy in Shakespeare's History Plays." In *Renaissance Genres: Essays on Theory,*

History, and Interpretation, edited by Barbara Kiefer Lewalski, 301–331. Cambridge: Harvard University Press, 1986.

Geertz, Clifford. *The Interpretation of Cultures.* New York: Basic Books, 1973.

Genette, Gérard. *Narrative Discourse: An Essay in Method.* Translated by Jane E. Lewin. Ithaca, NY: Cornell University Press, 1980.

Girard, René. *Deceit, Desire, and the Novel.* Translated by Yvonne Freccero. Baltimore: Johns Hopkins University Press, 1965.

———. *A Theater of Envy.* Oxford: Oxford University Press, 1991.

———. *Things Hidden Since the Foundation of the World.* Translated by Stephen Bann and Michael Metteer. Stanford, CA: Stanford University Press, 1987.

———. *Violence and the Sacred.* Translated by Patrick Gregory. Baltimore: Johns Hopkins University Press, 1977.

Goldschmidt, Richard. "Evolution, as Viewed by One Geneticist." *American Scientist* 40 (1952): 84–135.

Good, Graham. *Humanism Betrayed: Theory, Ideology, and Culture in the Contemporary University.* Montreal & Kingston: McGill–Queen's University Press, 2001.

Goodall, Jane. *In the Shadow of Man.* Boston: Houghten Mifflin, 1971.

Goodall, Jane, and Dale Peterson. *Visions of Caliban: On Chimpanzees and People.* Boston: Houghton Mifflin, 1993.

de Grazia, Margreta. "*Hamlet* before Its Time." *Modern Language Quarterly* 62 (2001): 355–75.

Greenblatt, Stephen. "The Touch of the Real." *Representations* 59 (1997): 14–29.

———. *Renaissance Self-Fashioning: From More to Shakespeare.* Chicago: University of Chicago Press, 1980.

———. *Shakespearean Negotiations: The Circulation of Social Energy in Renaissance England.* Berkeley and Los Angeles: University of California Press, 1988.

————. "Towards a Poetics of Culture." In *The New Historicism*, edited by H. Aram Veeser, 1–14. New York: Routledge, 1989.

Greenblatt, Stephen, and Catherine Gallagher. *Practicing New Historicism*. Chicago: University of Chicago Press, 2000.

Greg, W. W. "Hamlet's Hallucination." *Modern Language Review* 12 (1917): 393–421.

Green, David, ed. *Sophocles I: Oedipus the King, Oedipus at Colonus, Antigone*. 2nd Ed. Chicago: Chicago University Press, 1991.

Gross, Sabine. "Cognitive Readings: or, the Disappearance of Literature in the Mind." *Poetics Today* 18 (1997): 271–297.

Guillory, John. "Canon." In *Critical Terms for Literary Study*, edited by Frank Lentricchia and Thomas McLaughlin, 233–49. Chicago: University of Chicago Press, 1990.

————. *Cultural Capital: The Problem of Literary Canon Formation*. Chicago: University of Chicago Press, 1993.

Halpern, Richard. *Shakespeare Among the Moderns*. Ithaca, NY: Cornell University Press, 1997.

Harris, Marvin. "Anthropology and Postmodernism," in *Science, Materialism, and the Study of Culture*, edited by Martin F. Murphy and Maxine L. Margolis, 62–77. Gainesville, FL: University of Florida Press, 1995.

————. *Cultural Materialism: The Struggle for a Science of Culture*. New York: Random House, 1979.

————. *The Rise of Anthropological Theory: A History of Theories of Culture*. Updated ed. Walnut Creek, CA: Altamira, 2001. First published in 1968.

Hauser, Matt D. *The Evolution of Communication*. Cambridge, MA: Massachusetts Institute of Technology Press, 1996.

Hawkes, Terrence. "Telmah." In *Shakespeare and the Question of Theory*, edited by Patricia Parker and Geoffrey Hartman, 310–32. New York: Methuen, 1985.

Hernadi, Paul. "Literature and Evolution." *SubStance* 94/95 (2001): 55–71.

Herman, David. "Parables of Narrative Imagining." *Diacritics* 29 (1999): 20–36.

Hobbes, Thomas. *Leviathan*. Edited by Kenneth Minogue. London: J. M. Dent, 1994.

Hockett, Charles F., and Robert Ascher. "The Human Revolution." *Current Anthropology* 5 (1964): 135–68.

Holloway, Ralph. "Culture: A Human Domain." *Current Anthropology* 10 (1969): 395–412.

———. "Language's Source: A Particularly Human Confluence of Hard Wiring and Soft." Review of *The Symbolic Species*, by Terrence Deacon. *American Scientist* 86 (1998): 184–86.

Howell, Signe. *Society and Cosmos: Chewong of Peninsular Malaysia*. Singapore: Oxford University Press, 1984.

Hudson, Richard. Review of *The Symbolic Species*, by Terrence Deacon. *Journal of Pragmatics* 33 (2001): 129–35.

Hurford, James. Review of *The Symbolic Species*, by Terrence Deacon, *Times Literary Supplement*, October 23, 1998, 32.

Hurford, James, Michael Studdert-Kennedy, and Chris Knight, eds., *Approaches to the Evolution of Languages: Social and Cognitive Bases*. Cambridge: Cambridge University Press, 1998.

Iser, Wolfgang. *How to Do Theory*. Oxford: Blackwell, 2006.

———. *Prospecting: From Reader Response to Literary Anthropology*. Baltimore: Johns Hopkins University Press, 1989.

———. "What is Literary Anthropology? The Difference Between Explanatory and Exploratory Fictions." In *Revenge of the Aesthetic: The Place of Literature in Theory Today*, edited by Michael Clark, 157–79. Berkeley, CA: University of California Press, 2000.

Jackson, Tony. "Questioning Interdisciplinarity: Cognitive Science, Evolutionary Psychology, and Literary Criticism." *Poetics Today* 21 (2000): 319–347.

Johnson, Mark. *The Body in the Mind: The Bodily Basis of Meaning,*

Imagination, and Reason. Chicago: University of Chicago Press, 1987.

Jones, Ernest. *Hamlet and Oedipus.* New York: Norton, 1949.

Katz, Adam, ed. *The Originary Hypothesis: A Minimal Proposal for Humanistic Inquiry.* Aurora, CO: The Davies Group Publishers, 2007.

Kerrigan, William. *Hamlet's Perfection.* Baltimore: Johns Hopkins University Press, 1994.

Kerrigan, William, and Gordon Braden. *The Idea of the Renaissance.* Baltimore: Johns Hopkins University Press, 1989.

Knight, Chris. *Blood Relations: Menstruation and the Origins of Culture.* New Haven, CT: Yale University Press, 1991.

Knight, G. Wilson. *The Wheel of Fire: Interpretations of Shakespearian Tragedy with Three New Essays.* 4th ed. London: Methuen, 1949.

Kohan, Kevin. "James and the Originary Scene." *The Henry James Review* 22 (2001): 229–238.

Kuhn, Thomas. *The Structure of Scientific Revolutions.* 2nd ed. Chicago: Chicago University Press, 1970.

Kuper, Adam. *Culture: The Anthropologists' Account.* Cambridge, MA: Harvard University Press, 1999.

Lakoff, George. *Women, Fire, and Dangerous Things: What Categories Reveal about the Mind.* Chicago: University of Chicago Press, 1987.

Lakoff, George, and Mark Johnson. *Metaphors We Live By.* Chicago: University of Chicago Press, 1980.

———. *Philosophy in the Flesh: The Embodied Mind and Its Challenge to Western Thought.* New York: Basic Books, 1999.

Lakoff, George, and Mark Turner. *More than Cool Reason: A Field Guide to Poetic Metaphor* Chicago: Chicago University Press, 1989.

Lett, James. *Science, Reason, and Anthropology: The Principles of Rational Inquiry.* New York: Rowman and Littlefield, 1997.

Lewis, Wyndham. *The Lion and the Fox: The Role of the Hero in Plays of Shakespeare.* London: Methuen, 1951.

Lipking, Lawrence. "*Frankenstein*, the True Story; or, Rousseau Judges Jean-Jacques." In *Frankenstein*, edited by J. Paul Hunter, 313–31. New York: Norton Critical Edition, 1996.

Locke, John. *An Essay Concerning Human Understanding*. Edited by Peter H. Nidditch. Oxford: Oxford University Press, 1975.

Lodge, David. *The Modes of Modern Writing: Metaphor, Metonymy, and the Typology of Modern Literature*. London: University of Chicago Press, 1977.

Luckacher, Ned. *Primal Scenes: Literature, Philosophy, Psychoanalysis*. Ithaca: Cornell University Press, 1986.

Marlowe, Christopher. *Dido Queen of Carthage and the Massacre at Paris*. Edited by H. J. Oliver. Cambridge: Harvard University Press, 1968.

Marshall, David. *The Surprising Effects of Sympathy: Marivaux, Diderot, Rousseau, and Mary Shelley*. Chicago: Chicago University Press, 1988.

Maus, Katherine. *Inwardness and Theater in the Renaissance*. Chicago: University of Chicago Press, 1995.

Mauss, Marcel. *The Gift: The Form and Reason for Exchange in Archaic Societies*. Translated by W.D. Halls. London: Routledge, 1990.

Miers, Paul. "The Other Side of Representation: Critical Theory and the New Cognitivism." *Modern Language Notes* 107 (1992): 950–975.

Miller, Geoffrey F. "Sexual Selection for Cultural Displays." In Dunbar et al., 71–91.

Müller, Max. *Introduction to the Science of Religion*. London: Longmans, 1873.

Olsen, Stein Haugom. "Progress in Literary Studies." *New Literary History* 36 (2005): 341–58.

Patai, Daphne, and Will H. Corral, ed. *Theory's Empire: An Anthology of Dissent*. New York: Columbia University Press, 2005.

Pater, Walter. "Shakespeare's English Kings." In *Richard II*, edited by Kenneth Muir, Signet Shakespeare, 2nd rev. ed., 151–58. New York: Penguin, 1999.

Peirce, Charles Saunders. "Logic as Semiotic: The Theory of Signs." In *The Philosophical Writings of Peirce*, edited by J. Buchler, 98–119. New York: Dover Books, 1956.

Pinker, Steven. *The Language Instinct*. New York: HarperCollins, 1994.

Pope, Maurice. "Addressing Oedipus." *Greece & Rome* 38 (1991): 156–170.

Popper, Karl. *Conjectures and Refutations: The Growth of Scientific Knowledge*. New York: Harper and Row, 1963.

Pye, Christopher. *The Vanishing: Shakespeare, the Subject, and Early Modern Culture*. Durham: Duke University Press, 2000.

Richardson, Alan. "Cognitive Science and the Future of Literary Studies." *Philosophy and Literature* 23 (1999): 157–173.

Rollin, Bernard E. *Natural and Conventional Meaning: An Examination of the Distinction*. The Hague: Mouton, 1976.

Rousseau, Jean-Jacques. *Discourse on the Origin of Inequality*. Translated by Franklin Philip and edited by Patrick Coleman. Oxford: Oxford University Press, 1994.

———. *Reveries of the Solitary Walker*. Translated by Peter France. Harmondsworth, Middlesex, England: Penguin, 1979.

Rozik, Eli. *The Roots of Theatre: Rethinking Ritual and other Theories of Origin*. Iowa City: University of Iowa Press, 2002.

Ruse, Michael. "The Evolution of Symbols" Review of Terrence Deacon, *The Semiotic Review of Books* 9 no. 3 (1998), http://www.chass.utoronto.ca/epc/srb/srb/evolution.html (accessed February 19, 2001).

Sampson, Geoffrey. *Educating Eve: The "Language Instinct" Debate*. London: Cassell, 1997.

Savage-Rumbaugh, Sue E. *Ape Language: From Conditioned Response to Symbol*. New York: Columbia University Press, 1986.

Schneider, Matthew. "Problematic Differences: Conflictive Mimesis in Lessing's *Laokoon*." *Poetics Today* 20 (1999): 273–289.

Scruton, Roger. *An Intelligent Person's Guide to Modern Culture*. South Bend, IN: St. Augustine's Press, 2000.

Searle, John. *The Construction of Social Reality*. New York: The Free Press, 1995.

———. *Expression and Meaning: Studies in the Theory of Speech Acts*. Cambridge: Cambridge University Press, 1979.

———. *The Rediscovery of Mind*. Cambridge, MA: Massachusetts Institute of Technology Press, 1992.

Sebeok, Thomas. *Signs: An Introduction to Semiotics*. Toronto: University of Toronto Press, 1994.

Seyfarth, Robert M., Dorothy Cheney, and Peter Marler. "Monkey Responses to Three Different Alarm Calls: Evidence of Predator Classification and Semantic Communication." *Science* 210 (1980): 801–803.

Shakespeare, William. *Hamlet*. Edited by Harold Jenkins. The Arden Shakespeare. London and New York: Methuen, 1982.

———. *King Henry V*. Edited by T. W. Craik. The Arden Shakespeare. London: Thomson, 1995.

———. *King Richard II*. Edited by Charles R. Forker. The Arden Shakespeare. London: Thompson, 2002.

Shelley, Mary. *Frankenstein, Or, The Modern Prometheus*. New York: Signet, 2000.

Shils, Edward. *Center and Periphery: Essays in Macrosociology*. Chicago and London: University of Chicago Press, 1975.

Sosnoski, James J. *Token Professionals and Master Critics: A Critique of Orthodoxy in Literary Studies*. Albany: SUNY Press, 1994.

Stamenov, Maxim I., and Vittorio Gallese, eds. *Mirror Neurons and the Evolution of Brain and Language*. Amsterdam: John Benjamins, 2002.

Sternberg, Meir. "The *Laokoon* Today: Interart Relations, Modern Projects and Projections." *Poetics Today* 20 (1999): 291–379.

Stevens, Paul. "Pretending to Be Real: Stephen Greenblatt and the Legacy of Popular Existentialism." *New Literary History* 33 (2002): 491–519.

Stoczkowski, Wiktor. *Explaining Human Origins: Myth, Imagination and Conjecture*. Translated by Mary Turton. Cambridge: Cambridge University Press, 2002.

Tihanov, Galin. "Why Did Modern Literary Theory Originate in Central and Eastern Europe? (And Why Is It Now Dead?)." *Common Knowledge* 10 (2004): 61–81.

Tomasello, Michael. *The Cultural Origins of Human Cognition*. Cambridge, MA: Harvard University Press, 1999.

Tomasello, Michael, et al., "Understanding and Sharing Intentions: The Origins of Cultural Cognition." *Behavioral and Brain Sciences* 28 (2005): 675–735.

Tooby, John, and Leda Cosmides. "Does Beauty Build Adapted Minds? Towards an Evolutionary Theory of Aesthetics, Fiction and the Arts." *SubStance* 94/95 (2001): 6–27.

Turner, Mark. *The Literary Mind*. New York: Oxford University Press, 1996.

———. "Poetry for the Newborn Brain." Review of *The Symbolic Species*, by Terrence Deacon. *Bostonia* 1 (1998): 72–73.

———. *Reading Minds: The Study of English in the Age of Cognitive Science*. Princeton, NJ: Princeton University Press, 1991.

Turner, Mark, and Gilles Fauconnier. "A Mechanism of Creativity." *Poetics Today* 20 (1999): 397–418.

van Gennep, Arnold. *The Rites of Passage*. Translated by Monika B. Vizedom and Gabrielle L. Caffee. London: Routledge, 1960.

van Oort, Richard. "Three Models of Fiction: The Logical, the Phenomenological, and the Anthropological (Searle, Ingarden, Gans)." *New Literary History* 29 (1998): 439–465.

———. "The Use of Fiction in Literary and Generative Anthropology: An Interview With Wolfgang Iser," *Anthropoetics* 3 no. 2 (1998), http://www.anthropoetics.ucla.edu/ap0302/Iser_int.htm (accessed April 15, 2002).

Waal, Frans B. M. de. *Chimpanzee Politics: Power and Sex Among Apes*. New York: Harper & Row, 1982.

———. "Cultural Primatology Comes of Age." *Nature* 399 (1999): 635–36.

Watzlawick, Paul, Janet Helmick Beavin, and Don D. Jackson. *Pragmatics of Human Communication: A Study of Interactional Patterns, Pathologies, and Paradoxes*. New York: Norton, 1967.

White, Leslie A. *Ethnological Essays*. Edited by Beth Dillingham and Robert L. Carneiro. Albuquerque: University of New Mexico Press, 1987.

———. *The Evolution of Culture: The Development of Civilization to the Fall of Rome*. New York: McGraw-Hill, 1959.

———. *The Science of Culture*. New York: Farrar, Straus and Cudahy, 1949.

Wilson, Edward O. *Consilience: The Unity of Knowledge*. New York: Random House, 1999.

———. *On Human Nature*. New Haven, CT: Yale University Press, 1978.

Wilson, J. Dover. *What Happens in Hamlet*. 3rd ed. Cambridge: Cambridge University Press, 1951.

Wrangham, Richard, and Dale Peterson. *Demonic Males: Apes and the Origins of Human Violence*. Boston: Houghton Mifflin, 1996.

INDEX

aesthetic: capacity, 13; classical, 137, 153, 155, 156, 158, 206n.21; experience, 75, 118, 120, 125, 161, 189n.4, 192n.13; of irony, 48; neoclassical, 134, 147, 155; object, 99, 160-1, 202n.7; period, 74, 76, 107, 137, 190n.5, 192n.9; representation, 8, 9; romantic, 134, 151, 159, 204n.13; scene, 103, 138, 139, 147, 160, 206n.21
alarm calls, 6, 8, 46
Aristotle, 99, 100, 132, 154, 201n.4; Aristotelian, 96, 99, 100, 139; *Poetics*, 99
Austin, J. L., 75, 85, 96, 149, 194n.26; speech-act theory, 75, 194n.26
Arnold, Matthew, 76

Baldwinian evolution (See *genetic assimilation*)
Bateson, Gregory, 43, 45-6, 195-6n.33; double bind, 43, 195-6n.33
Bauerlein, Mark, 115-17, 191n.7, 192n.10, 198n.14, 199n.15; on new historicism, 200-1n.25
Baudelaire, Charles, 171n.3
Beckett, Samuel, 171n.3
Bickerton, Derek, 7, 13, 188n.3
Bloom, Harold, 113, 114, 126, 131, 201n.2; on *Hamlet*, 131, 201n.2
Boas, Franz, 184n.66
Bradley, A. C., 135, 146
Bruster, Douglas, 199n.18
Burke, Edmund, 150
Byron, George Gordon, 150

call systems, 6, 8, 81, 176n.27, 189n.1; of vervet monkeys, 6, 20, 21, 27, 46, 59, 71, 174n.13, 176n.31, 179n.38, 189n.1
chimpanzees, 4-5, 22-6, 41-3, 45, 52-61, 81, 88-9, 94, 101, 102, 109-10, 186n.76, 187n.83, 191n.8, 194n.23, 196n.35, 196-7n.5, 197n.6, 207-8n.33; Austin and Sherman, 22-6
Chomsky, Noam, 6; innate universal grammar, 182n.53
Christianity, 137, 143, 147, 154-6, 206n.21
cognitive: anthropology, 27; model of representation, 5, 9, 27; poetics, 3, 27, 172n.1; science, *xiii*, 3, 5, 26-9, 34, 35, 172nn.1, 3, 173n.4, 181n.52, 182-3n.56
Coleridge, Samuel Taylor, 133, 146, 157, 202n.5, 204n.13
collective memory, 97, 140
Collins, Randall, 171n.1, 198-9n.14
criticism, academic, 90, 114, 190-1n.7; aesthetic, 73, 107, 192-3n.13; anthropological, *xi*; cultural, 99, 107, 113, 128; culture of, 127, 128; literary, 72, 73, 76, 90, 91, 93, 113, 115, 116, 119, 178-9n.36
culture, origin of, 79-82, 88, 93, 94, 184n.66, 193n.17, 195-6n.33; theory of, 72, 76, 105, 107, 112-14, 128, 203-4n.10

Darwin, Charles, *xii*, 4, 40, 84, 112; Darwinian principles, 8;

Printed in Great Britain
by Amazon.co.uk, Ltd.,
Marston Gate.